Ess, Ess, Mein Kindt

(EAT, EAT, MY CHILD)

By *Harry Golden*

ONLY IN AMERICA

FOR 2¢ PLAIN

ENJOY, ENJOY

CARL SANDBURG

FORGOTTEN PIONEER

YOU'RE ENTITLE'

THE SPIRIT OF THE GHETTO
(*with Hutchins Hapgood
and Sir Jacob Epstein*)

FIVE BOYHOODS
(*with Walt Kelly, Howard
Lindsay, John Updike,
and William Zinsser*)

MR. KENNEDY AND THE NEGROES

SO WHAT ELSE IS NEW?

A LITTLE GIRL IS DEAD

ESS, ESS, MEIN KINDT

HARRY GOLDEN

Ess, Ess, Mein Kindt

(EAT, EAT, MY CHILD)

AUTHOR OF *Only in America*

G. P. PUTNAM'S SONS

NEW YORK

917.3
G618es

To the girls who married
our sons,
Doris, Bebe, and Judy.

Second Impression

COPYRIGHT ©, by Harry Golden, 1963, 1964, 1965, 1966

"The R.F.K. Aftermath" essay appeared in *Esquire*, "Protest in the Streets" appeared in *Crisis*, "Southern Hospitality" appeared in the *London Jewish Chronicle*; thirty-four other essays have appeared in Harry Golden's syndicated column, distributed by the Bell-McClure Newspaper Syndicate. Ninety-eight of the stories have appeared in the *Carolina Israelite*, published and edited by Harry Golden. One hundred and thirty-one essays were written especially for *Ess, Ess, Mein Kindt*.

Library of Congress Catalog Card Number: 66-20281

PRINTED IN THE UNITED STATES OF AMERICA

100078

Contents

6 CONTENTS

A letter to my readers

Ess, ess, mein kindt (plural: *kinder*) translates literally as eat, eat, my child. But it means much more. Its meaning is profound. *Ess, ess, mein kindt* is not only an expression of the love of a mother for her child. Along the Lower East Side of New York it was a rallying cry of survival.

Food, of course, is literally—survival. Among the immigrant Jews in the tenement districts of New York, Philadelphia, and Chicago, there was somehow always more than enough food. The poorest managed to eat—big. I was never hungry, nor were my sisters and brothers, nor were any of our friends or neighbors. All of us were sometimes cold, sometimes ragged, sometimes overworked, but not hungry.

The poverty and the pain of childhood are all forgotten, as they should be, but the joys remain in our memory—the silence in the ghetto on the eve of the Holy Days; your mother holding out a thick piece of rye bread covered with chicken fat when you came in from play, hungry as only a ten-year-old can be; the sheer delight of getting a paper bag full of that Christmas candy in millions of colors; the joy of visiting relatives "uptown" and being able to ride up and down the first "moving-stairs" (escalator) in America—on the 125th Street station of the subway.

I have received close to a half-million letters during the past ten years as a result of my recollections about New York's Jewish ghetto. (The word "ghetto" is used to denote a section of the city that is occupied, mostly out of economic necessity, by an immigrant or minority group, in this case, Jewish—not in the sense of a restricted prisonlike community). My correspondence has convinced me that there is much more involved in these recollections than nostalgia and sentimentality.

For sentimentality does not per se change the quality of life; indeed the chief objection to sentimentality is that it is a lie about the quality of life. The life I knew had a more hopeful quality, a richer texture, than the life the young folks see now stretching before them. On the Lower East Side in the early years of this century we came as close to any guarantee as life has ever offered. The guarantee was if you worked hard, went to school, studied and saved, you could participate in America.

Life offers no such guarantee today. There are millions of young people unprepared and unfit to enter the automated industrial society of today.

We were poor on the Lower East Side of New York, far poorer I suspect than the poor in America now. But we had a strategy for defeating poverty. And many of us did defeat it. Those who did not may have felt that life was fine and exquisite and brilliant or they may have felt life was hard and cruel, but they did not feel it was empty. Life today contains a major problem in the ever-increasing segregation of the poor and the elderly. In the ghetto of New York, grandmothers and grandfathers and crotchety maiden aunts were a part of life, included in the whole. The old were ever-present. This is by and large not true today. The elderly live lonely lives in one housing development, and the young lead frenzied lives in another. We have telephones and radio and television, but communication between the age groups grows less and less distinct.

To be truthful, these things are felt and understood only in retrospect and in retrospect I would say that I am happy to have grown up on the Lower East Side of New York. I believe it was a happier time to have grown to manhood.

In those days tuberculosis was endemic among the ghetto sweatshop workers. It was so prevalent that the Jews even joked about it. They called tuberculosis "Jewish asthma." The immigrant mothers learned that one of the first symptoms was loss of weight. And so they watched their men and their children. The mothers thought as long as they all ate heartily there was no danger. You may have weighed one hundred and forty pounds at the age of twelve and the kids on the block were calling you "Fatty," but if you once dawdled over your food, your mother was terribly distressed—"Look at him, nothing but skin and bones—eat, eat, my child, do you want to get sick?" The first question relatives and friends asked when someone returned from a vacation was, "How much did you gain?"

Now we didn't eat simply to ward off tuberculosis. Actually the offering of food by the mother of the household was the offering of her love. When her food was not eaten it was as if her love was rejected. Guests who may have just left their own dinner table valiantly ate everything the hostess offered. It would have been an insult to do otherwise.

This *ess, ess, mein kindt* tradition created its own culture; a hefty family was a happy family. And a *zoftick* (hefty) girl not only had sex appeal, but offered the best chance to a boy for the future happiness of a home. I remember girls and young women practicing postures to simulate heft, holding their heads in such a way as to give the impression of a double chin.

Heft in a male denoted not only a grasp on survival and life but good looks and affluence. All the cartoons of the day portrayed the rich man as a fellow with a huge stomach, a silk hat and a diamond stickpin.

I, too, was a husky kid and when I worried about it my mother consoled me with the observation, "In America, the fat man is the boss and the skinny man is the bookkeeper." I suspect the high bookkeeping stools of those days would never have accommodated some of the fat employers I knew.

No longer so young, but hefty still, I offer, with God's help, *Ess, Ess, Mein Kindt.*

As my readers know, I enjoy the offices of an excellent editor, Harry Golden, Jr., a topflight newspaperman on the Chicago *Sun-Times.* He has a fierce pride about his competency, gained after twenty years, and he has a fierce pride in his work on these books. It was enough for me to hear him say, "You have another good one."

—HARRY GOLDEN

Charlotte, North Carolina
July 1, 1966

PART 1

From Cleopatra to Computers

The new South

Down here, things have changed since the Civil Rights Act of 1964 was signed. Restaurants integrated so quietly that it seemed segregation had been forgotten. One of the girls in the office returned from lunch with the following account:

A timid, elderly Negro lady approached the downtown drug-store lunch counter, leaned over and whispered confidentially, "Do you serve colored here?"

The teen-aged white waitress looked blank. "Colored what?"

Will the computer end war?

If you feed the computer all the details concerning a given problem, it flashes back the answer. I've seen it at work, both at the dress manufacturing plant of Jonathan Logan and at Eastern Airlines.

Now if the machine were given details concerning the strength of two opposing forces, their equipment, their armed forces, the terrain, it should be able to calculate which of the two armies would win a war. There would then be no need to go to war, because we would know the result without fighting.

In response to this plan, a Jewish philosopher wrote me saying that it has been tried. He said that a general fed the computer all the statistics and asked the machine to tell him which side would win. The computer's lights flashed back and forth across its stomach and finally the machine said, "Yes."

The general asked, "Yes, what?"

The computer replied, "Yes, *sir!*"

Study the stars and how can anyone write editorials or sell insurance?

IT IS so vast, it bewilders me. I have often thought I would accept with nonchalance the news that there is intelligent life on other planets. It is silly for us to believe that out of these plateau after plateau of vastness, billions of planets revolving around billions of suns, only this speck of dust possesses the conditions which can support human life.

Women and forever

WOMEN KEEP the central core of religion in the face of man's combativeness. Women believe in survival beyond the grave. No woman believes for one moment that the child she bears is not established for all of what life there is to be, and in her endowment of her child she feels it is forever to live, advancing from perfection to perfection through eternity. Man takes over then, making contractual commitments to her deity for success in battle, good crops, and defeat of the boll weevil.

Think about this, when a woman is ironing her son's shirt she is serving immortality. It is hard to defeat the timeless patience of women and the smallest service is important if it partakes of forever. A man grabs for a sixteen-year-old chick. No woman in her right mind grabs for a sixteen-year-old boy. Her man is young, her sense of time keeps Maurice Chevalier a gay young blade forever and ever and ever. Now you know about women and love.

We're closer than we think

"SHOES ALONE know if the stockings have holes." Thus Haitians tell us secrets are known only to their keepers. Tribes in Africa say, "It is the sea only which knows the bottom of the ship."

"Three helping each other will bear the burden of six," say the Spaniards, while the Italians have, "A single finger can't catch fleas."

The English say, "God helps those who help themselves," and the Spaniards say, "God helps him who gets up early."

The quiet losers

I'M STILL thinking about the fellow who loved the pretty girl and who thinks of her at least once a week the rest of his life. In the meantime, she's had her hands full contending with her children, all of whom are dropouts, and has bad luck at all her bridge parties and never thinks of him at all.

The real losers in life rarely discuss their loss. I knew a man whose sole ambition was to be the youngest congressman in Washington. He did everything to realize this ambition except win the election.

By the time he did get around to winning an election, he was a pretty elderly state legislator and a very rich lawyer and a great advocate of "experience" in politics.

Our obsession with the female
mammary glands

OUT IN San Francisco, the saloonkeepers put waitresses on the floor naked from the *pipick* up. So far the cops have not been able to close the place down because the judge ruled the saloonkeepers are not kidnapping their customers who fork over good money for a look-see.

We have all of us waded through various analyses about the

American devotion to the female chest which represents both mom and sex to growing, red-blooded American boys.

There's more to it unfortunately.

We began developing the pinup culture since World War I. But I believe the pinup or the lounging girl with bared breasts photographed in a silk-lined boudoir represents nothing so much as she represents impotence. It has been remarked that the "Playmate" popularized by Hugh Heffner is a girl soft tonight and off your hands tomorrow and I am not sure that is what virility wants or demands.

It wasn't until World War II with the omnipresent photos of Betty Grable, Rita Hayworth, *et altera*, looking cozy but aloof, that we dedicated ourselves to the breast binge. I remember how we panned Howard Hughes's picture *The Outlaw* because Jane Russell was the first of the stars to open her blouse. In Britain, the reviewer for the *Times* said, "It's not much of a picture but the children will enjoy the shooting." And now look at us: silicone breasts and plastic faces.

I am sure the virile male wants something more than a poster or a picture in the center fold of a magazine, or even a naked waitress; but for so many others, impotence or the fear of impotence has provided the substitutions which satisfy.

I thought of Xanadu

I FINALLY spent two days in the Catskill Mountains of New York, the Borscht Circuit. I delivered a lecture on the evening of Rosh Hoshanah, the Jewish New Year, to the guests of the Concord Hotel.

It is hard to describe the Concord. Words like bewildering, fantastic, excellent, and magnificent, pale.

There are golf courses, swimming pools, solariums, sun decks, servants, food, bars, playrooms for children, card rooms for adults. There are two waiters for every table, the hotel serves three thousand people at one sitting. When you finish breakfast it's time for lunch. I thought of Xanadu and I thought of King Solomon in all his glory, and Solomon's Court seemed like Okies compared to the guests at the Concord.

In my speech I said that some of the audience would probably go home and complain to their organizations about the few "Gentile" hotels along the Atlantic Seaboard which still bar Jews. But I suggest we allow the "exclusive" fellows six or seven more such hotels if they promise to leave us alone at the Concord. Compared to the Concord, those "exclusive" hotels are one-arm roominghouses. And not only is there the Concord, there's also Grossinger's and The Pines, all of which boast three menu pages for lunch and four for dinner.

With every meal the two waiters bring you three different wines. They bring you a platter of dessert and after you've consumed one, they ask, "Would you like another?" And suppose an "exclusive" hotel like for instance The Vontzin at Sea Island, Georgia, finally decided to open it up to Jewish guests, it would be too much to ask of anyone to make the sacrifice and go there.

After my lecture, a lady arose during the question-and-answer period and said, "Mr. Golden, it's all right for you to talk about civil rights, but what have the Negroes ever done for us?"

"Madame," I said, "the minute the Negroes get themselves a Concord Hotel we will ask them to do something for us, and not a moment sooner."

And the food—the food is fantastic. Did I say that already?

Cleopatra and the moderns

THE WOMEN are angry with me. They say I have my nerve writing how their modern story is the same today as it was a thousand years ago. They say they have gone to college, they are sexually emancipated, they are better mothers, they stir up cultural activities in the community. And I say I'm sorry you're angry but the story is still the same as it ever was. A woman needs a man. Without a man who desires her, a woman has no visa.

Cleopatra and the Empress Josephine knew nothing about a college education. They didn't even know they were sexually emancipated. If they were alive today, they probably wouldn't know how to drive a car. But they both knew they had to have a man.

Two hundred years from today, some guy will be operating a computer the likes of which we can't imagine. He will be talking to people on Mars and throughout the realms of outer space and some little gal will say to him, "Never mind all that beeping and booping with outer space. Get over here now. I miss you." And he will get over there now. And she will have proved her worth to herself.

The big money

YEARS AGO, during a period of a steadily declining market, I remember a middle-aged lawyer pacing nervously in the brokerage house. The stocks he'd bought on margin kept dropping and his broker warned he'd have to sell him out unless he got up enough collateral to cover his losses.

The speculator said, "Let's wait for the next quotation on Baldwin."

"Okay," said the broker, "then you'll have to give me your decision."

The next quotation came over and Baldwin had dropped even more seriously. The lawyer quietly read the ticker and walked to the open window and dived to his death. Later, we found he had been "borrowing" from an estate over which he had professional control. We also realized that when he asked for that time to see the next quotation he was deciding that if the stock went up he would live, if it continued to go down, he would die.

The curious fact about the whole matter was that even after

his own estate was settled and restitution made by his two rich brothers, he still left some money.

What a compulsion that big money is! It has poured more good men down the drain than women, liquor, and politics combined. The trouble with money is that there is no such thing as too much of it.

The love of money is the root of all evil and so unfortunately is the lack of it. Samuel Butler wrote that money was the last enemy, the one we never subdue.

Among the very rich, I believe there is even a revulsion to money. More rich people have left their money to institutions than to another person. Money is so self-corrupting, people who have it often want to spare others. That would seem to be the reasoning behind their bequests, anyway.

They probably feel as Julius Caesar, who remarked, according to Voltaire, that the Romans used their soldiers to rob money, and with the money they paid their soldiers.

Soft sell for Prohibition

SOME TIME around 1942 or 1943 I went up to the public square in Charlotte to attend an Independence Day program. One of the local ministers gave the main address on the theme, "Mankind's Greatest Enemy Is John Barleycorn."

I remember that an old newspaperman named Bill Witter, who went with me to the program, was so moved, he reached into his hip pocket and threw away a half-full bottle of bourbon. Of course, Bill was a sucker for revival meetings and he had tossed away many a half-pint of whiskey only to crawl back in darkness and search for it.

But all of the old-time hellfire sermons about booze are old hat. Today, Prohibition has gone Madison Avenue. One of the new Prohibitionist leaders is Robert K. Squire of Smart Set International. His pamphlets are quite effective. He says, "Children are copy cats; if they see you do it, they'll try it."

Mr. Squire's arguments are models of the temperate approach. He does not urge national prohibition, but rather an all-out effort to redeem the casual drinkers. He says, "Non-drinking Pays! Give Yourself a Raise!"

All his material is handsomely printed and all of it in the soft-sell mood. I am for him. But I want to warn everyone I am probably in the category beyond salvation.

Apartments and brothels

WE HAD had books on the campus and sex, books on the single girl and sex, books on the bachelor and sex, ad infinitum. What we lack is a book on the big-city apartment house and sex. It is in the apartment house that the real sex goes on. It raises its beautiful head there because in the big cities people mind their own business.

In the fancy apartment nowadays, the management refuses to tolerate babies but they do allow dogs and cats.

Instead of a rowdy newborn babe, the tenants tolerate hilarious cocktail parties. The empty bottles and the crushed napkins and the broken glasses give semiweekly evidence of a big time. There are probably more respectable ladies of joy doing business in the big apartments in one city block than there are collected in Paris's Place Pigalle.

Yet this state of affairs was long ago predicted by New York's great mayor, William J. Gaynor, who told the vice-hunting Parkhurst Committee, "If you close the brothels which are now segregated from the rest of the population, the women will simply move next door to you. They will become the most desirable tenants because they will give the superintendent two dollars a day for his services while you will give him but fifty cents once a year at Christmas."

The old brothels were in a manner of speaking a bulwark of morality. For in the days when they flourished, one thought of extramarital relations in terms of the brothel and not in terms

of the average girl met socially or at work. The brothel protected
the innocents, and the compulsive sex-seeker was not about dis-
rupting the community.

Making friends

MEN HOLD onto the friends they make in school or when
they were unemployed because by and large they really don't
like the other men they work with. That is why the poker and
pinochle games usually include a motley group—there are games
which include truck drivers and brokers, small merchants and
golf pros.

But women are more ingenuous and make friends in a completely different manner.

One night at dinner, I discovered the pièce-de-résistance was
a huge bowl of green beans, garnished with water chestnuts,
from the center of which grew a regular hayfield of parsley. The
little woman informed me she had met this other lady on the
bus and this other lady had just won first prize from some can
company for this green bean recipe. Thereupon followed a
friendship as strong and as fast as Damon and Pythias except it
was based on the exchange of recipes. Unfortunately for my
palate and digestive tract this other lady was a veritable wizard
with vegetables and I have suffered through the delights of
celery stuffed with ground carrots sprinkled atop with paprika
and saffron and other gustatory marvels.

Not even moving from one state to another could cut off this
friendship. The recipes still flow back and forth with the regularity with which poker players exchange stories of the
last time they held a straight flush.

The women also make friends over such odd experiences as
reading books. Jessica Mitford's book, *The American Way of
Death*, has given us a whole new circle of lady friends who
spend their time shopping for the proper burial society. I am not
yet sure whether the American public thought funeral prices

outrageous or death itself. "Direct talk" about shuffling off this mortal coil chills me.

I want the doctor who signs my certificate to assure everyone it wasn't cirrhosis which did me in but simply the fact that my heart was too big for the body it inhabited, that my whole-hearted dedication to good causes weakened me.

Curiously, though most women deplore the gossip, it is invariably the informed gossip who has a whole cartload of friends. I have known plenty of gossips in my time and I have yet to see any woman avoid one of them.

Warren Harding: double disaster

WARREN HARDING sometimes appears one of the most benighted of all men. When he became President, he put his friends and cronies in positions of trust and they stole red-hot stoves and wet-paint signs. No Administration had the scandals poor Warren's had.

In addition, Warren had trouble with women, lots of trouble. Nan Britton accused him posthumously of having fathered her illegitimate daughter. She was very specific. She said she and Warren conceived the child in a White House closet. Now the historian Francis Russell has found two hundred and fifty love letters Warren wrote to a hometown paramour, Mrs. Carrie Phillips. Not only did Mrs. Phillips save the letters, but she blackmailed him, too.

Boise Penrose, the politician-journalist, once advised a friend of his, "Never write a letter to a woman you can't cool a beer on." And Soren Kierkegaard, the Danish philosopher who invented Existentialism, once observed the great trick with a woman is to get rid of her while she thinks she's getting rid of you.

Warren Harding was as inept a philanderer as he was a President. In fact, he was a disaster as a President, but I am afraid there are those who would whitewash him by claiming he was a disaster as a President because he had such bad woman troubles. This is a bum rap for some of the great men of the world.

There are great poets and great leaders and great musicians who carried on love affairs with everyone and never let love corrupt their work.

I would hate to be un-American enough to count up the number of Presidents who not only went through their terms of office but their lives as models of probity simply because they had the sense not to write an occasional lady-friend a letter and because they had the sense to know love affairs which last forever are no fun.

Social class and sex

MUST READING for me each day is the syndicated female "adviser" column. On several occasions I have met the most famous of these columnists and recently she awed me with the mileage she got out of answering so common a marital dispute as to whether or not the wife should undress in front of the husband. Forthrightly, she said he ought to encourage his wife.

Not only were her columns filled for the next successive series with letters from those offended and those applauding, but two Southern newspapers devoted editorials to the problem, one championing, one condemning.

I say the girl got mileage out of the problem because the pros and contras of such practice go back to the dawn of recorded history. I see, in fact, a troubled Pharoah consulting his soothsayers, asking, "What is it with this Queen? What kind of modesty is this for me, the Sun God? Tell me, sooths and sayers, is it me or is it the times?"

And the sooths and sayers probably told the Pharaoh, "Lissen, Yer Highness, the Sun God, we think you ought to tell the Queen to wise up or you'll start a crash program on her pyramid."

The daily advice to the lovelorn lady understands the times;

a naked woman is always big news these days. She is big news because naked she doesn't reveal her class status. The real truth is that our sex habit coincides with our income and educational levels, precisely as Professor Kinsey recorded. The modest wife is a lower-middle-class manifestation and the immodest wife an upper. The fellow who originally wrote to the advice column wants to find a mean between the lady who won't take off her clothes in the closet and the lady who wants to take off her clothes at the party. He should change jobs. Advertising or the export-import business will do.

Memo to Secretary Udall

A FITTING memorial to a great man, a man who should be remembered by all civilization, is a library, perhaps a school. These are institutions that last.

But I'm not so sure that I am ready to discard the old-time statue. The Romans, of course, went to extremes with statues. We are all familiar with the remark Cicero made when he and a friend were passing through the forum lined with statues of the living emperor and the senators and statesmen. The friend said, "How come you don't have a statue, Cicero?" and Cicero said something to the effect, "It's better for people to say, 'How come no statue for Cicero?' than to say, 'What the hell is this statue doing here? Who is he to have a statue?' "

The Romans overdid it, but statues should not be dispensed with. I think back to the immigrant boys and I remember the first statue with which we became familiar was that of Nathan Hale outside City Hall Park. I'm not sure where it is now, but we passed the statue constantly, memorizing the inscription. I'm not so sure it did not encourage a feeling about America, perhaps an impetus to study about its great men. I'm not so sure that a building with the name Nathan Hale on it would have been as effective as that statue with Hale's hands tied behind his back and his head thrust out saying, "My only regret is that I have but one life to give for my country."

We were also fascinated by the gold statue of General Sheridan at the entrance to Central Park. I remember, too, Garibaldi and Shakespeare and Verdi.

We used to go down to the New York *World* to see the base-ball game on an electric board and when the crowd was big we took up our perch on the pedestal of the statue of Horace Greeley.

Of course, nothing symbolizes America itself like the Statue of Liberty. Ask the soldiers who came home from the European wars or the millions of immigrants who first saw America as the land of opportunity to which the statue beckoned.

I have seen photographs of the proposed memorial to Franklin D. Roosevelt and I'm no architect or art expert but it seems to me that the statue of Roosevelt in London with that Navy cape, and his outthrust jaw, impressed me much more. I'm sure it will impress millions of British school children yet un-born who will pass the statue and say, "What did he do for us?" And they will find out what he did for them.

The topless dancers

ENGLAND RECENTLY held a Commonwealth Arts Festival in Trafalgar Square. Sierra Leone dispatched sixty dancers to demonstrate African ballet in native dress. In Sierre Leone ap-parently neither dancers nor observers wear brassieres.

Desecration hovered over Trafalgar Square.

An official of the Ministry of Public Works and Buildings ruled the sixty dancers could not appear in their topless cos-tumes.

The ballet master said, "If we are not allowed to appear in our traditional dress we will not appear at all. It would be en-tirely against the aesthetic appeal of our dancing."

One never knows the principles for which one must

eventually stand. It is one thing to urge the UN to get together, and perhaps the same to urge the Commonwealth to get with it.

While England is a land of freedom, like the United States, it cannot shed its hypocrisy about sex.

The moral climate in London these days is permeated with concern about homosexuality. Every theatrical performance refers to it and the fags themselves parade the streets.

Why the Ministry of Public Buildings and Works thinks bare-breasted dancers will corrupt Trafalgar Square and homosexuals will not is a mystery.

If I had a bit of advice for Londoners I would say the more bare breasts, the better.

Reading the newspaper

In *As You Like It* William Shakespeare listed the seven ages of man. Curiously, I have discovered newspapers are really sevenfold with a chief interest for each age.

When a little boy starts to read the newspapers he turns to the comic strips. It is impossible to conjecture how many advertising revenues have been raised simply because some child conceived a fondness for the adventures of a simple line drawing with continuity.

From the comic strips, of course, a young fellow graduates to the sports pages. Sometimes these pages are consumed with avidity the rest of his life and often the sports pages makes some men multiple newspaper consumers, as market research fellows love to put it.

He grows older. He wants to know whether or not he will be drafted. He reads the front page. He follows international developments. He is also interested in murders and in lascivious divorce-case conduct.

Reading the front page makes a fellow realize a paper has

something to offer. Sometimes he reads the rest of the paper. Human interest hooks him.

From human interest he will even discover how to read an editorial. And once he begins on the editorials he is ready for the financial pages, just as his wife is interested in the society pages.

The best part of reading any newspaper is when you come upon mention of your friends. It makes not only the world but the publishing industry a little homier.

But the sad part of the career of the newspaper reader is reading the obituaries. It is the last stage. The reward all of us get for reading or not reading a paper is that in those black-lined columns we, too, will one day be listed.

Life among the cookouts

IF YOU can get the tiger out of your tank, you can cook it on any one of ten different advertised grills. Some of the appliances cost as much as $500. Which shows there is no extreme to which the American public won't go for its own inconvenience and hazard.

The airline pilots tell me that winter flying is often dangerous. The runways ice up, the snow descends suddenly, the air currents move the plane capriciously. But these dangers are nothing compared to flying over the suburbs on a weekend. The fog is always immense. Except it isn't fog; it's the smoke from hundreds of thousands of grills over which a breadwinner in an expensive knee-long apron presides, cooking the spots right out of the tiger steaks.

I have always wondered just what it is that drives the folks outdoors to ruin their digestive systems. As a minor-league celebrity I've been at enough dinner tables to assure the American public that good food can be adequately ruined in any modern kitchen without the annoyance of a picnic atmosphere and attendant heat, flies, and smoke.

Anthropologists estimate it took man several thousand years to learn how to use fire. It took several thousand more years for man to figure how to get fire from the outside into the inside. Once he figured it out, then came the hearth and the kitchen and the middle class was on its way. Having gotten the fire inside, man is now intent on getting it back outside again, a development which will no doubt confuse generations of anthropologists as yet unborn.

About all that tempers the annoyance of a steak thickly encrusted by the gigantic grill is the amount of spirits served while the meat is leatherized. More than a picnic, the cookout resembles these days a séance, with the smoke belching, the séancees speaking more and more thickly as they nervously fidget with their paper plates and napkins, the host emerging from the swirling clouds, face blackened like a World War II commando.

There's a theory in America that any piece of meat retaining any red resembles only a cow that ain't hardly been hurt. The gigantic grills on the market will allay a lot of suspicion that the meat is still alive. In fact, the grill is all the forest fire you can use for a modest $500.

Feminine perfection

SOME YEARS ago, Ring Lardner wrote that his idea of the perfect woman was one with lockjaw. . . . Mr. Lardner was always dramatic.

The modern woman is not only not afflicted with lockjaw, she is the parliamentary master of the PTA meeting. Leave it to her to talk the community out of the clambake and into the fashionable ball where she and her pals can display their new gowns.

And in addition, she is now a sexual authority, writing best sellers and syndicating newspaper material about boys and girls.

W. C. Fields' idea of a perfect woman was one who would mow the lawn and put up the storm windows when December winds blew hard. Were Fields alive, I fully suspect I'd see him in the supermarket, pushing the cart filled with eggs, buttermilk, low-calorie cola and other health foods.

The American woman is constitutionally incapable of shopping alone. These days she sends Daddy to the supermarket. She stays home and tots up eggplant recipes.

"I can't, Papa"

AMONG THE Bedouins living in Israel's Negev desert, old Sheik Suleiman el Helzel is a legendary figure: he and his seventeen wives still live in tents, but he exchanged the camel for a Cadillac a long time ago. He is said to have more than one hundred children. One afternoon he saw a beautiful Bedouin girl walking along the road, told his driver to stop the car, and he asked the girl: "Would you like to join Sheik Suleiman's harem?"

"I can't, Papa," the girl answered.

A new lamb

AN ISRAELI visitor to Moscow was taken to the zoo, where his Intourist guide showed him with pride how the Russians did succeed in fulfilling one of the great prophecies of the Bible: there they were, a wolf and a lamb—together.

The Israeli was dumbfounded: "How do you do this?" he asked.

"Very simple," the Russian answered. "Every morning we give him a new lamb."

The lamented enemy

ONE OF the reasons for the growing boredom of the American housewife is that this society has taken away her natural enemies. For many years the housewife had a daily tilt with the butcher, for instance. And a most welcome bit of warfare it was. She looked forward to it even though she knew she would always lose. She would say to the butcher, "How come you gave me all that gristle yesterday?" The butcher grunted or opened his face in a display of wide surprise and shock at this betrayal of trust. But his histrionics never fooled the housewife.

She would make her new order and when the butcher began to cut it, she would stretch on her tiptoes and watch him with suspicious eyes. After he had cut away some meat and was prepared to weigh it, she would interrupt him. "No, never mind those cuts. Now start cutting."

She played the same high-spirited game with the grocer and the fruit peddler. Before eggs came blindly sealed in packages, there was a time when she held each egg up to the light.

Now there is no one to complain to, unless it's the clerk who didn't count out the appropriate number of trading stamps.

No housewife has figured out how to complain to a laundromat or an automatic vending machine. And, as I have said before, if babies came in packages like meat and cheese and apples do, the world would be full of waifs.

Some notes in passing

PUBLISHERS OF recent years seem to avoid the subject of poor people on the grounds that rich people are more interesting. The last *good* stories I read about rich people were *Pride and Prejudice* and *Hamlet*. In truth the best way to understand life is to live with the poor or with the insane. The common denominator they have is their humanity and because it is often all they have, they cherish it.

*　　*　　*

About the only professional who welcomes the drunk is the prostitute. Not only can a clever prostitute get payment two or three times from a drunk but sometimes she doesn't have to work at all, a secret both she and the drunk share.

*　　*　　*

Man is resourceful. He has always found a way. If there were ten billion people on earth instead of three, the drive for individual self-esteem would be that much more interesting.

*　　*　　*

There was a time when, if they wrote home at all, college students wrote, "Dear Dad: Please send money." All of that is changed. Students write home more frequently than heretofore but their letters read: "Dear Dad: Please send me a new tire for the Corvette."

*　　*　　*

The saloon is one of history's most decent institutions. Certainly it is far more decent than the pitch-black cocktail lounge, fit for assignations of the most sordid sort, or the speakeasies which from time to time proliferate in Charlotte.

*　　*　　*

Genteel philandering is much like our epidemic genteel alcoholism, you have to be quite successful to indulge it on a continuing basis. The ponies do more to devastate artistic talent and managerial enterprise than all the ladies throughout history ever did.

*   *   *

The *India Illustrated News* isn't widely read in this country, but it is a fresh, bright publication. Even its advertisements are instructive. Did you happen to know that under that exotic, luxurious sari there is a Maidenform bra?

*   *   *

There are always parents who exert pressures to prevent marriages, mixed or not. Wise children pay no attention to it. Nothing calms parents and dignifies them like a grandchild.

*   *   *

When Sigmund Freud left Clark University in New York to go home to Vienna, he remarked that America's great experiment was the liberation of its women. He didn't think it would work, though.

*   *   *

Americans fear death. Most Americans believe that if they live long enough, all the mistakes and sins of the past will dissolve themselves. Longevity is the ace in the hole all Americans hope they hold.

Parents and communication

ALL OVER the country I notice the lack of communication between parents and teen-agers. I don't mean teen-agers and parents don't communicate. I mean I, the guest, never see or hear the communication.

I hear parents tell their children, "Take a pill," and "Go to bed," and "Be sure and brush your teeth," and I hear children say, "I need eleven dollars," and "I want to use the telephone," and "I don't want to go to bed," and that's the end of it.

Real communication between parents and children takes place in those homes where the guest never sees the kids.

In my day, when a kid paraded out to play the piano for Mommy and Daddy's friends, you knew it was an unhappy home.

Tip to the lovelorn

I ONCE printed a letter from a girl who asked me what to do because her boyfriend disappeared leaving all his shirts, socks, and two pairs of pants at her apartment. I wrote her, "Honey, don't do anything about *him*. Just find another man who can wear the same size shirts, socks and pants."

Strategy for a crackdown

As LONG as I can remember I have heard sex myths. More than twenty fellows have told me how when they were young, out hitchhiking, three beautiful girls came by in a convertible and . . .

I have heard the story of the young boy and the middle-aged lady in the barn . . .

I have even heard the story of the brothel manned by local housewives . . .

Except the last was not a myth. For indeed the New York police busted up such a scandalous ring out on Long Island near the racetrack. I can only hope these hausfrau-madams don't give the betting ponies a bad name.

The cops in a city near Charlotte, North Carolina, have also heard that myth about the moonlighting housewives and for many years considered it just that. Nowadays they are searching the dark alleys high and low, trailing all housewives not carrying shopping bundles.

Far be it from me to give advice to police officers but the cops down here are on the wrong track. It seems from all reports that one or two of the ladies up in New York had husbandly consent. While milady was out adding to the family exchequer to buy another kitchen appliance, hubby was home tending the kids. The New York and North Carolina cops ought not to be looking for marauding non-shopping housewives but rather for dishwashing, baby-sitting husbands.

Get ready to live to 120

A SWEDISH authority on geriatrics, Dr. Carl Olson, declares that to take care of one aged person properly the services of five younger people are required. Many of these younger people can have some degree of disability and need not have high school diplomas. Patience, goodwill, a sense of humor, a sense of responsibility, are invaluable in caring for the elderly. When the old people are all properly cared for, jobs will be available for many who have become victims of technological unemployment.

Dr. Olson says living to be 120 will not be unusual, and we should get ready for it. Living to the age of Moses will present problems.

Knishes for the Chinese

THERE WAS a story in *The New York Times* not long ago about the youth of New York City's Chinatown. Under one of the accompanying photographs was the caption: *Chinese children readily develop a liking for American foods*. The children were at a stand bearing the inscription: KNISHES—15 CENTS.

There was a time when we immigrants thought that we could become Americans quicker if we discarded everything that belonged to us as Jews.

I'll admit that it is a matter of hindsight, but now I know how completely wrong we were.

Think of our advantages—knishes—varnishkas—blintzes—holishkas—sweet and sour meat balls—potatonik—and luckshen kugel.

We threw these things overboard like idiots, and deprived not only other Americans but ourselves.

America's two million truck drivers would today defend us to the death if they could stop off at a road café and order kasha varnishkas and coffee.

The kept lady

THE "kept lady" lived out her days on the quiet back street and is no more. The girls are all busy building up their own social security accounts and aren't waiting around.

The "kept lady" and the "lady under the protection of" were not the same. The protected lady was usually the social equal of the protecting male, the kept lady was usually of lower social strata. Each lady, regardless of social position, had a little dog, a canary, and a few house plants to take care of.

Other women had children, in-laws, and varied responsibilities, but the kept lady had only her poodle, her canary, and her petunias.

In many cases a warm friendship existed between the kept lady and her provider, a loyalty that sometimes left his family with the embarrassment of what to do about the inconsolable lady at Daddy's funeral.

In most cases a middle-aged uncle would figure out a solution and the kept lady kept her poodle, canary and petunias.

Shallow yesteryear

THERE ARE fifty percent more symphony orchestras than a decade ago and sale of classical records has jumped seventy-eight percent in the past three years. People took 6,700,000,000 books from public libraries last year, and millions more people are visiting museums than ten years ago. Many of these millions are young people who go hand in hand through museums, have dates to meet at the public library and enjoy companionship with good music as an accompaniment. They smile when their parents say they courted while they danced the Big Apple, and were crazy about boogie-woogie. It all seems very quaint to the young people.

No hiding place

SENATOR EDWARD V. LONG, the Missouri Democrat, recently presided over a hearing that sounded like the best science fiction, but is disturbingly factual.

Electronic experts described a transmitter that could be hidden in an olive, its tiny aerial doubling for a toothpick.

This contrivance takes all the freewheeling fun out of cocktail parties—who will know whether the pretty blonde snuggling close, glass in hand, is Operative 007 1/8 recording what he really thinks of the boss, the old crumb, or how cute he was figuring that schedule of depreciation for income tax purposes, or that his wife doesn't understand him. The dry martini proves there is no hiding place down here.

Why I believe in pride

EVEN THOUGH I know it is one of the deadly sins, I believe in pride in accomplishment, in family, in associations, in self. I do not wish to go Freudian on my readers, I do not know enough about it, but I believe the bigot is possessed of self-hatred.

I do not mean pride with a chip on the shoulder, or arrogance, or snobbery.

I think when we exercise this right to be proud of ourselves we have enough to spare to spread it around to others.

Plans for expansion

GOVERNOR EDMUND G. BROWN of California has opened an inquiry into why only one percent of working women earn over ten thousand dollars compared to thirteen percent of men. The Governor is puzzled but any woman can set him straight. She does not go out for the big money job for herself, being content to forego her ten thousand dollars a year and put the energy the job would take in rearing three sons who will each make over ten thousand dollars. She won't settle for less than thirty thousand dollars a year, is the way she looks at it.

The war on poverty

OUTSIDE the high school where I'm to speak are parked over 200 automobiles, all makes—Chevrolets, Plymouths, Fords, Jaguars—and station wagons. Some of the girls will go from the school to the beauty shop. Some of the boys will go home and

send their dinner jackets out to the cleaners, all this in prepara-
tion for the dance the following Saturday.

It would be extremely difficult to convince these boys and
girls that in my own lifetime I saw a mother take her handmade
shawl to the pawnshop to borrow a dollar in order to buy food
for her family.

What's life with no post office?

THERE USED to be a popular quiz about desert islands.
What would you take to a desert island if you could take only
one thing? One bright girl apparently ended the whole thing by
the logic of her request. She said she would take an ob-
stetrician. But the best answer is to take one United States post
office with Flag flying high and plenty of postage stamps.

The Pacific Union Club

THE Pacific Union Club in San Francisco is perhaps the
most famous of the private luncheon clubs in America.

One of the anecdotes I have heard about it comes from a
respected businessman of the city.

He is Jewish and his head auditor is a Christian. They have
worked together amicably for thirty years. Occasionally, they
leave the office together and go downtown. The auditor always
asks his boss to let him off at the Fairmont Hotel to meet relatives. And the boss long ago first stopped the car a block away
and through his rearview mirror watched his auditor sneak across
the street to the Pacific Union Club. A Jew is not welcome as a
member. The auditor is a good man. He's ashamed to ask his
Jewish employer to drop him off at the Club.

The more things a man is ashamed of, the closer he is to nobility.

The family of man

WHEN A child was ill, seriously ill, your mother always said, "*Mirr farr dirr,*" meaning "Me, instead of you." As you lay sick with pneumonia your mother kept chanting this phrase over and over, that if anything serious were destined to happen to you, it should happen to her instead.

This idea runs through the folklore of most races and peoples of the world and is symbolically dramatized by the old story of the boy who killed his mother and was carrying her heart and tripped and her heart spoke out, "Did you hurt yourself, my son?"

Another famous phrase was "*Meine kinder zultst du habben,*" "My children—you should have," which was her way of scolding you when you did not show proper respect or obedience. Or, "A *zay rett minn tsu a mommen?*" "Such a way you talk to a mother?" It was never "your mother," but rather in general terms—"a mother." She meant all mothers; the family of man.

Are scientists dull?

OUT AT the Stanford Research Institute there was a terrible wrangle between the boss scientist and his subordinate. The subordinate was suing the boss for two hundred ten thousand dollars, alleging that his work had suffered because the boss seduced his wife.

Two hundred and ten thousand dollars is enough to tax the ingenuity of any scientist and the boss replied in suit that he had no legal duty not to seduce the said subordinate's wife. Which is, indeed, one way of looking at it.

Up until 1939, said the boss, the California laws said he did have a duty not to seduce anybody else's wife. But then California removed seduction from the criminal code and at the same time unleashed the scientific mind.

Research, they call it.

The last sad rite

WHEN A beloved friend or relative dies, the funeral is very sad, but it is usually in the hands of trained people and is not so poignantly painful as the most final rite, cleaning out the desk of the departed.

The little things that expressed his personality—the trinkets, clippings, mementos, even a crumpled candy wrapper—express everything we found lovable and unique. Clearing away these things is the final farewell.

The attempted murder of James Meredith

WHAT THE bigots do not understand is that James Meredith, the Negro who integrated the University of Mississippi, loves the South. He loves Mississippi. The guilt of the white segregationist is so great he cannot understand this. Probably he will never understand it. All they could bring themselves to understand was that Meredith wanted to make trouble.

Without publicity, accompanied by a few friends, Meredith wanted to walk through his home state to help banish fear. On the first day, a murderer tried to kill him. That murderer, Aubrey Norvell, was one with the men who killed the three civil rights workers, with the men who murdered the children in that Birmingham church, with the assassins who have planted another 147 bombs in Negro homes and churches since 1954. These men are not really concerned with the South, nor with the South they imagine once was, nor even with maintaining racial segregation. They are simply consumed with hatred, so consumed they have advanced the cause of the Negro civil rights movement by at least a decade. Without them and their blood lust, it might have taken the United States of America at least another ten years to enact the civil rights legislation already enacted.

I heard a President of this country admit as much. When some civil rights leaders thanked the late John F. Kennedy for the proposals he had sent to the Congress to advance Negro equality, this young President said an amazing thing: "Bull Connor's dogs in Birmingham had as much to do with it as I did."

In 1956, in Savannah, I heard Dr. Martin Luther King tell an assembly of dedicated Negroes who were about to go into the field, "Always make sure you travel with a white civil rights worker. Remember they *look* for white bodies."

Fortunately, they now look for Negro bodies. They look for Negro bodies now because the whole country is on the search.

Is there a God?

JERRY LAWRENCE, playwright (*Auntie Mame, Inherit the Wind, Only in America*), tells a story of the new, fantastic IBM computer. The scientists gathered around and asked the machine the one big question uppermost in their minds: "*Is there a God?*" The answer came back: "There is—*now.*"

PART 2

Melodies of the Ghetto

Avenue M and the lark

YEARS AGO, I was riding a bus in Brooklyn on the way to see a girl who, if she hadn't lived so deep in Oyster Bay, would have been the mother of my children. The bus paused on the corner of Avenue M and Sheepside Street. On the corner stood a funeral home with the name MALLORY's spelled out along the canopy. The awnings on the window bore the emblem M.

At the back of the bus, a little boy turned to his father and asked, "Does that say 'M' because it's Avenue M?"

I would have said yes although at the time I was childless. But the father simply grunted "No." And that was that for scientific inquiry. I suppose the kid became an eventual dropout. This is one of the reasons there are more psychiatrists on any given block in New York City than there are in the whole of France.

I remember this incident when I was rereading Myra Kelly's *Little Citizens*, which recounts the adventures of an Irish lady schoolteacher among the new Jewish immigrants in 1905 or so. What makes one of Miss Kelly's teachers despair is the confusion the class one day suffers when a little boy confuses skylarks with lager beer.

"My papa, he has a lark. It's from a tin lark mit a cover. Und it's got a handle too. Und my papa he takes it all times on the store for buy a lark of beer."

Rivington Street

I WAS raised just off Rivington Street, the main thoroughfare of the Lower East Side of New York. Public School 20 covered one whole block of Rivington Street; across the street was the University Settlement House; two branch libraries were not far away. Carl Sandburg wrote a poem about Rivington Street and the pushcarts that lined both sides of this mile-long avenue.

Precisely because thousands of immigrants walked this street on their way into the open society, I have always thought that Rivington Street is what America is all about.

Rivington Street, originally Rivington Place, took its name from James Rivington, printer, publisher and bookseller who set up his establishment at a time when the Lower East Side was the center of New York's colonial life. Mr. Rivington was the arch Tory of the Revolutionary War.

In his newspaper, the *Gazetteer*, and later in his *Royal Gazette*, he published every conceivable calumny and libel against General Washington and the Colonial army. He had wide influence in British-occupied New York, and Tories in the other colonies sought to read his treasonable publications. In his book, *Prelude to Independence*, the late Arthur M. Schlesinger, Sr. (Vantage, 1958), quotes a letter from Governor Livingston of New Jersey to Gouverneur Morris: "If Rivington is taken, I must have one of his ears; Governor Clinton [of New York] is entitled to the other; and General Washington, if he pleases, may take his head."

Rivington was not vivisected. When the British left New York, James Rivington left with them. By the time Washington entered the city to be inaugurated President of the United States, Rivington was selling books in London.

The city began to grow in all directions, to become the largest metropolitan center in the world. The American patriots did not change the name of the street.

In fact, the Founding Fathers went to great pains to preserve Rivington's anti-American tracts. This to me has always been the most noble expression of the American Idea.

No one knows what Rivington thought on his sea voyage to England, behind him a victorious Washington and a new nation.

One thing he did not think of or even suspect was that, eventually on the site where he published his *Gazette*, there would one day stand a mikvah, the ritual bath for the immigrant Jewish women.

Birth and the Evil Eye

I REMEMBER that among Orthodox Jews nobody but the mother, father, and grandmother were supposed to look at the newly born child. If anyone else did see the kid, he was required to spit three times and say, "No Evil Eye."

If a weakly or sickly child was born, its parents gave it a nickname like Alter (which means "old") so it could live out its years by confusing the Evil Eye. Or the child could be called Chaim (which means "life") and by the same logic fool the Evil Eye. Another trick was to change the name of the child so that when the Angel of Death came it would not know whether it was taking on the right passenger.

Ess, ess, mein kindt was the basis of the Jewish upbringing. *Eat, eat, my child.* Here was a clear identification of food with survival. The greatest compliment a visitor could pay a new mother was to attempt to lift the child and say, "The baby is so heavy, I cannot lift it."

Recollections of an alumnus

THE Alumni Association of my Public School 20 on the Lower East Side of New York has just unveiled a memorial on the new building. It is a record of the graduates who made their way in the world, including Paul Muni, Edward G. Robinson, George and Ira Gershwin, Irving Caesar, Irving Maidman, Charles H. Silver, Edwin Goldwasser, and hosts of doctors, dentists, judges, writers, and big businessmen.

There is a strange fascination that grows on men who have come from the Lower East Side of New York. We did everything we could in our youth to escape the grinding poverty, the overcrowding, and the filth, but in our middle age we remember the ghetto with fondness.

Simpson's Pawn Shop, with its pendulous three gold balls, had a side entrance where the carriage trade from uptown could enter unseen and pawn heirloom silverware or necklaces after a tough day at the races. There was Lyons Restaurant on the Bowery and at one of the tables the fire commissioner sat every day, drinking. A little fire alarm on the table alerted him to fires in all five boroughs and outside in a red Winton, an automobile of the day, sat his chauffeur, ready to drive him at a moment's notice.

Opposite this restaurant was Dr. Kahane's Museum, where young fellows looked at posters portraying the female anatomy. A look-see at these posters cost a dime, probably the very dime a mother had handed over so a kid could go look for work. "Here's a dime, go look for a job," was a perpetual refrain along the Lower East Side.

After a tour of Dr. Kahane's the kids rushed over to Dr. Smith, whose advertisements in the museum promised a ready cure for acne. Smith got three dollars for three doses of distilled water and the kids still had their acne.

Our neighbors on the Lower East Side were the Italians. I have always had a deep affection for Italians because I remember the charm and gaiety of Little Italy. At least once a month during all these fifty-five years I recall to mind the little Italian girls dancing on the sidewalk while an organ grinder poured out the tarantella dance music. In Little Italy, a stillborn infant rated a complete funeral with white hearse and six white horses and a twenty-piece band playing "Flee Like a Bird to the Mountains."

On the patron saints' day, the statues of St. Anthony, St. Rocco, and Santa Lucia made their appearances outside the churches on thrones where the poor came to pay homage and leave their donations: bread, candles, a few pennies, sometimes a paper dollar. It was in this neighborhood that the famous detective Petrosino lived and worked. Petrosino was an enemy of

the Mafia and he jailed hundreds of hoodlums who exacted
protection from immigrant peddlers, laborers, and small merchants. He went to Italy to bring back a captured criminal but
the Mafia murdered him there. His death caused a great mourn-
ing throughout Little Italy and the Jews also grieved for
Petrosino, the man who was killed performing his duty.

Kids and blades of grass

EVERY ONCE in a while I receive a letter from a distant
land in which the correspondent is fascinated by my little story
about the Lower East Side kids who counted the blades of grass
between the cracks in the sidewalk. Is it an apocryphal story,
asks the letter writer? Is it symbolic?

Indeed not. During summer vacation we rushed out to the
street to water our blades of grass. We did indeed count them
in competition with other kids.

> The grass is up, my twenty-two blades
> Between one of the cracks in the sidewalk.
> I count them every day, it's lots of fun
> In front of Eldridge—one-seventy-one.

I wrote this poem during summer vacation, at the age of ten.
We lived at 171 Eldridge Street between Rivington and
Delancey streets. Several of us were in competition as to who
could grow more blades of grass.

I brought the poem to Miss Tibbitt's class when school
started again in September, 1913. She put it on the bulletin
board. Students and teachers read it.

The great thing in this story is that the plants did sometimes
crack the sidewalk. In retrospect I can see it suggests the people
in the ghetto who crashed out of their limited environment and
one way or another found a place in the sun.

There was the enjoyment of sharing and of each other's company in those days, and of storing up memories.

Mr. Unterman, Mr. Zwilling, and Mr. Schmier

I was impressed with the American Dream at an early age, even in the midst of poverty.

There was Mr. Unterman. He used to go around hauling in a little wagon, calling, "Rags, bottles," over and over again. The kids would approach him with the hoarded bottles and some old clothes and Mr. Unterman would pay us a few pennies and we had enough to see Bronco Billy Anderson at the local movie. Mr. Unterman went on to do pretty well when he opened a store years later. A grandson of his is a scientist at Cape Kennedy. This country never lost anything on Mr. Unterman and his offspring.

There was Mr. Zwilling, too, a friend of my father's, who peddled fruit from a pushcart. He never did well. The fruit spoiled when Mr. Zwilling found someone who would discuss theology with him. Every once in a while in the course of discussion he would take a nip from a bottle of slivovitz (plum brandy) he kept hidden under a piece of oilcloth. He once told me it was impossible to be a truly Orthodox Jew. He spoke with sadness because he felt it would be nice to be a truly Orthodox Jew, but there were so many laws and rules that it was impossible. But Mr. Zwilling was aware he should try a little harder. With this resolve he would take another little swig of slivovitz and sigh. Mr. Zwilling told me all these things not because he thought I understood but because he did not want to be talking to himself, which he was, of course.

There was Mr. Schmier with his little tailoring store. He did alterations and pressing and worked at his ironing board early and late. He was a lonely man who was glad a kid hung around for a minute to hear him out. He told me once that one of his shoulders was higher than the other because he had ironed ever since he was eight years old. His meals were hurried—and ascetic; a piece of fish and a slice of rye bread. Mr. Schmier was a dull man, ironing away in his dark little shop, but I knew a secret about him. His face would light up as beautifully as that of a bridegroom when he talked about his son, Morton.

Morton was away in college, learning to be a lawyer. The scanty meals the father ate, the long hours of work, were all for Morton. Some years later I read that Morton Schmier was up at Albany, the state capital, fighting to get a law passed to make it impossible for manufacturers to sell imitation ice cream as the real thing.

I looked up Morton Schmier, and told him about my friendship with his father. The man was touched. He told me his father had lived to eighty-six surrounded by loving grandchildren in a comfortable home.

What kind of sentimentality and nostalgia am I talking about with these true stories of Mr. Unterman, Mr. Zwilling, and Mr. Schmier?

We might as well say the story of Winston Churchill's battle for Britain was sentimentality. In a sense Mr. Unterman and Mr. Zwilling and Mr. Schmier were expending blood, sweat and tears; for them it was an epic struggle to provide for those who were to come after them.

The retirement of Hymie

THE Jewish Court of Arbitration was set up by the immigrant Jews some seventy years ago. Since its establishment, it has saved the State of New York many millions of dollars because the Jewish litigants who come to Arbitration sign an agreement to abide by its decision. The Supreme Court of the State of New York has on several occasions upheld these agreements when losers have tried to back out. I have served on this board of arbiters two or three times and on one of these stints I read the story of Uncle Hymie, a sixty-nine-year-old widower.

Uncle Hymie was living in the lap of luxury, or at least what immigrant Jews considered luxury fifty years ago. He had a furnished room, paid for by his son and son-in-law, and an allowance of four dollars a week. His married son and his married daughter were poor people. The son worked as a pants presser and the son-in-law also labored in a sweatshop, and between them they didn't make fifty dollars a week. But they still shelled out seven dollars and fifty cents a week to support Uncle Hymie because of Uncle Hymie's threat: "I'll go to the Bowery Mission."

Uncle Hymie was highly intelligent and he had divined the great possibilities in what he called "this American Idea," as it was exemplified by the Bowery Mission. The threat of going there kept his children in a panic. For them it meant the shameful admission they had a father on charity, which in those days was a terrible tragedy. Then there was a second horror about the Mission, that of an elderly Jewish father singing the Bowery Mission's theme song: "What a Friend We Have in Jesus."

Hymie sported a cane, a beard trimmed like Robert E. Lee's, and was seen every pleasant afternoon disporting himself along the park, discussing with other old codgers the news about Tudder Roosevelt. He also thought himself something of a dramatic critic, and convinced many of his listeners that David Kessler was a greater actor than Jacob Adler. And many of the neighbors, looking upon him as a sage of sorts, asked his advice on sundry matters like, "Should I change jobs?" or "My daughter wants to use face powder . . . should I allow it?"

But the day came when son and wife, daughter and husband could take it no longer. They brought the old gent before the Arbitration Court and told their story of being held in virtual bondage because of Uncle Hymie's threat: "I will go to the Bowery Mission."

Four judges ruled that the four dollars' spending money should stop at once but that the young people should continue paying three dollars and fifty cents a week room and board until Uncle Hymie was admitted to the Jewish Home for the Aged, application to be made immediately. The Court, in fact, would draft a letter urging his speedy admission.

When Uncle Hymie scoffed at the ruling, the Court said it could play rough. If he persisted, the Court said, it would recommend his children apply to the New York Supreme Court to issue an order committing Uncle Hymie to a state institution. This was an "American Idea" of which Hymie had not heard. He accepted the first decision.

Uncle Hymie died in 1938 at the age of eighty-seven. During his eighteen years at the Jewish Home for the Aged, he was the envy of all because of the attention his son and daughter paid him and because his five grandchildren visited him often. He also continued his mission to convert everyone to the notion that David Kessler was greater than Jacob Adler.

The hotels in ambush

ONE BY one the famous hotels are dropping behind the New York horizon. They are falling like lonely settlers ambushed by Indians. The Savoy Plaza, on the east side of Fifth Avenue, is going. So too are the New Weston, the Madison, the Park Lane and the most famous of all, the Astor.

The major city newspapers have long been running commentaries upon the hotels' demise. They are not a profitable investment since rehabilitation costs are so high. The land they occupy can be more profitably utilized for offices. Little can be done to save these places. The great hotels are simply a reminder of another way of life. The Hotel Association has reminded us that once upon a time a businessman spent three or four days in the city settling his accounts. Now he flies in and flies out the same day. People do not use railroads and check in at the nearest hotel. They come by plane or car and use a more convenient motel.

It is more than a pity that so many of these elegant places

crumble under the wrecker's ball and are replaced by office build-ings with papier-mâché walls and imitation marble lobbies.

But I am an old hotel man and I remember those days. The Markwell Hotel was not fancy. It was not well-appointed. But, as I have mentioned often before, some great actors lived there and some wonderful people occupied its rooms. In the depths of the Depression, there were actors and actresses who found refuge in the Markwell and bided their time until things im-proved (i.e., a job on Federal Theatre Project or a social work-er's position out in Akron—and for the lucky few, a Hollywood contract).

But that kind of acting life has vanished, too. By the time a young singer is nineteen, the theatrical agencies and the movie operators and the television directors all know whether or not he or she will be a star. One role in an off-Broadway show is enough to make an assessment on actors these days. And the actors themselves tell me they were able to gauge accurately very young whether they would spend their lives making com-fortable television commercials or whether they would be dra-matic performers. No one waits around anymore. The nature of modern society absolutely forbids indecision or vagueness about careers.

When I was a night clerk at the Markwell, around midnight I always adjourned with the policeman on the beat for a session of double-deck pinochle in the room off the lounge. Hotel work-ers today are college graduates and every moment behind the desk is filled with some duty. Every week, there are delegates from a convention where in the early 1930's we only saw Shriners and American Legionnaires and saw them only every three or four years.

They were better days. You didn't find two plastic glasses wrapped in sanitizing paper in your room; you rang room service and got a real glass and ice.

Election bonfires

IT'S BEEN many years since they had the big bonfires in the metropolitan cities on Election Night. It was the big event on the Lower East Side of New York. The bonfire was carefully planned weeks in advance. The kids from eight to twelve began to accumulate wooden boxes and every scrap of wood they could find in empty homes and sometimes in homes that weren't empty.

When the polls closed they built their fire. On Election Night the entire Fire Department was alerted and you heard the sirens and the fire bells all over the city far into the night. The kids started the fire, which was pretty big. The Fire Department put it out. But then the older fellows took over—the fellows between fifteen and twenty. They had vast stocks of lumber and they built the really big bonfire. In my day they had these bonfires on Delancey Street, which was probably the widest street on the East Side, and they were brilliant sights to behold.

The big bonfire on Election Night probably came from the English colonists who first settled America. I find that on the coronation of a new king there was always a huge bonfire, and while I'm not sure of this, nor have I ever seen the connection anywhere, it seems reasonable that the American English continued the bonfire when they were electing new Presidents instead of shouting, "Long live the King!"

Early memories

WHAT A thrill it was to see Thurston. I believe the act was called "The Great Thurston." I do not believe that any other magician had an act as dramatic as Mr. Thurston's in those days. Part of the thrill, too, was that we ordinarily saw few interesting things, and part of it was that we were young.

There was a cage suspended from the ceiling of the theatre on a heavy chain. In the cage was a woman playing the piano. From the stage, Thurston fired a rifle at the cage. When the smoke cleared there was no woman and there was no piano. Just an empty cage. Of course it was a trick but I still don't want to know how it was done. I'd rather remember it as it was.

Because of the tremendous role played by the Metropolitan Opera and the great singers, Caruso, Scotti, and others, there has been no writing on the lesser operatic troupes that came from Italy and performed at various theatres on the Bowery. It was opera at a dollar tops, and thousands of people who could not afford to stand in line to hear Caruso went. These operas had to be good. The singers came from small Italian cities where they wouldn't tolerate anything but major league opera.

There was the Windsor Theatre not far from the Thalia, where I saw Thurston. The Windsor Theatre played melodramas such as *Nellie, the Beautiful Cloak Model,* and *Bertha, the Sewing Machine Girl,* and *King of the Opium Ring.* Some of us got in free because we distributed posters to stores. If a man put the poster in his window we gave him a ticket, and for our work we received two tickets and ten cents.

Chuck Conners was the mayor of Chinatown. He wore a pearl derby and a pearl-gray suit and had pearl buttons. For a fee he would take the tourists on through the opium dens of Chinatown. Three or four elderly Chinese lay around with pipes in their mouths looking ominous. After the tourists went out, the Chinese brushed themselves off and went back to the produce store where they were packing chow-mein mix to be shipped around the country.

A half-mile farther up on the Bowery was beautiful Atlantic Beer Garden for the Germans who had already entered our middle class. They came in horse-drawn phaetons and threw you a dime for watching the horse. These big fat men and their portly women sat inside for hours eating the schnitzel and drinking Rhine wine.

Each place had a special clientele. Steve Brodie's saloon on the Bowery was the hangout for newspapermen. The Occidental Saloon was where the Tammany politicians met—Charlie Murphy, Sheriff Jim Culkin, Pat McCarren, and Jimmy Hines. Farther uptown was another saloon, frequented by a handsome song-and-dance man named Jimmy Walker of the Huron Tammany Club.

Canfield's was the most famous of all gambling houses in New York. I once owned an authentic set of ivory poker chips that Canfield used. I befriended an elderly woman who was all alone when she was taken to Bellevue. She was a guest at the Hotel Markwell where I was a clerk. After she died, one of her friends took care of her effects and found a note in which she said that for my kindness I should have the Canfield chips.

Miner's Burlesque Theatre was along the Bowery on Delancey Street. Some of the people we knew in our time performed there: Bert Lahr was one of them; Eddie Cantor worked there once as a stooge for a juggling team, Bendini and Arthur. Eddie was a blackface comic. At Miner's also appeared Maggie Cline singing "Throw Him Down McCloskey" and "Who Threw the Overalls in Mrs. Murphy's Chowder?"

On the fire escapes of the tenements in the Italian district were signs reading MIDWIFE and in the Jewish districts there were two signs—one, MIDWIFE and another, MOHEL (Circumciser). There were also plenty of witch doctors. This is by way of advising my readers that we Jews are quite normal, like everybody else. Everybody in history had witch doctors. So did we.

An old aunt lived with us shortly after she arrived from Roumania. She must have been in her late eighties and I remember a witch doctor sitting by her bedside when she was very ill. The witch doctor recited all sorts of incantations, pasting amulets around the pillows and on the curtains and windows. The family's idea was to get her out of there before the doctor came. We merely indulged the old aunt, but in an enlightened household the presence of the witch doctor could be embarrassing. But one time our verein doctor, Dr. Julius Frankel, came to see the old aunt before we could get the witch doctor out. He was a great man, Julius Frankel—he knew. He said, "Let her be. The old woman has pneumonia and right now the witch doctor can do her as much good as I can." Those were the days when you waited for "the crisis." That's all science could do at the time—wait for the crisis.

The coal stove

THE BLACK coal stove was a kitchen fixture in the homes of the Lower East Side of New York. Since those days, there have been innumerable jokes about keeping coal in the bathtub, but this indeed is where it was stored in many homes, including my own.

Bathtub installations were innovations back then. We didn't always need the bathtub because we had become accustomed to other facilities. Every neighborhood had a fair share of public baths provided by the settlement houses.

There was the public *mikvah*, the ritual baths for the women; and Turkish baths proliferated throughout the whole section. Once a week I went with my father to the Katz's Turkish Baths. A few years ago, in Copenhagen, I went to the hotel's baths and after a few minutes in the steam room, I climbed to the top bench. The attendant was deeply concerned and tried to wave me down, worried about the intense heat the higher you go. But I was accustomed to it from my days in the steam room of Katz's Baths.

Washtubs were most commonly used for baths at home. The bathtub, in the first few decades of its life, was a luxury. Instead of keeping coal in the burlap bag in which it arrived in fifty-pound lots, we dumped it into this most convenient container.

Above the black iron stove was a shelf where my mother and countless others kept the can of Vulcan Stove Polish. The black brush had bristles on both sides, one with which to apply the polish and the other for rubbing.

We always kept one of the lids unpolished. This was for toast. We made toast before any of us had ever heard the word. A heavy slice of rye bread on the lid and on top of the bread a heavy flatiron. You turned it over when the first side was done and then we spread *schmalz* (chicken fat) on the toasted bread and rubbed garlic on the crust. A dandy meal.

Melodies of the ghetto

How RIGHT Oscar Levant was to recognize *Porgy and Bess* as the great American Jewish Opera. While I am no musician or musicologist, the voices and sounds I heard all my life still perambulate through my head. Much of Gershwin's music I heard in the Jewish ghetto of New York City.

There were beggars on the Lower East Side of New York in the days of mass migration from the pogroms in Europe. There was one special beggar who stood on the corner of Stanton and Orchard streets every Friday. Before the Sabbath, people sought him out to drop a coin in his hand. After all, they needed him more than he needed them. Charity on the eve of the Sabbath is a good deed recorded in heaven. This elderly beggar repeated a phrase over and over in a singsong voice: *Shenkts a nidduvah, yiddishe kinder!* (Be charitable to me, ye children of Israel!) That phrase was identical to the first two bars of "Summertime."

Pasteles Calientes

JOE BERNSTEIN was probably the first Jewish prizefighter and he owed his fame to the fact that he was able to stay in the ring for fourteen rounds with Terry McGovern. Bernstein's father was a pious man with a patriarchal beard who was always

in Joe's corner. The old gent never took his derby hat off because
he did not want the crowd to see the yarmulka (skullcap) which
he wore beneath it. It was Joe's father who coined the phrase,
"Hit him in the *kishkes* [stomach]."

Years later, even when an Irishman like Slattery was fighting
a Pole like Sharkey, you heard the cry from the balcony, "Hit
him in the kishkes."

Miner's Burlesque Theatre on the Bowery had Sliding Billy
Watson. Also such famous teams as Smith and Dale, the Em-
pire City Quartet, Weber and Fields, Eugene and Willie
Howard, and Bert Lahr.

Mr. Miner was a decent man. He permitted the amateur con-
testant to remain on stage long enough to pick up all the coins
thrown to him by the audience before removing him by means
of a long hook.

Now I hear many good people in New York complain about
the Negroes and the Puerto Ricans—their bad-smelling tenements, they hang the wash out on the line, they leave the baby
carriages in the hallways, and I answer: "That's what they said
about *your* mother forty years ago."

The names on the mailboxes have changed but the human
story remains the same—hope and the drive for self-esteem
and a better life.

On Delancey Street where I was raised there is now a hot dog
stand with the advertisement, PASTELES CALIENTES, which
means, "Puerto Rican knishes."

The boy adults

THE JEWISH BOY of my era, like the peasant boy and the
boy of the lower economic classes of all eras and of all national-
ities, was turned loose on the world almost immediately after
he was weaned. A Jewish boy became a member of the congregation at thirteen, but he had already savored much of the adult
world for at least six years before that. He listened to all the

talk and often participated in the important decisions of the family.

What would have happened to me and to every Jewish, Irish, Italian and Polish boy of my generation had we suddenly announced to our mothers, "We ain't happy"? No mother would have comprehended such a statement. If finally one mother did understand what the boy meant, she would have taken whatever she was cooking and dumped it over the kid's head.

Conceivably there was a mother who said, "My son is unhappy because he has to use crutches," but she would have been, at that, an ultrasensitive mother.

Sex existed. But there was no overpowering Biblical sense of guilt about it. We all saw the book *Man's Mission on Earth*, soft black cover, one dollar, and we all read it and hid it and passed it on. Sex was in the brothel on Fourteenth Street. While there is no doubt that sex figured prominently in marital plans, it was not troublesome.

All the boys I knew—and I mean *all*—made their own decisions. At fourteen or fifteen, a boy told his parents, "I think I'll go to law school," or "I intend to stay in the hat factory and become a salesman."

Today's fictional hero can make no decision or make only wrong ones. I think that is because our novelists do not recognize that the bourgeoisie has dealt itself a new hand. Like the clerk and the manager, the college professor does not feel guilty when he seduces the dean's wife. He is much more worried about his tenure, his scholarly publications, and whether or not he should sign his name to a "Stop Escalation in Vietnam" petition.

No one in the middle class is scandalized about sex. They are scandalized and scandalous only when they set out to defend their status and their property. The American nightmares are about collective bargaining, calories and Communism, probably in that order, with body odor not far behind.

The Jewish bourgeoisie is, of course, doubly exposed. That is the Jew's burden. He is a capitalist and a Jew, a radical and a Jew, a banker and a Jew. This double exposure is all-important and it forever contributes to his sense of alienation. In the affluent society, the Jew has as many dilemmas as the Gentile, but he has several additional worries. Will he get into the Country Club? Will he be accepted as a Little League manager?

Or maybe I've been traveling around another planet for the past twenty years.

Broadway Rose

No ONE ever wrote a musical comedy about Broadway Rose, I suppose because she looked so seedy. Broadway Rose was an habitué of what we liked to call the Great White Way. She was, when I knew her, perhaps forty years old and so homely as to be interesting. She reminded me of Lion Feuchtwanger's Ugly Duchess who attracted men by virtue of being repulsive.

Broadway Rose wore shoes like Charlie Chaplin's and her stockings were always in tatters and hung unfashionably from her knees. The coat she wore in the winter smelled so that you were constrained to keep a breathing space of four yards between you and it. Her black hair straggled to her shoulders. She had everything in that hair except hairpins. She had no front teeth at all.

But she had invented a profession all her own. She would come into the lobby of a good but small hotel and plump herself in one of its upholstered seats and start waving one of those Chaplin shoes as she crossed her legs. She cleared out more lobbies faster than any fire that ever raged anywhere. When the desk clerk walked over and asked her to leave, she started hollering.

Since I was a desk clerk at the theatrical Markwell Hotel on Broadway at Forty-ninth Street for several years, I too was subjected to her fits. After a while you caught on to her system. You walked over and gave her a dollar and said, "Here, Rose. Now don't come back for a week." Invariably she lived up to her end of the bargain.

She also hung outside the chic restaurants and when some folks in evening clothes exited she would go up to the man, throw her arms around him and ask cozily, "Honey, where you been?" This gambit was good for a dollar at least, sometimes five. Any stubborness drove her to terrible extremes. If a fellow tried to disengage himself, Broadway Rose started screaming, "This is my husband who deserted me, who made me what I am today, who left me with four children, all with mouths to feed."

There were times when this touching scene attracted a crowd and often the people would start scolding the hapless fellow.

I signed a concordat with Broadway Rose. She agreed never to sit in the lobby if once a week I gave her a dollar when she approached the desk. I took the dollar out of petty cash and charged it off to public relations.

The worries were dandruff-free

ONE OF the television commercials that absolutely enthralls me shows a bride in her white gown brushing dandruff from her daddy's lapels. She is quite worried that these specks will doom her wedding, which obviously takes place soon.

Comes the morn and as the lissome bride descends the stairs on her way to the altar, newly installed in the living room, Daddy proudly points to his speck-free coat and daughter smiles happily and strides toward her groom, content and sure of her marriage.

I forget which lanolin syrup sponsors this happy epiphany, which I suppose means a million dollars' worth of copywriting down the drain, but I am wondering if the hair-oil manufacturers suppose this is literally the way things are. Or do they simply hold the television watchers in absolute contempt?

I have myself received invitations to weddings which assured
me that a hairdresser would be in attendance the day before
the ceremony at such and such a place.

Maybe I am wrong and the advertising agencies are right, but
if the bride no longer blushes at the prospect of her wedding
night, a lot of creative literature is out the window. Or maybe
the bride in this episode is only formalizing a relationship which
has existed for quite some time.

The television wedding surely isn't like the Jewish weddings
I remember from the Lower East Side of New York. The last
thing in anyone's mind was Daddy's dandruff. I have written
how everyone at a Jewish wedding cried but how everyone was
thinking of something else.

Daddy's big worry was controlling the neighborhood crashers
who would deplete the feast. By the time he married off
a daughter, the immigrant father had survived a battery of worries that would make modern worries over dandruff seem de-
lectable fantasies. To get the youngest girl, who was pretty, married, Daddy had to marry off her older sisters first and this was
no easy task. To get a plain daughter off your hands often meant
promising some serious fellow you'd help him get started in a
business of his own. You finance an inventory like that
and dandruff will never again occupy your thoughts.

And no matter how fortunate daughter was, still she came
home with an extra mouth to feed after the ceremony.

There were no honeymoons in those days. Couples didn't set
up by themselves. They moved in.

The landlord and the commissar

WE SHOULD be proud to call England the Mother Country. When a prime minister like Lord Home loses an election,
he remains in the House of Commons, the leader of the loyal
opposition. Unless a Presidential candidate holds elective office in America, once he loses he is out.

And in Russia, once you lose office you are dead. If not literally, you are dead in the sense that your name and your face and your term of office are simply erased from history, from the newspapers, from the billboards. This is not an easy thing to do. In fact, to accomplish this, the Russians terrify the world whenever a new leader ascends to power.

The only event comparable to changeover in the Kremlin that I can remember was when the landlord changed janitors along the Lower East Side of New York. Most of the landlords of the ghetto were absentee owners. The existing property was administered by a serf we all called the janitor. Usually, the janitor and his family occupied space on the ground floor, laughingly called an apartment. From there his power was as absolute as that of any commissar. He collected rent with the vengeance of a commissar collecting party dues. Undoubtedly, landlords instructed janitors in a prescribed set of duties. What they might have been, however, I cannot tell. As the janitor interpreted those instructions, they dictated that the tenants were never to disturb him.

He chased the kids who played stoopball. He chastised the housewives for their untidyness. He thundered against anyone brave enough to ask plumbing repairs. And when a new tenant was rash enough to move a piano into the tenement, the janitor went on a four-week sulk, like Mahatma Gandhi used to do when the British tried disciplining him.

Eventually, we tenants learned to live with him and keep peace. But then came the agonizing day when he was replaced. Maybe there was a burying ground for janitors like there supposedly is for elephants. At any rate, they used to disappear every decade or so and a new janitor moved in. He used to promise us a new five-year plan now that he had deposed our nemesis. The halls were going to be cleaner because every family was going to pitch in. There was going to be less noise because he could instruct mothers in the disciplining of errant children. Rent collections would be prompt because our new janitor swore he would make but one trip a month up the tenement stairs. We tried to grasp the change that came over our lives much like modern Russians, except we didn't have big parades to help accustom us to it. Ah, if we only had the parades!

My advice to Jewish college boys— become a rabbi

THERE WAS a time when everybody felt sorry for the rabbi, and sorrier still for the *rebbitzen*. The folks of the congregation brought food to the rabbi's house and the ladies of the sisterhood brought a made-over dress or a winter coat for the *rebbitzen*. Often the men spent Sunday doing volunteer repair work on the rabbi's bathroom fixtures or repairing his leaky cellar or plastering a hole in the wall. Those days are gone and gone forever.

By any vote of the sophisticated the best-dressed woman in the congregation today is the *rebbitzen*. Today the rabbi lives in an air-conditioned house and he has an air-conditioned car with cruise control and push-button windows with electric vents. He also has the latest stereo–hi-fi equipment so he can listen to a tape recording of the Torah portion for the following week. And now the rabbi brings food and stuff to his members. Often after a vacation trip he brings back cans of exquisite tidbits for the four or five members who had originally "called" him to the pulpit.

Recently one congregation passed a resolution, without opposition, to air-condition the rabbi's garage.

There was a time when the Orthodox would pray for one of their sons to become a rabbi. Of course this was at a time when learning and spiritual leadership marked status in the community.

Then there was a sharp decline. The boys wanted to be doctors or lawyers or sales managers or manufacturers. We live in a money economy and money is status rather than learning.

Now it will go back to the old days. Parents can take their son on a visit to the rabbi's house and whisper, "See, that's what I call living, get on with it, go to the seminary."

No more broken windows

THE REAL mischief we indulged in as kids, I suppose, was breaking windows during stickball games. Every now and then a foul ball curved with exactly the right velocity and the ball game and players evaporated. Since all of us were recognizable, that evening individually we all played George Washington: "I cannot tell a lie. Us Ludlow Streeters broke the window."

But I never hear of a broken window anymore. All the games for kids are organized now. Not that I want any little roughneck smashing mine, but it does seem a shame that not one window is ever broken anymore as the result of a batted ball.

I live on Elizabeth Avenue in Charlotte, North Carolina, which becomes the racetrack for the soap box derby in Charlotte in the late spring. Some of the judges station themselves on my porch and they always give me a pith helmet made of plastic on which is stamped SOAP BOX DERBY OFFICIAL.

On the Lower East Side we didn't have an organized soap box derby but we had races all the same. We used to tack a pretty solid two-by-four under an orange crate. We made a scooter out of this by screwing onto the two-by-four the front and back ends of a discarded roller skate. And we were off—trying to beat the trolley car to the crossing.

Life as a hotel clerk

SOME YEARS AGO, in *Only in America*, I wrote about Koppel Berger, my uncle who owned the old Hotel Normandie on

Broadway. Koppel Berger deserves more than an essay. If I were younger I would do a whole book on him. With a vocabulary of less than one hundred words of English he amassed a fortune in the hotel business.

On West Thirty-eighth Street, the Normandie was a theatrical hotel with about two hundred rooms. Koppel really started making money in 1914 when there were few hotels in the city. The big hotels that dot Midtown Manhattan now were nearly all built between the two world wars. In the days when Koppel obtained his first lease there were only two kinds of hotels: the very best—like the Waldorf, Plaza, Vanderbilt, Astor; and flophouses. One of the good ones between the two extremes was the Normandie, which advertised ACTORS ACCOMMODATED. In those days, the fancy hotels did not take on actors.

With World War I, the Normandie became a bonanza. Because it was patriotic, the fire inspectors allowed Koppel to fill the hotel halls with cots which he let to young soldiers pouring into New York City to report to the embarkation points.

One morning a weekly guest came down to the lobby and complained to Koppel that he had a lot of trouble exiting from his room that morning because a cot with a sleeping figure atop it blocked his way.

In a deeply considerate voice Koppel asked, "What room you have?"

"Room 314," said the man.

"Ralph," barked Koppel to his cashier, "Room 314 is checking oudt!"

The weekly guest grabbed his key from Koppel's fervid grasp and pleaded, "No, no, no. Please, everything is fine," and he made a hasty retreat.

Around this time my brother Jacob was also managing the Hotel Taft, not the big one now called the Manger, but a little theatrical house of sixty rooms on the corner of Sixth Avenue and Thirty-eighth Street. I believe it is still there or was the last time I passed through the neighborhood. I remember Bert Lahr lived there and so did Ed Wynn. I was just a kid then, over a half-century ago.

LIFE AS A HOTEL CLERK

It was my brother Jacob who literally gave currency to one of the famous New York wisecracks. One night a fellow came in for a room.

"That will be two dollars," said Jake.

"You've got a dollar and a half on your sign," complained the prospective guest.

"Go sleep on the sign," Jake answered.

In the early thirties I too was a hotel clerk at the Markwell, another theatrical house about one hundred feet west of Broadway on Forty-ninth Street. What always amazed me were the extremes to which some of the guests would go to get out of paying their room rent. Then there was the ingenuity of the family groups over Labor Day. They would steal you blind. Towels, sheets, and blankets are not too difficult to steal, but we always lost three or four medicine cabinets. How did they ever get them past the elevator man and room clerk? It was always a mystery.

I remember a guest who was the advance man for the rodeo or circus playing up the street in Madison Square Garden. He checked in and gave me an envelope with three hundred dollars to deposit in the hotel safe. During the next two weeks, the bellhops and outside bartenders and waiters made appearances at the desk with signed slips from this advance man instructing me to give the bearer ten dollars or fifteen dollars. Our guest was spending the money on booze up the street. (The hotel operated no bar or restaurant.)

He checked out two weeks later and his envelope contained nothing but signed slips for his three hundred dollars. I presented him his bill, the room at two dollars a night, which came to twenty-four dollars, and he stood at the desk and argued with me for an hour, insisting he should pay only $1.50 a night. He argued about a difference of six dollars after spending three hundred dollars on whiskey.

Believe it or not, a hotel clerk is engaged in a hazardous profession, one which demands he be alert. One night my relief man was behind the desk and I was sitting in the lobby when a girl came in and asked for a room. We took in single girls only if they were members of the National Vaudeville Artists or Actors Equity. We needed no identification for this one. We knew her. She was a Broadway streetwalker.

I nodded *no* to my relief man and he told her we were filled for the night. I thought she had not seen my signal but I suppose her profession trained her to see everything. She turned around and affably enough she said, "Harry, could I talk to you a minute?"

I walked toward her and when I was about a foot away from where she waited, still smiling as though readying herself for a plea, she swung that heavy pocketbook from her hip and fetched me one flush across my face.

Luckily the doctor at the Polyclinic Hospital saved my eye, though he had to remove a sliver of glass from my spectacles which had broken.

Under the clock

THE FIRM of Minskoff & Sons, which purchased the famous Hotel Astor of New York, got a real bargain. They paid a little less than eleven million dollars for sixty-five thousand square feet of land between Forty-fourth and Forty-fifth streets on Broadway. That is a rate of one hundred and sixty dollars a square foot. Once the Astor is razed, a forty-story office tower will take its place.

A few blocks to the east, the Hotel Sheraton East brought five hundred and twenty dollars a square foot. The price of twenty million encompassed only thirty-seven thousand, five hundred square feet.

In 1929, the Irving Trust Company, flushed with that gorgeous optimism of the late 1920's, paid seven hundred dollars a square foot for a plot of land at the corner of Wall Street and Broadway. This is the all-time high.

To come back to the Hotel Astor and Sheraton East,

although they are separated by five long city blocks, both hotels stand on land which once formed part of the Eden Farm, which included a substantial part of Midtown Manhattan.

William Waldorf Astor bought the Eden Farm in the early 1800's for one hundred and ten thousand dollars, lock, stock, and barrel.

The story of the Eden Farm has been told before by the American economist Henry George. Mr. George pointed out that the appreciation of the Eden Farm from one hundred and ten thousand dollars for its acreage to two, three, and four hundred dollars a square foot, was brought about by the increase in population, and not by anything the owners contributed. George called this the "unearned increment of land values" and proposed a single tax on such unearned increment.

The Astor has a great history. The girl I was dating lived in Elizabeth, New Jersey. I lived in the Bronx. Each week, by letter or by telephone, Rosie and I exchanged the immemorial directions: "I'll meet you under the clock." Those words were passed between hundreds of thousands of couples who were going to meet each other in Manhattan. "I'll meet you under the clock" meant "I'll meet you in the lobby of the Hotel Astor."

What Peacock Alley in the Waldorf-Astoria Hotel was to society ladies and Wall Street tycoons, "under the clock" was to ordinary folks—to the clerks, stenographers, housewives, their husbands, and high school seniors. And if you were really flush you had dinner on the Astor Roof where Ted Lewis doffed his battered top hat and yelled, "Is Everybody Happy?"

Once this area of New York was the most romantic and most glamorous place in the whole world. But in the 1940's it began to decline and soon the smaller merchants decorated Broadway with their soft drink stands, discount record stores, sexy bookshops, shooting galleries, and dance halls.

There is no need to spell it out but "under the clock" was no longer a fit place to meet a fiancée or a wife, and the folks began to go eastward or farther uptown—but it will never be the same.

Beer and clams

UP IN New York City the big drink is the egg cream. The egg cream is a combination of chocolate syrup, milk and seltzer; in reality it is a "for 2 cents plain" with the difference that, instead of a little on the top, it has a little on the top and a little on the bottom. The true secret of the frothy egg cream is freezing cold milk.

I have never had an egg cream in the South. Since many parts of the South have yet to catch up with rye bread, that is not surprising. The big drink down South is the shake. The shake consists of milk, ice cream, a powder of some kind, all blended together into a creamy thickness that is with some difficulty sipped through a big colored straw.

It is such differences that add spice and variety to our American way of life, particularly our politics. Although the hamburger is fast displacing the barbecue, every Southern politician sticks with barbecue. Perhaps this is because the friendly political get-together goes by the name of, say, Dan K. Moore's Barbecue or Zeno K. Ponder's Barbecue. Invariably these conventions open with an invocation, since any astute Southern politician can spy a minister or two milling around with paper plate. Afterward the candidate addresses himself to the major issue of the campaign, which is the plight of the tobacco growers or the plight of the Outer Banks fishermen, depending, of course, in which part of the state he is staging his Barbecue. Everyone then joins in a couple of choruses of "What a Friend We Have in Jesus," looking straight at the candidate, and then off to the tables groaning with barbecue, which is chopped pork highly seasoned. Along with the barbecue the folks help themselves to hush puppies (corn bread) and right smart slaw.

The Tammany appeals of my youth were conducted in quite a different manner. In the first place, most of the Tammany men never heard of barbecue, hush puppies, or slaw. They had beer and clams. Sometimes they had raw clams and sometimes they had clam fritters. Whatever their expenses, they were one-half those of the Southerner. Everyone eats the barbecue but the Tammany men knew the Jews who came to the get-together didn't eat the clams. At one of these beer and clam conventions the speech of Congressman "Big Tim" Campbell, representing the Bowery district, is preserved for posterity. Campbell's opponent was named Rinaldo. As some of his colleagues rolled in the beer barrels, Big Tim addressed the assemblage:

"There is two bills before the country—the Mills Bill and the McKinley Bill. The Mills Bill is for free trade with everything free; the McKinley Bill is for protection with nothing free. Do you want everything free or do you want to pay for everything? Having thus disposed of the national issue I will now devote myself to the local issue which is the dago Rinaldo. He is from Italy. I am from Ireland. Are you in favor of Italy or Ireland? Having thus disposed of the local issue and thanking you for your attention, I will now retire."

Big Tim Sullivan was the man famous for having told the President of the United States who objected to one of his measures on the grounds that it was un-Constitutional, "What's the Constitution between friends?" On another occasion when one of the New York papers accused him of having one million dollars in his bank account at a time when his salary was four thousand, four hundred dollars a year, Big Tim answered this canard by saying, "The New York papers are against a man saving his money."

But the Big Tims have disappeared from the New York scene as well as the free beer and clams. Neither has been replaced by the egg cream get-together probably because an egg cream is so hard to make. I suspect when barbecue goes really out of favor in the South, politics will be conducted on a higher, more abstract plane and the plight of the tobacco growers will be slightly worsened since they won't even get the barbecue, hush puppies and slaw during primary and election time.

Playing marbles

MARBLES WERE a big deal when I was a kid. We played marbles everywhere. All we needed was a patch of dirt and we scooped a hole out with our heel.

Today, I understand the best kids do with marbles is fry them. Literally. One of the women's magazines ran an article on what to do with a kid on a rainy afternoon. Buy them a bag of marbles, put the marbles in a frying pan, ignite the electrical burner, the heat makes the marbles crack, and, presto! the kid has an aesthetic experience.

What the kids do with the marbles isn't so clear. Some of them use these fried agates to make earrings, others make Daddy a tie clasp with a fried marble in the middle.

Well, I suppose rainy days make all of us a little balmy.

When I was young, marbles were migs and agates and we fried neither. A mig was the cheapest, a solid-color piece of clay. An agate was glass with the beautiful swirls inside. For a penny, I suppose, we got ten marbles which included eight migs and two agates.

We paid off our losses in migs but were always tight with the agates. There was a game we played where you rolled a mig quite a distance and if you could hit the agate, you won it. Your opponent kept all the migs that missed. There were also giant agates, say twice as big as your fingernail. Everyone put one of these near the hole and if you could budge this marble with a mig, you won it. The giant agate, I believe, was worth ten migs or two ordinary agates.

Marbles were the first medium of exchange among young boys on the Lower East Side of New York. Marbles I thought at one time were really money.

I played marbles with the intensity a bridge expert plays bridge. I remember being wiped out and I also remember coming home, my pockets laden with glass and clay.

The kids don't shoot marbles anymore, though any who want to can use my clay-packed back lot for a game.

Marbles went out of style when pants began to cost so much.

Ellen Terry on the East Side

THE MOST memorable events on the Lower East Side of New York were the visits of Theodore Roosevelt and Ellen Terry. Theodore Roosevelt came to eat a dinner at the Little Hungary Restaurant on East Houston Street, some time about 1905 or 1906. All the Jews turned out to see him. They remembered when he had been police commissioner and later Governor. Roosevelt knew the Lower East Side, of course, but his visit was more political than nostalgic. A candidate for the mayorality of the city accompanied him.

That was all right with the Jews. My father had always insisted that if you had a choice between two men, one an amateur and one a professional politician, vote for the professional. The professional has earned his spurs somewhere along the line, winning some support because he attended a Bar Mitzvah, some more because he defended an Italian peddler, and more because he went bail for some misguided youth. It rubs off on the professional.

Ellen Terry wasn't running for anything. She came down to the Neighborhood Playhouse during one of her American tours because she hoped to perform Shakespeare before an audience which ordinarily wouldn't get the chance to see her.

The Neighborhood Playhouse was the first American theatre to produce Shaw's *Major Barbara*, and it did several plays by Ibsen and Sudermann. It was a perfect place for a one-night stand by England's greatest actress, and Ellen Terry came to it on the night of Shakespeare's birthday, April 23, 1915.

To say it was a memorable evening is an understatement. She stood in the center of the stage behind a table covered with spring flowers. She wore a red gown with sleeves and never looked more beautiful.

J. P. Morgan lent the theatre his copy of the First Shakespeare Folio, and the first quartos of A *Midsummer Night's Dream* and *The Merchant of Venice.* A museum lent a fine Shakespeare portrait, and the artist Gordon Craig hung his paintings in the lobby.

Ellen Terry read several of Shakespeare's heroines, concluding with Portia. She brought England and high culture to the Lower East Side and the Lower East Side returned love and attention.

Everyone belonged

NOWADAYS we say, "He's a good neighbor, he minds his own business." It was just the opposite on the Lower East Side of New York among the Jews, and in Little Italy among the Italians, and in Hell's Kitchen among the Irish. Everybody knew when someone lost a job or someone got another or someone was promoted.

"No baby yet?" was quite a natural question to ask of a young woman who had been married a year. "When is your sister getting married?" was commonly heard. There was no conjecture and no one made up any stories. They asked, and they always got an honest answer.

The grocery man Mr. Solomon was blind. My mother would say "go to the blind one." She meant no insult. The blind were called blind and the lame were called lame; they were all part of the community because of this directness. The afflicted felt a deep sense of belonging. There were no outsiders.

The first English words

SEVERAL OLD-TIMERS dispute me on the first English words learned by the immigrants. "Post No Bills" is my selection. I remember also when the folks played around with the word "café." It took us years to learn the French pronunciation. We always pronounced it *"kafe,"* the Litvak word for "purchase," and for a long time that's what we thought a "café" was.

I suspect, though, that in a general sense, the first English words all immigrants—Jews, Italians, Poles, Russians, Greeks, Hungarians—learned and knew thoroughly were son of a bitch. They heard it on all sides, heard it said in anger and in jest, heard it said contemptuously. They heard it also as a term of endearment. Your closest friend would get up and pinch-hit and win the whole thing for you and you'd say, patting him on the back, "Ah, you son of a bitch."

At first you couldn't understand how someone would insult your mother in that way. But it began to dawn on you that it wasn't like that at all. You went to a concert and heard a master violinist and you heard yourself say, "Son of a bitch, he can sure play." And then you realized the significance of the exclamation, and then you also realized that you, too, were finally an American.

It wasn't all *ess, ess*

EACH DAY after school the mother sent me down with a large basket to buy some fresh rolls and bagels. I remember walking down Avenue A to Essex Street and over to Broome Street to a large bakery. On a broad plank outside were the pastry, the rolls, the cakes, from which we picked what we were sent to buy. On the way home I ate part and got a good bawling out.

Would-be millionaires

REMEMBER when we wanted to be rich millionaires so we could buy anything we wanted in the fifteen-cent store? We were nose-high to the counters, our eyes on a level with the rubies, diamonds, pearls, toys, pencil boxes, and every desirable treasure.

Tiffany's should look so good to us today.

I remember a fifteen-cent "gold" ring with initials, and plenty to pick from to find your initials.

Coffee of a childhood

THE SCHOOLTEACHERS in P.S. 20 appointed two of us each day to clean up after their lunch in the science room. I got the point a few years later. We thought they had "neglected" a couple of pieces of cake and two, half-full cups of coffee, but of course they wanted us to have it, without actually calling it to our attention. "Saving face" was a big thing on the East Side. The coffee was a treat and I recall the bag, marked ARBUCKLE COFFEE, and have always recalled the name with reverence. In our home the coffee was made with chicory. The chicory came in lengths about the thickness of one-inch pipe, and a piece of it was broken off into the grinder with the coffee beans. For lunch at home I had a big cup of that coffee and bread and butter. The bread was called "Tip-Top" and cost five cents a loaf. I usually ate the loaf with the cup of coffee.

The one-cent tuition

THOUSANDS of men throughout the country who were immigrants or children of immigrants during the early part of the century will be forever grateful to the "uptown" German Jews who founded the Educational Alliance on East Broadway on the Lower East Side of New York. I do not know of any other organization that contributed more to bridging the difference between the Old World and the New. It did not take you long to become an American if you went to the Educational Alliance for two hours after public school. More than knowledge, the Educational Alliance brought greater dignity to our religion, a finer sense of responsibility, and related America to our own cultural values.

Quite frankly, the old-time *melamed* (Hebrew teacher) was often an unpleasant fellow who knew nothing about teaching and even less about the handling of young boys. It was never a happy time with him, although I still feel sorry for the old gent walking up five flights of stairs to instruct a kid for a twenty-five-cent fee. Many a kid hid under the bed when he heard the *melamed* was coming, and there was screaming, scolding, and punishing, all designed to make a boy sit down with the fellow who taught him. You learned Hebrew words by rote and a few sentences in singsong fashion that had no meaning for you and it all seemed terribly out of place.

The Educational Alliance, however, helped solve this problem with learning and above all—with dignity. You attended classes after public school, five times a week, and they were all interesting. There were capable teachers who understood not only how to teach but how to teach young boys, and classes were conducted in Hebrew and in English. This is not to imply that you were never whacked over the knuckles with a twelve-inch ruler. The Educational Alliance had no nonsense about it, nor was it beset by PTAs demanding the teacher instruct the "whole" boy. The teachers did not instruct the "whole" boy. They taught English and Hebrew. "Wholeness" you had to get at home with your parents or with your uncle.

The tuition, I believe, was one cent a week. It later increased five hundred percent—to five cents a week. There were many happy times; the Hannukah parties and the Purim treats and the once-a-year excursion up the Hudson River to West Point and later a picnic in New Jersey.

The sidewalks of New York

THE FANCY suburban subdivisions do not provide side-walks. It is a status symbol not to have sidewalks, I guess.

The poorest of us used to play hopscotch which we more usually called potsy, little girls skipped rope, boys noisily played marbles. We all played tag—all because we had sidewalks.

Now in the absence of sidewalks you've got to buy the little darling a Jaguar, and the little girl instead of skipping rope is teasing her hair and watching TV.

Brooms to the ceiling

THE FOLKS on the East Side used a white gadget called a mantle to cover the gas jet and disguise it so that it looked like one of those new electric lights. The mantle cost ten cents and it was a status symbol. They burned out often, however, and the folks bought spares when the fellow was calling on your sister.

This mantle was very delicate, it cracked easily if you turned up the gas flame and if you slammed the door it collapsed and ten cents was a lot in those days. The mantle also brought a great deal of frustration to the kids. Up to the time the mantle made its appearance on the mass market, kids could do as they wanted in the tenements. They could roller skate through the rooms, play cowboys and Indians, or hide-and-seek through the tenements. Noise was a constant of tenement life. But when the people began buying the mantle, the kids upstairs were always breaking it through reverberations of the play. So the people downstairs, sadly surveying the collapsed mantle, used to grab a broom and pound on the ceiling yelling for the kids to be quiet.

The sad thing was after electric lights came into wide use, the people downstairs didn't give up the broom or the pounding. It had become a habit, one that has never been broken.

Mothers at mealtime

I NEVER remember my mother sitting back on her chair. She always sat on its edge. I don't believe she ever ate a whole meal. But when I was older and asked her why, she replied, "I sit on the edge of my chair six nights a week so that on the Sabbath I am the queen." Her experience was duplicated and reduplicated hundreds of thousands of times.

The old folks are becoming a problem

THE OLD are becoming a problem. What's happening today is nothing compared to what is yet to happen ten years from today.

I noticed that in all these attempts to build an old folks home the first thing the loved ones say is: "Remember, it's not a charity institution, it's a home where they meet their own and play games and meet people with the same interests, etc."

And the nice matron sits in her front room and says to me: "My mother loves it there. She's so happy."

Our segregation of the Negro and the poor finally caught up with us. Someday we'll have to *desegregate* the elderly too.

PART 3

Sixty Million Widows

Don't blame the Cotillions

HERE IN Charlotte, the Junior League or the Confederate Dames or some such tax-exempt organization sponsors a Cotillion at which the fifteen- and sixteen-year-old boys and girls disport themselves. The boys wear dinner jackets and look twenty-five and the girls wear evening gowns and look very nice. The kids all seem to have a good time, but a lot of anxiety attends the parents. The mothers think, "I didn't have an evening gown until I was in college. If my daughter has an evening gown at fifteen, what will she want when she is twenty-three? What's left? Maybe she will get tattooed?" The fathers worry, too. They say, "He has a dinner jacket at fifteen. I didn't even get to drive the car until I was out of high school. What are we coming to?"

I have no intention of allaying these fears, except to remark that the tattoo parlors are virtually a thing of the past. I am not at all sure that my sister was a better person for having done piecework in a factory when she was fifteen instead of parading around a dance floor in a new gown. If American life is suffering from a corruption, I don't think we ought to blame the Cotillions.

Some years ago many experts were of the opinion that television was enfeebling our youth. But many of the kids that watched Superman and Milton Berle are in the Peace Corps or fighting in Vietnam. Television didn't make them scared.

We have changed from an immigrant and pioneer society into an affluent one and the quality of life in an affluent society is appreciably different. The affluent life cannot help but frighten people by its very comfort.

Half our attention can devote itself to preparing a child for a Cotillion and the other half worry about the famine that approaches India this winter. No matter how radical he may have been in his youth, none of us in middle age wants to give up that which he feels he has earned.

For all this futility, we have made some improvements in our attitudes. In the midst of the Depression I remember important men believing that other men were unemployed because they were lazy. No one now believes that poverty programs are a sop to the lazy. Most of us believe mass unemployment is a terrible disaster and that it results from a combination of environmental and economic factors.

Sex and Social Security

WHEN THAT misplaced minister, Woodrow Wilson, saw the income tax become law, little did he wot how it would change the moral caliber of the American culture.

Did anyone ever realize some of the men who would cheat and lie and short-change the Government would lose their freedom? Did anyone realize in 1916 the cohorts of lawyers who would devote all their time simply to filling out income tax forms for the well-heeled, the lawyers themselves joining the ranks of the well-to-do by the hundreds of thousands? Did anyone realize how convenient the penalties for income tax evasions were to prove to a harassed Government which, except for its provisions, could not deal with syndicated crime?

As if the income tax weren't bad enough, look what the Social Security laws are doing to our morals. Authorities in Miami recently expressed national outrage at the number of the elderly living together out of wedlock, or as some of the young might put it, shacking up, simply to hold onto their Social Security benefits.

You see, a widow gets eighty-two point five percent of the payments due her dearly departed. Thus, if her late husband was entitled to payments of one hundred dollars a month, his survivor gets eighty-two dollars and fifty cents. Should she remarry, however, the Government immediately subtracts all of that eighty-two dollars and fifty cents and gives her one-half of what Number Two draws. Thus, if Number Two is entitled to one hundred dollars a month, the remarried widow draws fifty dollars. True, it improves his position somewhat, but she is losing thirty-two dollars and fifty cents. Is it fair to penalize love? And supposing he draws only forty dollars a month: then she gets only twenty dollars. Can connubial bliss be worth sixty-two dollars and fifty cents each and every month?

Max Friedson, according to the dispatches, head of the Senior Citizens Councils, told reporters of the earnest efforts of a rabbi who gave unofficial blessings to such unions, which may not have reduced the sin but at least reduced the thinking about it. That's moral moonlighting.

Any rational disquisition about the inequities of the Social Security law falls on deaf ears. Most Americans feel the elderly are lucky to get it, forgetting, of course, the elderly paid for it. Nothing brings Americans to the framing of an ordinance or the passage of a prohibitive statute like the prospect of regulating sex.

The children's hour

ONE OF the recent suburban vogues to which I have been subjected is to let the eight-year-old attend the cocktail party. Dr. Spock, of course, advises against intoxicants for children. Deprived of sampling the spirits, Junior perforce will have to badger one of the guests to read the Atlas with him or tell him a ghost story or, if he's precocious as indeed all suburban kids seem to be, play cribbage. This is precisely what anyone who has spent nine or ten hours in the shop or office wants to do.

Junior's presence will also give Daddy the opportunity to bark nastily at his best friend, "Watch your choice of subjects" gesturing meaningfully to Junior's cocked ears.

The real style-setters let Little Missy come to the cocktail party. She is six and not only precocious but an absolute genius at interrupting. One more word and a rather decent chap discussing a profoundly interesting subject might have gotten someone's attention. Little Missy to the rescue. She zips in there with an Indian yell to show Mommy the scratch on her knee she picked up yesterday noon. After a detailed examination during which Mommy and Daddy assure themselves Little Missy will survive, they devote the next ten minutes to shrieking, "This is adultsville!" Then back to the chap with the egg on his face to ask, "What was it you were saying?"

These days most cocktail parties reach the conversational summits of reciting the deeds and doings of Little Missy or Junior during the past forty-eight hours.

There are, sad to say, unmistakable signs that the cocktail party is vanishing from the face of the suburbs. I myself do not go to cocktail parties unless I am assured that the host and hostess are grandparents whose progeny live in remote areas like Oklahoma City or Scranton. I see no way of reversing this trend easily. The cocktail hour might be salvaged if someone would come along with the companion to Dr. Spock about the care and handling of adults. Conceivably it could make being a grown-up once again popular.

The balanced budget

WE ARE once more off on the never-ending search for the balanced budget. This search for "fiscal responsibility" is a lot like the search for the buried, lost city of Atlantis. None of the hunters is ever sure there is an Atlantis, but it would be awfully nice and rewarding if there were.

What is most amazing about the call for regulation of government spending is the response it elicits from a large portion of the electorate. The plea that no one, least of all the United States Government, should spend more than they or it take in is absolutely against everyone's self-interest. Every four years however, all the Republicans go down to the shore and wave good-bys for another sailing party, armed with harpoons and fishnets, off for another try at raising the Atlantis of the balanced budget.

How many of the enthusiastic shore party have two thousand, nine hundred dollars at any one time with which to buy a new car? If new cars were sold only for spot cash, Detroit would long ago have become a ghost town. The very men who pompously announce the virtues of the balanced budget are the ones who invented deficit spending. They are perfectly willing to trust anyone with a down payment, perfectly willing to bet that anyone with fifty-six dollars and fifty cents this month will have fifty-six dollars and fifty cents every one of the thirty-six months ahead. They'd even bet he'd have fifty-six dollars and fifty cents forty-eight months from now, except that after thirty-six months the car is not worth fifty-six dollars and fifty cents.

How many Americans who praise the majesty of the balanced budget would have a home if they were restricted to spending only the amount they own? Of course, it takes most folks a lifetime to pay off a mortgage. Invariably they have paid as much interest as they have paid principal, their equity in a house is roughly two-thirds of what it costs, but at least they have a home, which is more than seven-eighths of the world's population has. No mortgage bank has ever condemned imbalanced budgets.

The deficit finance the Federal Government incurs is moreover not even borrowing in the way borrowing from a bank is borrowing. When a family or a business cannot meet its obligations, it faces serious trouble. But the debt of the United States is money we owe to ourselves, and the interest we pay, we pay to ourselves. The key to this situation is the gross national product. If that continues to grow, or remains high, the increased government debt is no problem at all. It is a good thing.

The folks in Texas and Southern California are fed and clothed and housed by virtue of the missile race. The missile race is financed by the purchase of Defense Bonds, taxes and government borrowing. Yet these are the people most insistent on controlled government spending. And they must mean let's control everything except missile spending on borrowed money.

Where are the diners?

WHAT HAPPENED to the diners at which we used to grab a quick bite? They were all over the place during the 1930's and 1940's and now there is hardly a one to be found. One wouldn't complain if the short-order places which replaced the diners were an improvement, but not even the restaurants are an improvement except in isolated instances.

The diner resembled a railroad car with entrances at either end. A long counter stretched the length of the place and stools lined up beside it. What made it an attractive place to eat was that any customer could see all the food prepared in front of him for the range, and the icebox and the cutting boards lined up behind the counter. I can even remember the exceptionally sturdy water glasses that the waitress or owner set before you as soon as you entered. In fact, it was in one of these diners that I first saw a paper napkin.

The diners encouraged a certain camaraderie that is lacking in the drugstore restaurants or short-order places of today. There is little joviality today, eating at a plastic-top table with some sullen clerks from up the block. The food is all prepackaged and it is rare these days to see a slab of meat. Most of the sandwiches are some sort of salad—chicken salad, turkey salad, egg salad.

At the beginning of the war, I remember a counterman I used to talk to daily about life and love. He had written a song which he hoped to publish. He called it, "You Have Liberty in Your Hand, Now Hold It!" It was a long title and as I remember, it never did make the Hit Parade, although he sang it all day for the benefit of his clientele. Eventually he sold his diner and back lot to a building developer who squeezed thirty-eight houses in the space, and neither he nor that developer needed hit songs after that.

Maybe that's what happened to the diners.

Passenger trains

IT MAY well be that in the near future there will be no more passenger trains. The New Haven Railroad is petitioning for the right to stop hauling passengers from Westchester County to New York City. Two other major Eastern railroads have threatened they cannot continue their runs unless they can merge. All over the country the same complaint is heard: the railroad men say they cannot compete with superhighways built with public funds.

Freight still turns a profit for some lines. A lot of that, however, comes from "piggyback" hauling—hauling loaded trucks over long distances. Even the companies which manufactured toy electric trains have fallen on hard times, the victims of an age in which children prefer rocketry and spacecraft.

Imagine an America without trains! Imagine the most mechanical country in the world without locomotives. My father could not conjure so bleak a vision. He was an immigrant from Galicia in the Austro-Hungarian Empire. He saw very little of America, only the Lower East Side of New York City and, in the last decades of his life, the reaches of the Bronx. My mother never saw Grand Central Station. But they knew all about railroads. The elevated trains were all around in those years. And like most Americans, my father and mother always had a love affair with the romantic trains. Now the elevated trains are gone. The Third Avenue el came down ten years ago to make way for the Second Avenue subway which is still fifty years away.

The railroads will die for lack of profits. Lack of profits is the hallowed American excuse for abolishing anything. Passenger rates, no question about it, do not produce profits.

The passenger railroads will probably go. It is a sad thing. It is even sadder to realize, as Lewis Mumford once remarked, that fifty years from now we will have to reinvent them.

How to make money

THERE ARE several easy ways to make money in America. Of course being a teacher, a newspaperman, or an artist is not one of them.

The easiest way to coin a buck is to invent a new diet, the goofier the better. I remember when the banana diet was the vogue. And then there was a diet where you counted toothpicks. And then there was a diet where you counted calories and one where you didn't count calories. There is the drinking man's diet and the diet which commences on Tuesday in case the dieter has a hangover on Monday.

A good friend of mine who worked on a reputable magazine once confessed that whenever their circulation dropped, which naturally affected their advertising rates, they immediately dug up a diet and headlined it the next month, usually choosing words like "miracle," "wonder," or "painless." Circulation always increased.

In a diet-conscious country the manufacturers of bathroom scales are always due for luxurious retirement.

Feminine apparel seems to have a market with no tomorrow. There are men who make money at this by inventing clothes women can't even wear, like the topless bathing suit. I wish I had the royalties that accrued to the fellow who invented the big hat with the sunglasses attached.

Women buy clothes, lingerie, and nightgowns to look at themselves in. If you are a manufacturer of mirrors, you will probably be able to play golf with the manufacturer of bathroom scales when you are old.

And anything that will distract a kid, other than new books or piano lessons made easy, will make a fortune. A Davy Crockett hat or an astronaut's helmet or an educational toy or a television show with well-disguised violence or a kiddie car with a real motor or a harmless tranquilizer will endear you to the small fry. And you will make so much money you can blackball the mirror and scale men from the country club if you've a mind to.

True short stories

SAM RUBINSTEIN used to wait for little Mrs. Sadie Hyman and they took long leisurely walks through the park, each telling the other of life before they were widowed and of their loneliness.

Everyone thought it would be nice if this pair of lonely people got married. Finally, they got the idea and their married children gave them a lovely wedding and their blessing. Months later, they admitted it was the mistake of their lives. In those long walks Sam didn't tell Sadie he liked his meat rare and lots of it and she didn't tell him she was a vegetarian. He didn't tell her he had to have every window open and Sadie didn't tell him the slightest draft was a hurricane to her.

They sadly filed for a divorce on grounds of incompatibility and next thing you know they were again walking arm and arm in the park.

*   *   *

Nothing so fills a man with pride as moving his family into a first-class neighborhood. Barney Goldman bought an almost palatial home next to the town banker, Throckmorton Bidwell.

Barney found out how the other half lived. Throckmorton's son was a hi-fi addict and subjected the neighborhood to sound blastings daily. He had records which reproduced boiler factories and runaway railway trains of which he never tired. Throckmorton's daughter had run off at sixteen with a gypsy used-car dealer and was back at age thirty with six bright-eyed young predators who knew no boundaries.

Barney sold out to a Billy Graham disciple, figuring the neighborhood could stand a little missionary work, and moved back into the cramped apartment over his drugstore.

* * *

Morrie Bernstein became alarmed when Miss Higgins, his mother's companion-nurse, called to say that every morning his mother was slipping out of her penthouse apartment with a suitcase full of clothes and in the lobby waited for a taxi that took her to parts unknown. She always came back at four o'clock but where did she spend her day? Morrie was a good son who provided lavishly for his mother and always had Friday-night dinner until his ulcer acted up. Where was Mama going? Was she pawning her clothes to play the ponies?

A man of decision, Morrie instantly called a private eye to trail his mama. The report came in: subject took a taxi to the Neat 'n' Clean Laundromat and put clothes in washer. Then served cake and coffee; set hair of one young woman; advised another what to do for diaper rash; admired snapshots of children shown her and told what a terrible time her son Morrie had in teething; exchanged recipes with another woman and demonstrated a knitting stitch to still another—subject seems to know all the patrons and is held in esteem by them. At 3:30 P.M., said her son expected her home to cook dinner. Left for home in a taxicab.

Morrie realized his mother, for all her wealth and comfort, was lonely. He decided to drop in every afternoon and ask what was for dinner, and find more time for his mama.

The wide-open spaces

ALL TELEVISION and newspaper pictures of the recent New York blackout showed mile-long lines of automobiles trying to inch their way toward northern New Jersey, Westchester

County, Connecticut, and Long Island. Millions of them.

It all started way back yonder with the man or his wife saying, "It would be nice to raise the children in the country wide-open spaces." And all that stuff.

When the Negro began to move about with greater freedom, this movement to the "wide-open spaces" was accelerated to the point of a little Exodus. All over the country.

And now there are millions in the "wide-open spaces" who leave the house at six in the morning and return at seven at night. Either they take the train or they drive, and the highways are jammed with a million enormous cars each containing only one guy.

Some day all Long Island, all of Connecticut, all of West-chester County, and all of northern New Jersey will be covered with asphalt and serve as a parking lot for the metropolitan area.

What's this big deal about how good it is for children to grow up in the country in the wide-open spaces? By the time every-body moves to the "country" it's another suburb from which Daddy leaves at six in the morning and you know the rest. The leisure time which everyone worried about is spent commuting. Meanwhile, at least one generation is growing up with no idea at all what the adults do all day in the big city.

There was a time when Daddy came home for lunch or at five in the early evening, and he came home from the drugstore where he worked or which he owned, or from a retail dry-goods store, or from the office or factory, and everybody was in on it: the kids, the wife, the grandparents, the aunts, the cousins, and even the neighbors. If something really important happened during the day, everybody in the family knew about it—often everybody on the block.

But today the kids haven't the faintest idea what their daddy does to maintain the Establishment in the wide-open spaces. By the time he comes home at seven in the evening he's tired, reaches for the martini, and if he should dare open his mouth she says, "Don't bring the office home with you," and if she asks a simple question, he says, "Let's not talk about business"— here in the wide-open spaces.

Organizational crisis

THE CRISIS among the Communist leaders in Russia about whether to push ahead with armaments or turn to consumer goods no doubt has its moments of acrimony. I suspect that members of President Johnson's Cabinet often lose their tempers in discussion about money.

This acrimony is nothing compared to flaring tempers and the harsh words that transpire in the community organization as it tries to decide how it will raise its money.

Say the PTA wants to send all the school kids to the Shakespeare Theatre in Stratford, or the Republican Town Committee wants to raise money for campaign expenditures, or the golf association wants to install a new sprinkler system on the course, they will decide upon an event.

Unfortunately, all of these organizations can decide on three events: a theatre party, a ball, or a clambake.

It would be nice to have all three. But for all the population explosion, most of it is children who are unable to buy tickets. That leaves just their parents, and three events spreads it pretty thin.

Theatre parties rarely win out. The men instantly oppose them. Most of them are sure they will be lured to the ballet. And if not to the ballet, to some wholesome musical chock-full of children.

At moments like this, a lottery would carry the day.

Reclamation

FOR MANY years John L. Lewis of the United Mine Workers was the *bête noir* of American conservatives. He was Satan, the bogeyman, and Benedict Arnold rolled into one. He once so outraged Captain Eddie Rickenbacker during the war years that Rickenbacker recommended that all the miners forthwith be drafted and sent to the front lines.

John L. Lewis, however, knew something then that we are only discovering now. All during those years that businessmen and conservative editors were reviling him, the coal operators, engineers and promotors were stripping coal out of Pennsylvania, West Virginia, Illinois, and Kentucky. They opened no mines, they simply took bulldozers and dredges and gouged the earth, denuding the land of forests, streams, and habitation. It was cheaper that way. For when they were through, they simply moved on and left behind them the gaping holes and tortured earth.

No one ever mentioned this process when they begged the Federal Government to put John L. Lewis in jail or behind a rifle. Not only did they not mention this, they also never paid taxes on the profits they made from the holes they left on the land. We do not even know the corporate names of those who desecrated the earth and abused the principle of equity.

Now the Government is coming along with a few billion dollars to try to reclaim this scarred land. There is some money appropriated, too, to help the miners who have been unemployed for the last twenty years. Of course the miners won't cost as much as the reclamation because they do not need to be wholly reclaimed.

Search in the lobby

I WAS at the Americana in New York one night reading the afternoon paper in the lobby when I saw a little kid going around the lobby investigating the easy chairs and couches. Obviously his people were guests at the hotel. He was well-dressed and polite but quite feverish about this investigation.

He came to where I was sitting and asked pleasantly, "Would you mind getting up a minute, mister?"

I was curious. I got up.

The kid pulled away the chair cushion and ran his hand all around the outlines of the chair and came away with a nickel.

"Do you think you might have lost this nickel from your pockets, mister?"

"No," I answered, "I don't think so. Tell me, how many nickels did you find in the lobby today?"

"Yesterday I found two dollars and seventy-five cents. Only sixty cents today, though. One Christmastime I found four dollars in the chairs at my grandma's."

Probably I found some money when I was a kid. Maybe a penny or two over the years. And I suppose in the day long-dead beyond recall I found a nickel in a phone booth. When I did find that money I spent it forthwith at the candy store. These smart hotel-lobby kids, I suppose, are saving their money to pay their way through graduate school or buy a 1976 Mustang.

Commercials will endure

LET US grant it is nobody's fault. Some artistic media give out, just like we ourselves do at fourscore and ten.

These thoughts came to me the other night as I watched television. Already television shows signs of age. It has long instituted the summer programming, which consists of repeating the winter program. I wondered what dandy aspects of television are going to be saved.

It came to me. None of the shows, save baseball's World Series, deserves preserving. But the advertising is timeless. The ads and the commercials will live on and on.

And why not? For, as I said, these thoughts were inspired by a commercial in which a booming voice promised that some product had more vitamins than any given pound of liver. What in the world could such a product be? Who in the world eats liver anyway? What does the human body do with such vitamins? Any commercial which sets the mind to this sort of per-ambulations has impact.

Certainly we would want to preserve the kitchen ads which so happily interrupt the daytime soap operas. The folks in the commercials are generally prettier, their homes are nicer, and they have memorized their lines better than the folks in the drama. We would not want to sacrifice such effort, would we?

Best of all, however, are the cigarette ads wherein we can watch two charming people partaking of the joys of the fresh air while they smilingly blow the smoke puff by puff—the most beautiful enactment of a suicide pact in all history of the theatre.

Credit for kids

IT IS helping the economy but ruining some boys and girls for life. High school credit, some jewelry stores call it. Teen-credit, say some of the sports stores.

They make it easy. Come and get it—weejuns, London Fog coats, madras shirts, the whole bit. Some of the stores charge eight percent on the unpaid balance. At the end of four months the kid has paid three hundred dollars for two hundred dollars' worth of merchandise which is worth ninety-five dollars to be-gin with, and which was already out of style. One store adver-tises, ALL THE CREDIT YOU WANT, and the kids buy and buy.

They have all discovered that kids between thirteen and eight-een are ready for exploitation. In addition to the credit, the kids also have an allowance.

The great joy of an allowance, of course, is not reserved for the small fry. Rather, it is the parents who dole out the money who pleasure themselves with reminiscences of how, when they were young, they didn't get an allowance but had to mow the neighbor's lawn or run errands.

My classmates and I on the Lower East Side of New York received an allowance of two pennies a day, back there in 1908-

1914. One penny was for lunch at one of Mr. Nathan Straus's free milk stations. For a penny you could drink all the milk you wanted. And it was pasteurized. Mr. Straus was a pioneer in the pasteurization of milk. The second penny was for candy, and there were vast possibilities in those days for a penny.

Today the little girl next door gets a five-dollar-a-week allowance and so does her sixteen-year-old brother, but he also has a secondhand car which cost six hundred and ninety dollars. His father says, "Tommy is paying off his car, a dollar a week—isn't he wonderful?" Papa had raised Tommy's allowance one dollar a week to take care of that weekly payment to him on the car.

But back to the allowance. According to the *Wall Street Journal*, which not too long ago ran a front-page story on kids as capitalists, the true crisis of the allowance is when the eleven-year-old wants to subscribe to *Playboy*. After all, the allowance is his money.

Hamburger and pizza

TOURISTS DRIVING from Charlotte to Asheville will see Lake Lure and pass through the beautiful Sapphire Mountains. In Asheville they will see the palaces of the rich. But more than anything else, the tourists will see the hamburger palaces which line the highways.

An alert tourist could probably eat three hundred different varieties of hamburgers between here and Asheville. There are Big Boy hamburgers, which come between three slices of roll and contain two enormous patties. There are fishburgers and stroganoff burgers. There are hamburgers stuffed with olives and hamburgers served with blue cheese.

What presses the hamburger, what has made the hamburger dress up, is the pizza. The pizza has always been as varied as the hamburger. Down here in Dixie we have always been able to avail ourselves of the eggplant pizza, the meatball pizza and the sour-dine pizza, as Southerners put it. Along that highway between Asheville and Charlotte a tourist can buy as many varieties of pizza as he can hamburgers. And in the supermarkets, he can buy frozen pizzas and pizza mixes.

In Shea Stadium, a ball fan can buy a pizza as readily as he can buy a hot dog, but it is my impression that hot dog devotees stick to hot dogs while hamburger devotees are switching.

While the pizza is Italian in origin I am willing to bet more pizza is consumed in South Carolina in one day than in Tuscany in a month. In fact, there's a pizzaburger stand outside of one South Carolina town that has yet to construct a library.

Sixty million widows

TODAY THERE are among us almost four million widows over the age of fifty. A female born in the 1950's, say the insurance statisticians, may expect to live to seventy-five, while a male can look forward to only sixty-six years. The gap is getting wider and wider. Fifty years from now, in the year 2115, the United States of America will be a matriarchy ruled over by some sixty million widows.

The widows will hold many of the political offices and most of the civil service jobs. Perhaps one will be President. There will be a bevy of governors and a bevy of senators.

On their summer vacations in magnificent hotels on distant space platforms, the widows will exchange experiences which will tell the story of the terrible competitive stress that makes a new widow every hour on the hour, around the clock, year in and year out.

The chitchat will go something like this:

"The first time I was here was right after my first husband won the top-man-of-the-year button from his sales outfit."

A second widow:

"Yes. I had the same tough break at about the same time. My Jim was so happy when he got the thirty-year watch from his firm, but he went a month later just like that, sick, dead and buried in a week."

A third widow will join them at the atomic-reducing pool:

"Only a month after my husband finally met his quota and was due for a regular drawing account, he collapsed right on the street—heart. I didn't even know about it till after midnight. Poor dear, always worrying about that quota, and him so well-packaged.

"I remember when he asked me to read to him from a book he brought home. It was called *What Salesmen Should Know About Clothes* and I read him to sleep every night; the book told all about the kind of hat brim a good salesman must wear, and things like that. He was very conscientious. Whatever he started out to do day or night, first he'd say to himself: 'Does it sell Flippo?' That's what he sold—it was a dog food—poor dear, he tried so hard."

The Establishment

THE Southern Establishment, which includes the bankers, the contractors, the branch managers of the national concerns, has never really been against opening all public accommodations and public schools to the Negroes. They would make Martin Luther King mayor of the city if he would guarantee them no collective bargaining, no more unionization, no Medicare, and no laundry worker to get above a dollar an hour.

The Establishment in many cities desegregated the restaurants when the Negroes threatened a demonstration. Each of the community leaders took two or three Negro leaders to lunch and that was that. No fuss, no bother. No one can say the Establishment isn't quick to learn what loses money and what makes money.

It is the sub-Establishment—the sheriffs and the white-collar workers—who fear that Negro equality will shut them off in social oblivion.

The big Establishment accedes to this request the sub-Establishment makes: continue the pipe dream that segregation will come back to industrial twentieth-century America.

Our leisure

ALL THE anxiety about tennis permits and overcrowding on both the children's swings and the grown-up golf course comes about because we all have so much more leisure. In some suburban towns and even in civilized cities the argument about who will or who will not be entitled to go swimming on the local beach reaches the proportions of an embittered civil war.

In my youth, the big worry was whether the kosher butcher was indeed completely kosher. This worry was engendered by the amount of time the folks spent in the synagogue. Out in New England, there was terrible anxiety about whether some of the sports were drinking beer on Sundays for the same reason. And in the Bible Belt, anyone who danced was a fit subject for Hell.

The minister could drive out there to the oak grove, drink himself a glass of well water and wonder aloud if any beer had been consumed on the premises lately. The old-time rabbi used to go around and spy on the butchers, which is certainly easier than having to write a book every so often and manage a rummage sale as the modern rabbi must do simultaneously. Today, the Arthur Murray and Fred Astaire studios are institutionalized, like fins on the back of cars, and a minister who would prohibit dancing is like a minister who prays for a Depression.

Once upon a time, leisure consisted of those precious hours between waking up and going to work and coming home from work and going to sleep, and whether the golf course had a sprinkler or not was as far removed from most men's minds as whether or not the moon could be irrigated.

And as far as schools went, parents entered them at their own risk, either to register a child on his first day, or claim a child who was ill. A teacher's salary was a secret matter, just as J. P. Morgan's personal fortune was a secret matter (though we knew it was considerable). Today, of course, the PTA bruits the teachers' salaries all over town, trying to convince folks they are underpaid, insisting they, the teachers, deserve a one hundred dollar per year raise, beginning next year.

White liberation

TWENTY YEARS ago I wrote a piece, "Why I like the South," in which I said that the South is on the threshold of the greatest news story of the twentieth century: the changing of its social order. The Negro will soon be entering the middle class, coming into the mainstream of the American society.

The way I see it now, any young man who comes south will be in the same position as the man who went west seventy years ago. The victory of the Negro will bring an even greater victory to the white Southerner. What held the Southerner back was racial segregation.

In 1929 a city councilman in a large Southern town was able to defeat an appropriation for a new white high school by stating: "If you build that extra high school for the whites, you're going to have to do something for the Negroes, under the 'separate but equal' law." So the city did not build the necessary school for the white children.

The South was once the most politically creative section of America. Out of the South came Jefferson, Madison and Mason. From South Carolina came the Congregationalist Reverend Tennent, who went to the Constitutional Convention and said: "The first requirement is freedom of religion." Gouverneur Morris replied there was nothing to worry about with men like Jefferson around. Tennent said, "The hearts of men doth change." Reverend Tennent was right. Fifty years later, Americans were killing Baptists in Virginia, burning Catholic convents in Massachusetts, and chasing the Mormons across the continent. But Americans put it in writing in 1789, which is the miracle. The law was on the side of equity and justice.

That Covenant which Moses brought down from Sinai has not yet produced the results in human relations he had hoped for, but the Covenant still stands, at least. In essence, Law is a curriculum for the management of life.

It has always puzzled me that the *most* Anglo-Saxon people in America, the Southern Protestants, have so often frowned at the legal foundations which they, more than anyone else since the Hebrews and the Romans, helped perpetuate.

The South was creative—the Anglo-Calvinist Society gave us the ballot, habeas corpus, and the free public school. But after Southerners segregated the Negro, the South fell into economic and intellectual stagnation.

The Negroes, entering into the mainstream of America, will liberate the white Southerners who will finally be able to go about their own business for the first time in this century.

States' rights, to my mind, is the greatest political hoax of the century. The only time Southerners have raised the issue is when it has involved the Negro. They did not talk of "states' rights" when the United States Supreme Court, in Plessy v. Ferguson in 1896, sanctioned racial segregation.

And the Southerners demanded the cooperation of the Federal Government in administering the Fugitive Slave Law. When the Federal Government brought back an escaped slave from Ohio, it was fine. When the same Federal Government says Negroes shall participate in our public facilities, the Southerner begins to talk about "states' rights."

But the fakery of this issue is evident on all sides. What are they talking about "states' rights"? Actually the South has been a sort of federal preserve for the past thirty years, like Yellowstone National Park.

Southerners talk against the Federal Government but take

anything that's not nailed down. They take with both hands from sunup to sundown, every day, except Sunday, the year 'round: cotton payments, peanut payments, Soil Bank Program, Commodity Credit, pensions, hospitals, laboratories; army camps, airports, veterans' benefits, Social Security; no use going any further, look it up, there are forty-three separate federal agencies pouring money into the South, but when it involves the black man, Southerners holler "states' rights," and many people who are otherwise perfectly rational take them seriously.

In New York, at fashionable hotels, sit the several Bring Industry to Our State committees, each with a huge budget. One day they entertain a few men from Troy, New York, another day from Erie, Pennsylvania. They wine and dine them, tell them of the wonders of their Southern state, the good climate, the kind people, the free taxes, the free water rights, and no labor unions.

The "Bring Industry . . . committees" have helped bring compliance. They send word to their governor, "Let that Negro in . . . any bad publicity like barred doors, and federal sheriffs will kill our program." It has happened that way on numerous occasions.

So the Governor calls in the top segregationists and says, "Boys, here it is, we've got to let him in." And they say, "Okay, let him in." When the aristocracy says, "The time has come," it has come, and the message goes all the way down the line.

In Alabama, in Birmingham, the first one to desert the cause is the merchant—if he can get away with it.

Benjamin Disraeli had been a precocious child. At the age of nine, he could recite from Kant and knew Macaulay's *Lays of Ancient Rome*.

In his day as Prime Minister of England there was a kind of do-good movement called "Young England." It was a project to extend the franchise to everybody, not only those who owned property. Disraeli, the Tory Prime Minister, was favorably inclined. So he called in the leaders of the movement and told them that in the Anglo-Saxon world, no social reform is possible without the aristocracy. He said: "Get some of the nobility interested."

And that's how they succeeded and that is how integration is now headed for success.

My mother and God

I WAS thinking of what my mother's reaction would be to the "God Is Dead" movement. She would have used one of the few English words she commanded. She would have said, "Foolish." Maybe "God Is Dead" was all right for some of the Protestant scholars, but how could she have cooked, fed her children, known they were safe, without God's help?

My mother never even saw a cookbook but her specialties were the best I have ever had. Yet she never took credit for her skills. Everything she did was with "God's help" even the chicken soup, or the dress she made for a neighbor's daughter.

If I told my mother God was dead she would have smiled in sympathy for such an attitude. She would have been very sad for the people who believed such a thing, and she would have repeated a favorite passage from Joshua:

> . . . be not daunted nor dis-
> mayed, for the Lord your God
> is with you wherever you go.

The best-dressed woman

THE EASTERN European Jew who came to America between 1880 and 1914 contributed much to the self-esteem and happiness of the American woman. He made her the best-dressed woman in the world.

The remarkable thing is that he did this even before he learned to speak the language.

In the 1880's the wife and daughter of the average working-man wore a shawl over her shoulders. The evening frock, except for the rich, was practically unknown. Even a woman in the middle class had one special dress which she had had made for her wedding and which she continued to wear on special occasions all her life. In 1885 a Fifth Avenue store advertised a silk-lined cloak for sixty dollars, the equivalent of two and a half weeks' wages for the skilled mechanic in 1885.

When the Russian, Austrian, Roumanian, and Hungarian Jews came to America, the needle trade was in the hands of the German Jews who had preceded them by a generation. But the German Jews were already beginning to "relax" within the middle-class society of America. Now the eastern European Jews were to inject that driving enthusiasm "to get ahead" that most newly arrived immigrants possessed. It was not merely ability and the drive to work. It was also imagination and an ingenuity which combined to change the American way of life.

In the first place they discovered the advantage of the division of labor, thus making it possible to "retail" their products at prices within the reach of all. At least fifteen years before Henry Ford established the first assembly line in the motor industry, the garment manufacturers had trained their workers to perform specific jobs rather than to follow the system of the old country where the tailor made the whole garment. The industry was divided into pattern-makers, designers, cutters, operators, basters, finishers, and trimming-women. On Sunday they discreetly "followed" rich women on Fifth Avenue and at the fashionable summer resorts, and copied the Paris styles of cloaks and suits worn by the women of the Astors, Vanderbilts, and Morgans. A week later—out of some dingy shop on Division Street would come—the same thing, "to retail at fifteen dollars." This was the important thing, "to retail at fifteen dollars."

Today the International Ladies Garment Workers Union has over four hundred thousand members who are divided into the following divisions: blouses, children's outer-wear, coats, suits, skirts, dresses, corsets and allied garments, infants' wear, knitted outer-wear, knitted underwear and nightwear and cotton garments. It was once sixty-six hours for an average wage of twelve dollars to fourteen dollars a week. Today it is thirty-two hours for an average of fifty-five dollars to ninety dollars a week. And today the sewing shops employ a majority of Italians, Puerto Ricans, and Negroes. The eastern European Jews did this for the American way of life.

Crying in the suburbs

I REMEMBER my mother crying at funerals. But as far as I can recall, my mother cried only on one occasion that was not in the synagogue during prayers for the dead. The tears were over an ordinary fifty-cent piece. She had misplaced the money for her weekly installment on the sewing machine. My mother was a seamstress, an expert dressmaker. Often she worked ten and twelve hours a day. She had a sewing machine for which she paid fifty cents a week, I believe, as long as she lived. Because the same collector came throughout the years, my mother used to remark that she and the Singer Sewing Machine man grew old together.

But one week, she lost the fifty-cent piece. She cried, and I suppose the tears were also for the thought of what that fifty cents meant to her family in those days.

Looking back, it seems to me, the ordinary pressures of life did not reduce the immigrant women to tears. I suspect the pioneer women never cried frivolously either. They went about their work, as did the immigrant women a century and a half later—the early-American women with water bucket, ax, and sometimes rifle, and the immigrant women with sewing machine and library card.

But more crying goes on in the fancy suburbs today than in

all the history of recorded sadness. Which proves what my mother always said: "It's bad when things are too good."

I have a friend who confided in me that at least once a week his wife rouses him in the wee hours of the morning to ask, "Why do you let me sit here crying?"

To which he invariably asks sleepily, "Why *are* you crying?"

"Because," she answers, "that's what's wrong with our marriage. You let me cry all by myself."

In one of his plays, Moss Hart, I believe, had his hero remark, "She cries over card tricks," which is a sort of seismographic indication of how popular tears have become.

There are women who cry over pretty Christmas wrappings and others who cry at family picnics. They cry when they burn the roast and some of them literally go to pieces when *dotter* comes home from kindergarten with twelve of her classmates moments after the cleaning woman has finished the house.

L. B. Mayer, the junk dealer

"What's Joseph P. Kennedy doing in the movie business; he's not a furrier."

—MARCUS LOEW

WHY SHOULD I write about Louis B. Mayer now? The Hollywood tycoon has been dead for some years. I have my reasons, however. It is a good opportunity to make a point which has been on my mind for many years. A particularly excellent opportunity precisely because I have never heard anyone speak a kind word about the man. He was irascible, I take it, and vulgar, and greedy and crude. What in others inspired praise, in Louis B. Mayer inspired condemnation. He tried to gather for himself what he thought were the supreme values of our society, but what the poor arrogant fool did not know was that in a Louis B. Mayer it doesn't work.

In fact, I myself, as often as I thought of Louis B. Mayer, was amused. I was amused at his posturing along with William Randolph Hearst and the leaders of the Republican National Committee, and I was amused at his attempt to reflect the attitudes of the D.A.R. and to propitiate the American Legion. I was amused because I understood him and his needs, his hunger, his longings.

But in recent years I think I've acquired affection for L. B. because his memory is so universally damned. The late movie mogul fascinates me to the extent that I ask about him of all and sundry when I visit Hollywood. They say he was *nouveau riche*, that he was arrogant, crude, Jewish, and had an accent.

But it is not all that simple. Take Bosley Crowther's *Hollywood Rajah*, for instance. Mr. Crowther (*New York Times* movie critic) is a man of great awareness and even he did not get the point.

The facts and details Mr. Crowther relates about this Hollywood tycoon of course are correct; nor do I question Mr. Crowther's conclusions. Yet this biography could have been a work of humor instead of an unrelieved hatchet job.

Thus, I'd like to issue a minority report on the late Mr. Mayer. I go to all this trouble because the point involved is what my readers and I have been discussing for twenty-five years.

The L. B. Mayer-haters always bring up the fact that L. B. Mayer was a former junk dealer. I was surprised that Crowther makes so much of this and usually refers to it in comic terms.

I'm not oversensitive in these matters. I believe these critics go all out in relating Hollywood tycoons, who built a great industry (at one time it was the third largest in the United States), to their earliest beginnings: the former junk dealer, the former pants presser, the former cloth sponger, and the former glove salesman. When you add to this emphasis Mr. Crowther's few hundred insistent adjectives like "greedy," "wily," and "devious," you cannot help but feel he is not only desecrating the foundation of the American success story, but using an underhand method to relieve himself of a usual phobia.

It seems that a Hollywood director or producer, I forget which, once waved his finger at John Barrymore, scolding him for some infraction of a studio rule, and John struck a pose and said, "Don't wave that finger at me. I remember when it had a thimble on it." This story was repeated all over and everybody laughed.

In the American culture, success is the only substitute for a knighthood or dukedom. There is a story in every Sunday supplement which relates the history of a success who delivered newspapers when he was four years old, whose mother worked in a jute mill, and who used to sober up his father every night. Now he is a success; he is the local distributor of Coca-Cola. And because of his success we think him an admirable man.

This is the classic American dream—except when it involves a Louis B. Mayer or another ex-pants presser, or an ex-cigar maker, or an ex-cloth sponger.

When Louis buys racehorses, Crowther says he bought them so he could make more money breeding them. Of course, no one else—Vanderbilts, Whitneys, Sinclairs—ever bred horses to make money. They are sportsmen: L. B. Mayer is a breeder for money. Crowther makes us weep for those wage slaves in the studios getting two thousand dollars a week when Mayer tried to cut their salaries. He sounds shocked.

Mr. Crowther turns all the virtues that we accept into Mayer's sins.

Mayer insisted on keeping his old father with all his broken English and sad table manners in his Hollywood mansion and introducing him to everyone that came. Now I think this is a very wonderful thing to have done. (I know at least three fancy pillars of society who visit their old parents in a nursing home: "My father loves it there, he has everything.")

Crowther is skeptical about the whole business. He searches high and low for some angle to it. When Crowther doesn't find anything, he leaves this poor old fellow dangling in the air and with a bit of disgust. It would have been nice to know something more about the old fellow's reaction to the Hollywood splendor, but Crowther seems to consider it an intrusion. Crowther says that even though the old Mayer "hawked and coughed" and had crude manners, "yet Mayer maintained his father in the bosom of his own family."

Of a reception for Mayer's daughters, Crowther writes, it "was fraught with embarrassment, incidentally. Trunks containing the new dresses of the Mayer girls did not arrive and they had to appear before the Republican politicians wearing their grubby traveling clothes." Does Mr. Crowther really imagine two daughters of a millionaire are happy about wearing "grubby traveling clothes"? (I remember that a very famous wedding was held up five hours because the gal's special handkerchief could not be located, and the newspapers told this story with compassion and understanding; the parents, of course, were old-stock Episcopalians, not more recent immigrants.)

This fellow really takes the life of an important man of our times out of the context of the American experience. The motion picture industry—founded by pants pressers, glove salesmen, and junk dealers—probably gave more pleasure and joy to more people than any other industry of modern times.

When we think of steel, oil, automobiles, and even newspapers (and here I remember Mr. Crowther's anger at Louis B. Mayer's hiring away some star and I thought back to the days when William Randolph Hearst hired away the entire staff of Joseph Pulitzer's World), the former junk dealers were conducting meetings of the Epworth League. Compared to all other American industries in their days of piracy, in the days of Rockefeller, Whitney, Russell Sage, John W. Gates, E. H. Harriman, and Daniel Drew, the former glove salesmen and pants pressers were men of the highest vision and of the noblest character.

I think the time has come to stand up and applaud these ex-junk dealers, ex-pants pressers and ex-glove salesmen because in the industry they created no one was killed, no strikers were shot down in cold blood, no copper company got up one morning and said, "There's no more copper" and left three thousand, two hundred families in little shacks stranded as though there had never even been a relationship between employee and employer, and no ten-year-old children were trained to stand on special platforms to fix the looms as they were in the Anglo-Saxon cotton mills of the Old South. Some of the folks I interviewed and (Mr. Crowther too) complained that Louis B. Mayer once propositioned Myrna Loy and Jeanette MacDonald. This too is considered bad? In fact, it was precisely at this moment that I acquired an affection for that poor old immigrant who was trying so desperately to be an amateur Gentile.

Mary, Mary, quite contrary

A FEW years back, Mary McCarthy published a novel about the class of Vassar, '33. The novel enjoyed a wide popularity, a popularity so wide that the moviemakers snapped it up and produced a picture changing nary the title, a word, or, more importantly, the ending. I saw this movie recently. Fortunately, I had forgotten the book.

As the movie ends, the members of the class of '33 gather at a pier to welcome home one of their number who has been away for several years. Lakey has been living in Europe, still a bachelor girl, or spinster, if you prefer. The other members of the group are now all young marrieds. They have had their share of "life." They have been, not collectively, raped, seduced, beaten, abandoned, dehumanized, and a few of them have committed adultery. One of them spends all her day counting her kid's bowel movements. They are blowsy, they have hips as big as a fireplace, they dress carelessly, they worry about the infidelity and bestiality of husbands, but Lakey's arrival cheers all of them.

Lakey is the lesbian. She disembarks trim, beautiful, self-possessed and humorous. She says the only things worth saying in the book and movie, she is the only one with an iota of kindness left. In short, she is a beauty, a philosopher, a sophisticate, to say nothing of the flat tummy and the magnificent grooming. She is the envy of the group who have all, to their misfortune, enjoyed the "normal" experiences of life.

Does Mary McCarthy really believe this? Or is she heaping contempt upon her pals who believe she has written the story of the 1930's, sans Roosevelt, Father Coughlin, Harry Hopkins and Henry Wallace?

Before the lesbian became a fit subject for serious literature, which is roughly between the time of Sappho and Miss Mc-Carthy, the rest of us used to call her a "woman lover." But just what she did in terms of love was a mystery, and it was a long time, personally, before I knew how the thing worked.

But then I am still better off than a lot of people because I was a clerk in a theatrical hotel on Broadway and I had occasion to meet lesbians.

Of all our permanent guests at the Markwell, they were the most desirable. They were not drunks, they did not make noise, they did not entertain men who might get drunk and make noise. There was one lesbian couple with whom I became quite friendly. The three of us went to the Metropolitan Opera two or three times. The older woman was roughly fifty, tall and angular, and the younger woman was no more than twenty-five, short and fat, with a pretty face. They worked in the same office, both of them city employees in the Municipal Building. Every morning, the older one, the one we would call "Butch" today, the bull dyke of the duo, came to the desk and intercepted any mail due to the younger. During the years from 1932 to 1938, I was behind that desk every day and the older one never missed, even though the younger girl received a missive about once a month. What a bore it must have been! What terror! And what a poor soul to be thus enslaved!

I knew another lesbian who took to heroin at thirty-nine and killed herself at forty-one. It was I who provided the facts for the reporter from the *Daily News*. "Former Miss Wyoming Found Dead: Leaves Notes." It was a small item on page 29. I picked Wyoming because it was a small state far away and they probably wouldn't bother to check on the "Former Miss Wyoming."

But no Lakey she.

Woman trouble

No TROUBLE in the world is as acute as woman trouble. Alcoholism or kleptomania involves only one person, but woman trouble always involves two persons—the one in trouble and the woman. Sometimes it involves the one in trouble and two women.

One of the attractions of being sixty is that the likelihood of getting into trouble diminishes every hour.

Brave men who commanded whole quartermaster depots twenty years ago, patent lawyers who have secured the rights to important textile processes, champion card sharks, are reduced to tears like children over woman trouble though, unlike children, they cry not because they are deprived but because they have surfeit.

I remember an old Thurber cartoon in which the analyzed, rising on the couch, says to the psychoanalyst, "I do everything you say, Doctor, except I keep thinking about this one girl—"

You can tell an embezzler to turn himself in or you can run down to the airlines terminal and get him a one-way passage for Brazil; the alcoholic can be directed to the local AA chapter or we can assure him he is not an alcoholic—he is only drunk. There is very little you can do for a man with woman trouble.

The big spenders

THE BIGGEST spenders are not the do-gooders in government. No sirree! The big spenders are the balance-the-budget boys who, through their lobbyists and their public relations offices, decry welfare measures and militate against all social legislation which destroys the moral fiber of the old pioneer stock.

No one in our society spends the money they do. They pour it out like rain. I know one lobbyist who buys one hundred tickets on the fifty-yard line for the big football game every year. I have known conservatives who think nothing of airplane jaunts for their ace salesmen. A state legislator who is forever demanding a balanced budget treats every one of his colleagues, once a year, to an outing complete with sirloin steaks and cases of whiskey.

The out-of-town buyer who arrives annually gets, at a snap of his fingers, what luxuries he craves. And the seller who counts the pennies when he haggles with the union shop-steward, is happy to plaster the money around nightclubs.

They never think of what they are doing to the moral fiber of the buyer—hotel suites, theatre tickets, telephone numbers. And send up more ice and soda!

And the joy of it is, all of it comes out of the income tax. Out of your pocket and out of mine and out of the pocket of the union shop steward, who does not get to deduct his beer and bowling expenses.

Sometimes the company doesn't get the order but it perseveres in pouring out the money for public relations. And no one can spend it like the conservatives from Texas who dump millions into radio programs of questionable value, who subsidize publications preaching the gospel of thrift, plus the maintenance of the oil-depletion tax exemption.

No one, in the American 1960's, spends money like a balance-the-budget man and no one deducts it from his income tax faster.

Southern hospitality

THE SOUTH insists on a cavalier culture before the Civil War, a culture of slave owners, dueling pistols, blooded horses, hoopskirts, and magnolias. But the defeat in the Civil War was the greatest boon to the average Southerner. Less than fifteen percent had been part of this cavalier culture, but the disaster of defeat enabled all the rest to become plantation owners, retroactively. Even the small cavalier culture could not have been more than sixty years old at best, for it could only date from the invention of the cotton gin.

But the charm and hospitality of native-born Southerners is one of the boasts of the South that is not a myth. The people who populate the old Confederate states have an unfailing devotion to charm and politeness.

But I do believe that the politeness and consideration so much a part of the Southerner's nature was acquired from his Negro slaves and later from the segregated Negro society. For two hundred years, the black man had been in perpetual service to the white society. The slave helped the master on with his coat, he cared constantly for the children, he learned the protocol for an elegant dinner ritual, and from morn till night the words most commonly on the lips of the slave were, "Yes, sir," and "No, ma'am," always uttered with a slight bow of the head.

The Southerner could not help but be influenced by this obeisance he himself demanded, and so in time he borrowed these, as eventually he was to borrow his slaves' music and dances. This politeness is everywhere manifest in the South. It will take the Southerner, both white and black, another generation to adopt the rough, cold impersonality of churning, whirling, industrial America.

Then, too, the natural beauty of the land contributes to the soft manners. A drive up the Shenandoah Valley, the valley Thomas Jefferson loved so much, is breathtaking. A tourist can begin this drive at the base of the Smoky Mountains in North Carolina—the first mountains, the geologists tell us, to bubble forth from the earth—and by traveling north-northeast, traverse the whole of the Shenandoah into Virginia to the city of Charlottesville to see Monticello, where Jefferson lived, and the University of Virginia which he founded.

Past Charlottesville is Mount Vernon, George Washington's home, still to the south of the nation's capital. Four miles eastward is Arlington Cemetery, once the estate of Robert E. Lee, the commander in chief of the Confederate Army.

No tourist or traveler, however, should miss the example of the new South. There is a new South and its exemplars are the cities of Charlotte, North Carolina, and Atlanta, Georgia.

Today, Negro lawyers hurry along these busy streets taking their daughters to dancing school. Negro bus drivers have savings accounts and Negro businessmen are on the board of directors of the Community Chest. The one-family farm is slowly disappearing, replaced by factories and airports.

Racial segregation may not yet be dead in Charlotte and Atlanta, but it is dying. The social, educational, political and economic compulsions which kept the Negro securely segregated have been banished by the new laws passed by the Kennedy and Johnson administrations. Within a generation the federal enforcement of these laws will change the South, its face and its character.

The Negroes are now moving toward the open society, just as all the other immigrant groups moved into the wide American middle class. Probably the native-born Southerner will not be so considerate in the future, probably not so polite, but at least he will be more equitable. For the first time in a century, the Southerner can tend to his own business: he does not have to worry whether the Negroes are moving to the back of the bus, he does not have to worry whether Negroes are uppity, as he likes to put it, or whether the Negro is toeing the segregation line.

If America had both a frontier and an immigrant tradition, now it also has a new South tradition, a tradition spawned when twenty million Negroes began moving from the margins of society into the center of full participation. And the Negro, like all former newcomers to the wondrous American middle class, is beginning to buy everything he does not need—in fact, two of everything he does not need.

As a lifelong adherent of the civil rights movement, I admit some drastic sacrifices are necessary. The old-time hospitality will perforce disappear. The South will no longer live as leisurely nor as generously. Some of the most beautiful acreage in the world will go under the bulldozer's plow. But justice will live in the land.

The brown-bagging sorrow

FOR TWO long weeks the city of Charlotte, North Carolina, suffered through a "brown-bagging" sorrow.

What was the "brown-bagging" sorrow?

Well, Charlotte has state-controlled liquor stores. No drinks may be sold, anywhere, by the drink. So when the folks go to clubs, restaurants, hotels, or sports arenas, they carry the bottle in the brown paper bag used by the state-controlled liquor stores. The restaurants and nightclubs charge from 75¢ to $1.50 for setups; i.e., soda, ice, lemon peel, etc., and everybody has a good time.

But after many years of "brown-bagging," the Attorney General of the state suddenly decreed that it was a violation of North Carolina's liquor laws. The only time it was legal to possess liquor other than in your home, according to this new interpretation, was when booze was being transported home from the liquor store, seal unbroken. And violation of this law, he said, was a misdemeanor, the violator subject to up to two years in prison, or a fine, or both.

The restaurant and nightclub owners immediately hired a lawyer to see what could be done. Some stated that they would have to close up unless the restriction on "brown-bagging" was lifted. The Chamber of Commerce estimated a loss of two million dollars in canceled conventions.

But just as both state and county police were ready to crack down on all brown-bagging, a Superior Court judge saved the day. The lawyer for the restaurants argued a petition and Judge H. L. Riddle enjoined the police, the Attorney General and the officials of the State Alcoholic Beverage Control Board from enforcing the law against brown-bagging. The Judge took the position that the State Legislature which meets again in January, 1967, should clarify the state's liquor laws.

And for the present, Judge Riddle has given the green light to continued "brown-bagging," and Charlotte, the restaurant and nightclub operators and the convention committee of the Chamber of Commerce are happy.

Some optimists thought that the whole controversy was an attempt to create enough agitation for the enactment of a law allowing the sale of liquor by the drink. But such a proposal would have a rocky road in the state legislature. The rural counties, which hold the balance of power (pre-reapportionment), would continue to resist any liberal expansion of the liquor laws. Liquor-by-the-drink would have little chance of overcoming the combination of rural counties, Methodist and Baptist clergymen, bootleggers, and Tar Heels in the hills who make the white liquor.

The folks will continue to carry that brown bag, the skin-tight bag for men, and the larger roomier one for the ladies. The liquor stores, manned by Southern gentlemen, place the bottle for a female customer in a larger, fluffy brown bag, so that people will think she's carrying knitting—or her husband's overalls —or canned food for her pets.

The American way of life

THE American way of life is an Idea in the minds of men and women. The American way of life is the opportunity for each man to burgeon out for himself and achieve whatever his character, talent, and ambition will permit. The American way of life is the destiny of the unknown—forever meeting the new challenge for which there is no precedent.

Life in the middle class

WHILE there is some controversy over the war in Vietnam, most of that controversy rages among a few college professors, fewer newspaper columnists, and a handful of college students.

It is true the PTAs of America are concerned about many things in the scheme of educational values, but the chief worry of the PTA is that the college board examinations are too hard.

The John Birch Society raises hob with the liberals, but it is also true that the Birch Society has to distribute its books free of charge to the folks and the number of people who read the literature, so called, is miniscule.

The newspapers reproduce the anxiety about teen-agers and rock 'n' roll and I suppose any fellow at a bar can work up an argument about Lyndon Baines Johnson or Martin Luther King.

But what really exercises the folks, what brings them out in vast numbers, is the proposal of the city council to cut a road through a residential area or to re-zone twelve acres to accommodate a shopping center.

Never mind the threat of a Negro family moving into the neighborhood, the folks can take care of that themselves, with their real estate agents and brokers. But re-zoning and road building are horses of two different colors.

The hearings usually take place in a setting of virtually paralytic hysteria. Hundreds of folks crowd the chamber where the harassed city councilmen or county commissioners conduct what is laughingly called a parliamentary proceeding. The poor, banded in their little association, always have a lawyer with them. The rich bring twelve lawyers.

Ah, the dialogue! "We don't need or want a shopping center!" Applause. "That is no place for the new road. The new road belongs over on the north side." Applause and tears. "We do not want the road widened—it is beautiful as it is." Exultant applause.

Eventually they sue, but they have won the battle right there in the chamber. All of them have votes and if public officials can do one thing, they can count noses pretty accurately. The angriest ones are the ladies, dressed in their finery, shouting down the member of the city council by reminding him not only that they are citizens, voters, and residents, but MOTHERS too. The only way to clear the chamber is to encourage the folks with some kind words and assure them nothing is going to happen immediately.

Of course when the city council in its ignorance and innocence passes an ordinance requiring all dogs be leashed, the wellsprings of emotion geyser skyward, too.

Leash a dog! Man's best friend?

The folks sit there in dismay, shaking their heads in wonderment at such cruelty. "I can understand though not approve leashing maybe a wolf. But to leash a collie? A Weimaraner? A little Chihuahua?"

Anyone on that city council or county board of commissioners who wants to be President or even a member of the state legislature is going to move to table the ordinance until the town can hire a few experts to look into the matter of roads, shopping centers, and penned animals.

A kind word for Cassius

CASSIUS CLAY, the world's heavyweight champion, expressed himself rather illogically, perhaps even unpatriotically, when he was informed his draft board was reclassifying him 1-A. But what Cassius Clay said, hot off the cuff, was mild compared to what thousands of college students and professors are saying.

We would be naïve if we didn't acknowledge that there was great pressure to get this fellow out of circulation. If an offbeat journalist in North Carolina who enjoys no connection with government, army, or prizefighting receives a few letters every week asking, "Why isn't Cassius Clay in the army?" we can well imagine the letters which must have poured upon draft board officials, army officials, and government clerks.

In 1966, Cassius Clay is in the same position Jack Johnson was fifty years ago. But the emphasis is entirely different. People hated Jack Johnson because he had married a white woman. The public clamored for a "White Hope" to recapture the heavyweight crown "for the White race." Today, such a clamor is taboo. Sammy Davis, Jr., enjoys great popularity and he is married to a white girl. Harry Belafonte is married to a white girl and he is a most respected concert artist. Cassius Clay knew they hated him when he told the Negro Floyd Patterson, "You are now the white hope." No one hates Cassius because he is a Negro.

It would be easy to say the folks resent Cassius because he is a loudmouth and a wise guy but that is too simple. The loud-mouths in sports are admired and respected. Leo Durocher is anything but retiring and Ty Cobb was anything but sports-manlike. People don't hate Clay because he promises a knock-out in the fourth round. Babe Ruth pointed to the stands be-fore he hit a home run and the crowd rose and cheered his trip around the bases. When a reporter told Babe he received more money than President Hoover, Babe replied, "I hit better than him." The folks revered Babe. I revered him even after listening to his language while he was playing pool with a teammate up in Doyle's on Broadway.

The truth is America really should love Cassius Clay because he is a living symbol of Puritanism, old-fashioned Puritanism. He doesn't drink, he doesn't smoke, he doesn't take the Lord's name in vain and he divorced his wife because she wore slacks and outraged an orthodox tenet of Puritanism. The Hebrews had originally made it a crime for a woman to masquerade as a man and the Puritan and the orthodox Anglo-Calvinist tradi-tion of America and England took over this idea.

Moreover, Cassius is religious. We don't by-and-large approve of the Muslims, but none of us takes them seriously. And anyway, how many fight fans are up on their theology and have read the Koran? As a matter of fact, the most glamorous delegates to the UN are Moslems with turbans. I once suggested to the Israeli ambassador that he wear a turban so all the high school kids would ask him for his autograph. In those two personal habits which forever haunt the American soul, sex, and religion, Cassius Clay is everything we say we are but ain't. His Puritanism evokes huge areas of guilt. And I think that is why we hate him.

The older girls

THE AIRLINES have insisted on a contract which makes stewardesses leave the airplane upon reaching age thirty-two. Eight stewardesses involved in contract negotiations with American Airlines said this was unfair and a discriminating labor abuse.

Airline officials said the average age of their stewardesses was twenty-two, that most of the girls worked about twenty-six months, and the reason most of them left was because they got married.

I had hopes as I began the story that these airline officials would finally reveal what grievances they had—or thought they might have—against girls past thirty-two, but no soap. Some of my best friends are over thirty-two.

The airlines invoke no such serious age requirements on pilots. In fact, pilots are always agitating for the Government to allow them to fly until they are in their late sixties. Since I am over sixty and believe I shouldn't even be a passenger anymore, I hope the Government doesn't accede to this request.

But thirty-two for the girls! Is there a specific reason for thirty-two? How does it differ from thirty-three or thirty-one? Are the airline stewardesses like certain trees which can only be cut down at a certain age?

Let me ask the airlines this: how old was that stewardess who sat on the pilot's lap? There's your reason for the older girls, so-called.

Jewish names

To the immigrant Jew, the most English of all names was Shirley. Sheldon ran it a close second. Today, every novelist who wants to write about a Jewish girl calls her Shirley. When the Jews adopted Shirley and Sheldon en masse, the Gentiles dropped these two names like hot potatoes. Now the Jews are dropping them and Shelly is gaining popularity along with Robin and Penny.

Down in the South, names like Herschel and Mendel persevere among the Presbyterians and the Baptists but the Jews are going to Jonathan and Scott.

The surname Schwartz was as Germanic as the surname Bismarck. The Russian Jews who came to America with the surname Chornee met with immigration officers who couldn't spell it.

"What does it mean?" asked the inspectors.

"Chornee means *schwartz* [black]," was the answer, naturally.

So the immigration officers did the Jews a favor. They translated black into Yiddish—Schwartz.

Among the rigorously Orthodox Jews, the Cohanim are the priestly caste. To the immigration officials, Cohen was as good and easy a Jewish name as any, so many the Litvak who welcomed the immigration shorthand which transformed him immediately into a man of the highest standing in the synagogue.

Judge Samuel Leibowitz tells the story about his name being Leibow and a neighbor advising the family to Americanize it into Leibowitz. At Baltimore, the immigration inspector ran out of names one morning and the last Jewish family that day was hurriedly catalogued as "Baltimore." The family of Joseph Baltimore eventually became prominent in Maryland.

The attempt to shed every vestige of Jewish life extended to the language. Some of the folks stopped talking Yiddish. My uncle was one of these. When my mother talked to him at a time when at best he knew but eighty English words he still pretended he didn't understand her Yiddish. He would turn to one of us and ask, "Vot did she sed?" and we always translated for him.

One lady lost a suit in court because she would not surrender her pride and speak Yiddish. She had brought suit against a storekeeper who had refused to repair the sidewalk in front of his place of business. She fell, sustained painful and costly injuries.

During the trial, the lawyer asked, "Where did you fall?"

She replied, "Offn sidewalk," which in Yiddish means "on the sidewalk," but translated was "off the sidewalk."

The lawyer repeated the question.

Again she answered, "Offn sidewalk." She wouldn't budge.

She lost.

Only in America.

Madalyn Murray

MADALYN MURRAY, the embattled atheist who sparked the controversial Supreme Court decision banning school prayers, is battling another appeal to keep from being extradited from Hawaii to Baltimore, where she is charged with assaulting police officers and resisting arrest. I have no idea whether these charges against her in Maryland are reasonable or not. I doubt seriously, however, that anyone can deny she has indeed been harassed.

She has been harassed because she is a self-declared atheist, probably the No. 1 atheist in America. How many "secret" atheists there are is anyone's guess. There are probably millions who silently share the skepticism Madalyn Murray expresses openly.

Madalyn Murray is a victim of these perilous times. Less than fifty years ago, it was possible for Clarence Darrow to travel up and down the country speaking in every city, challenging the local divine to a debate on the subject of whether or not God exists. Darrow, of course, always took the negative.

People packed these debates, paying fifty cents for a ticket.

They asked questions pro and con. And Darrow, after chasing God out of heaven, used to go out to the coffeehouse, arm-in-arm with the priest or the rabbi or the minister and they would argue some more. And everybody had fun.

But there is no longer any relaxation about religious faith. It isn't that atheism has become unfashionable. Nor do I believe atheists are reviled because Russian Communists profess a disbelief in God. I believe atheism is suspect today because our churches have become secularized. The Protestant Church is secularized and the synagogue and temple are secularized and even the Catholic Church, albeit to a lesser degree, is secularized. The laymen have taken over.

When a layman is secure in his faith, he worries about nothing. But alas, there is no more security and the laymen worry about everything.

Does anyone think my mother, a pious Jew, worried a whit about my father and his cronies talking about Eugene V. Debs and Clarence Darrow? She smiled as if to say, "They are mere children." She had God, she knew He was there, she was secure.

But the situation is changed now. The clergyman has lost his classical function. He is no longer the teacher, the spiritual leader. He is there to deliver the invocation and the benediction and compile credits with his board of trustees for having visited the Kiwanis, the Rotary, and the Chamber of Commerce, or as the Jewish laymen like to boast, "The rabbi does wonderful interfaith work." It's always "wonderful."

So these laymen now take to harassing Madalyn Murray. They send her obscene letters and make threatening phone calls and cheer the bully-boy cops who try to arrest her. These laymen and many Americans generally have only the faintest idea of what a religious observance is and what demands religion makes. They are guilty about their ignorance. The only way they can express their guilt is to raise hell with Madalyn Murray and to denounce the Supreme Court for banning a prayer constructed by the Board of Regents in New York from the philosophy of the Hindu Rabindranath Tagore.

Harassing Madalyn Murray is the new piety.

I often laugh at the tremendous religiosity of the Baptist, Methodist, and Presbyterian brethren in my home city of Charlotte. Charlotte has more churches per capita than any other city in the world save Edinburgh, Scotland. I smile when I watch the clergymen on television discussing premarital intercourse, drug addiction, and juvenile delinquency.

When I was a boy the minimum requirement was three prayers a day and you washed your hands before you sat anywhere. You invoked God's protection for every step you took. My mother began preparing for the Sabbath on Thursday morning and she worked until sundown Friday. If our Italian neighbor wasn't nearby, my mother didn't even cut the string on the laundry bundle on the Sabbath.

Now our churches, shules and congregations, for an hour and a half a week, are filled with "civic leaders," all straining to get at them there atheists.

Without a job

A LETTER from a reader in Tucson, Arizona: "What do people do when they get to be fifty-six years old? . . . I've been a competent musician all my life, but now I am too old for a job. . . . Do we all have to send our wives to work to support us? . . ."

It is not much better, emotionally at least, among the highly paid executives.

One of the giant advertising agencies in New York recently revised the way it billed one of its clients and in the process had to let go forty-six employees. Their yearly salary was an aggregate of some six hundred thousand dollars. That represents some six hundred thousand dollars' worth of demoralization.

Being without work in this highly competitive, affluent society is about the worst that can happen to a man. True, life will deprive him of his parents and some of his friends and he will have to bear this grief. But when he is without work he is deprived of his very purpose.

There is no harder job than looking for a job.

Think of the strong men, the most individualistic in the world, reduced to mill-daddies. I've seen them sitting on the porches of their shacks, waiting for the factory whistle so they can take the lunch to their wives and daughters in the mill.

Any man who is employed or who owns a business will get ten calls a year at least from fellows who want help. Sometimes they just want to come into the office to talk, to be near people working; sometimes they want advice about making a contract. It is always painful, though once in a while you help a man connect.

A man needs a place to go in the morning, just as a woman probably needs children. There are men who trotted the streets during the Depression, watching construction work, sitting through dull movies, so that at night they could return and create the illusion that they were in action. A man must have a place to go to in the morning.

Firecrackers in Dixie

WHAT SURPRISED me most when I first came south was the sound of firecrackers on Christmas Day. Down South there were no firecrackers on the Fourth of July, even when they were legal. But you heard them popping off all over the place beginning on Christmas morn.

I have found out why.

The story goes back to a big Alabama plantation before the Civil War. At that time, which we like to call the antebellum society, the Southern cavaliers and younger gentry did indeed shoot off fireworks on July Fourth. One day, the year was either 1841 or 1842, a rather literate Negro slave came up to the big house and asked about the fireworks.

"Old Sam," said Mr. Gaylord Thurmond, "that shootin' and shoutin' is to celebrate today, the Fourth of July."

"Massa Gaylord, what's that?"

"Sam, the Fourth of July is Independence Day. The day the colonies won their freedom from England."

"Massa Gaylord, how did you all win this freedom from that Massa Englan'?"

"We fought for it, that's how we won our freedom."

"Massa Gaylord, you mean you can get freedom by fighting for it?"

"Old Sam, isn't it time you were back there pickin' cotton? Nothing for you to worry your head, Sam, the good Lord will take care of you—see to it that you get to heaven. . . ."

But Gaylord Thurmond did not take this lightly. That very night he sent word to all the plantation owners for miles around, to come to a meeting the following Sunday. At the meeting Gaylord Thurmond told of his conversation with Sam and it was agreed all around that there was considerable risk in the July Fourth business.

The committee sent letters to planters all over the South, alerting them to this danger. And so they began to shoot fireworks on Christmas Day to remind the slaves that the good Lord will take care of them in heaven and they forgot about doing any shootin' and hollerin' on the Fourth of July.

Public vs. private schools

WHEN I was a boy, attending Public School 20 on the Lower East Side of New York City, the big debate that every

class held annually was: "Resolved: Living in the city is better than living in the country."

The city always won. That was not because no one in the
school, debaters, audience and referees included, had ever so
much as seen more than a brief glimpse of the country, if that.

The debate is over now, I suspect. Some of us moved to the
country in the suburbs, some of us to the real country in the
West and Southwest, and some of us even to the Northwest
where the great timber grows.

The debate that rages now is: "Resolved: Are private schools
better than public schools?"

One of the metropolitan papers recently conducted a private-
school census in which it estimated that in New York City there
were twenty thousand students in attendance. Catholic and
Jewish parochial schools were excluded from this figure.

What the folks mean by "better," of course, is not hard to
figure out. By better they mean: Is the education more personal?
Is it easier to get into college from a private school? Does one's
child have a chance to associate with other students equally and
universally as genteel?

The answer to these and similar questions is a resounding yes.
It is easier for the private school graduate to enter college. The
educational techniques are often more advanced and more ex-
perimental in a private school and the classes always smaller.

But—and it is an important but—by virtue of their equal-
itarian nature American middle-classniks never tolerate an elite
for long. There are twenty thousand private school kids in New
York City, which is about what we would have guessed was the
population of the rural countryside when I was young. Twenty
thousand is an elite. All one has to do to start a race to the death
is show one American an elite and he is off running to catch up.
The private school will soon start proliferating like the pro-
verbial toadstool, growing everywhere. Once we thought we
were imprisoned forever in the city save for that one day a year
when we went on the Annual Boat Ride and Picnic to Bear
Mountain, sponsored by the local Tammany district leader.

The day will come when no suburb will dare call itself

a suburb unless it boasts a private school as well as a public
school. The result will be that we shall be the first three-school-
system country in history—public, private, and parochial—but
I do not think this portends the day that the majority of graduates forty years old and over can divide fractions.

Sex for convicts

CLINTON T. DUFFY, the warden of San Quentin Prison,
and Al Hirshberg, a journalist of prolific talents, have forwarded
a revolutionary proposal for convicts in the October, 1965, issue
of *Coronet* magazine. They make an interesting point in trying
to abolish the evils which result from men confined without sex.
Those who are not corrupted by homosexuality are often corrupted by a traumatic bitterness and hatred.

The Latin countries are much more practical about their
prison systems than we—and spend considerably less. They long
ago instituted the privilege of conjugal visits between convict-
husbands and wives and between bachelors and mistresses.

North Carolina recently instituted Released Time which gives
a convict a furlough of sorts at home in return for exemplary
behavior. It is a partial answer to the question of how to avoid
the brutalizing effect of imprisonment, and Released Time works
best for prisoners with short terms who have indicated they will
not become recidivists.

I doubt seriously if the puritanical American society would
ever really underwrite the visit of a convict to his home for sex
or the visit of his wife to prison for the same purpose, but then
we are very clever at pretending sex doesn't exist at all which
is precisely what Released Time does. It was inaugurated by
our own Mr. Randall (now prison head in Oregon), and it saves
Tar Heels and a few other states millions of dollars as well as
preserving some human beings who will probably prove useful
to law-abiding society.

The federal penologist, J. V. Bennett, one of the greatest prison men in America, knew how important sex was as an elementary drive, and he did the only thing society would allow. The federal prisoner is kept in constant motion, up and down the stairs, over and over again, marching, or trotting in and out of corridors—constantly, plus a full eight-hour day at work, so that by the time of "lights out" at 9 P.M., there is nothing the prisoner wants more than a night's sleep. They have reduced to a bare minimum the idle moments for thoughts to wander.

This system is not followed in most of our state penitentiaries where men simply sit idle in cells. As I see it now Randall's Released Time idea was the greatest development in prison science since Thomas Mott Osborne of Sing Sing took the stripes away, brought an "outside" baseball team to a prison yard, and abolished the silent system.

Thomas Mott Osborne, Lewis E. Lawes, J. V. Bennett, Clinton Duffy and George Randall are the great scientists of this sad, sad discipline. It is the tragic American institution, involving some three quarters of a million Americans who have no vote and are thus wholly dependent upon the rare public servant who dares utter a word above battle.

A charcoal world

THE North Carolina Supreme Court handed down a decision that a restaurant could use "Charcoal Steak House" as part of its name. The Charcoal Steakhouse, Inc., has sued Staley's Charcoal Steak House, charging an infringement on its prior rights. The Supreme Court said no, anybody could say Charcoal Steak House.

It figures.

The advertising agencies are fighting with each other over television and radio and in the newspapers with ads boasting which cigarettes have more charcoal.

I have a vague recollection from my boyhood in the ghetto of pregnant women chewing on charcoal to ease heartburn.

We live in a charcoal world.

The vanishing drummer

THE DRUMMER—the fellow who set up in the local hotel for a couple of days and brought the town all the news and gossip from the area—is vanishing from the American scene.

They are gone, gone with the smoking car. In their place are the manufacturer's representative, the sales engineer, and the buying office. You can still see traveling men at Chicago's O'Hare or at the Atlanta or Dulles airports every Friday night, shoes still gleaming, suit neatly pressed, attaché case stylishly setting off their whole outfit. They travel these days by air and by automobile, often averaging more than a thousand miles a week, and they sell everything from heavy machinery to housedresses.

But statistically there were more drummers when the gross national product was a tenth of what it is today. There were more drummers when we had ninety million people than when we have one hundred and ninety-one million. The development of buying offices, national advertising, and the computer have seriously decimated the numbers of the traveling men. The big firms now wait for the chance to retire the fellow who makes thirty thousand dollars a year so they can hire college boys at one hundred dollars a week, who become order-takers.

I report all of this in sorrow. I have always loved the traveling salesman.

Problems of urban living

THERE'S A new problem afflicting the tenants of high-rise apartments. The mezuzah, which traditionally is mounted on the "doorpost" with nails, can't be attached to the metal door frames.

A company is now manufacturing magnetic mezuzahs to solve this problem.

"Our Negroes are wonderful people"

In one of my books I wrote that the happiest Jew in the entire world is the lone Jew in a small Southern town. To the Gentile community, he is "our Jew," and they guard him like they guard the Confederate monument in the square.

Now "our Negro" is approaching the same happy status. The Protestant churches of the South now fall over one another to get a Negro family to join, and when they succeed there is a great feeling of pride: "We are an integrated congregation, suh," they say, "our Negroes are wonderful people."

The fight game

On January 19, 1865, Patsy Foy and Harry Cooper fought a boxing match near Virginia City, Nevada. The fight went sixty-four rounds, which took two hours and twenty-eight minutes. Both men were badly bruised and Cooper was knocked out. The purse was one hundred and eight dollars. History does not record whether it was divided or if winner took all.

Patriotism

Every now and then, one of our professional super-patriots rises to the moment and denounces the times. We are never as patriotic as we should be nor as we once were. In his time, he says, people praised the Flag unashamedly. They sang the patriotic songs with fervor and love.

I shrug off such complaints.

The vast majority of Americans are patriotic enough to pay their taxes, federal, state, and city, on time and with little fuss. The vast majority answer the call to the Colors when security of the country is threatened or the Congress declares war.

The immigrant never heard of states' rights nor did a rendition of "Dixie" stir him. All he knew was America and the Flag and there were more flags on the Lower East Side of New York on any given day than there were in the whole South on the Fourth of July. The immigrant felt a compulsion to prove his loyalty while the native-born citizen knows you are born with loyalty just as you are born with blue eyes or black hair. The fellow who says we're not as patriotic as we used to be is unaware of the fact that he is talking about us ground-kissing immigrants of 1880 to 1920.

Urban renewal

TODAY America is on the move. Everything is temporary. "To Grandmother's house we go" has given way to a mere place to flop. When asked for his address, many a tenant has to open his wallet to find out.

This tremendous mobility is, of course, part of our great industrial expansion and the complete urbanization of our culture. Of itself this development is not bad; it provides us with creature comforts once undreamt: the inside toilet, the ice-machine, television and the air conditioner. But we would be fools if we did not honestly acknowledge that we are paying a price for them.

Perhaps urban renewal will mean something entirely different to the "do-gooders" who come after us. The uprooting of the slum areas, which moves people from their accustomed surroundings and uproots them, may give way to the happier solu-

tion of rebuilding, modernizing the houses, and providing mod-
dern facilities, leaving some "roots" intact instead of trans-
ferring the folks to an institutionalized project.

We have one clue about the old slum sections. We older types
tried so desperately to get OUT and now our grandchildren are
on the waiting list trying so desperately to get IN.

Visitor from Mali

THE GENTLEMAN from Mali sat in the rear of a Dr. Martin Luther King, Jr., rally. He quietly observed that he was gathering material for a Ph. D. thesis, "The Curious Customs of the
White Natives in the Hinterland of America."

The discothèque

A DISCOTHÈQUE is a night club. The people go there to do
those variant dances on the twist. While the customers writhe
on the floor, a girl in a suspended cage writhes above them. It is
just the kind of an evening Grandma wouldn't understand. But
that's only because Grandma has better sense than most of us.

The Mets and TV

THE NEW YORK METS played a twenty-three-inning baseball game with the San Francisco Giants. Earlier in the day they
played a nine-inning game. From 1:05 on a Sunday afternoon
until 11:23 Sunday night these two teams toiled for victory.
Everyone interested by now knows the Giants won 8-6 on Del
Crandall's twenty-third-inning double. Everyone also knows
the Mets won the television rating for the day.

That is probably the most interesting part of the story. Think of the number of children who reached sudden maturity when they realized Daddy was not going to surrender the set for *Lassie*. Think of the wives and sons and daughters who suddenly said in a shocked whisper, "You mean we're not going to watch Ed Sullivan?" Think of the wailing when some of the folks cried, "But *Bonanza* is passing us by!"

Phenomenon at the Fair

OUR AGE is a computerized age and the New York World's Fair was no exception. Computers on the turnstiles not only totaled the folks who passed in but the folks who passed out. On one Saturday when the glamorous computer checkers toted up the respective totals, they found 209,198 persons had entered the Fair by pass or payment but 211,176 had exited. Wrote *The New York Times* reporter, "No one had an explanation for this phenomenon." This you call a phenomenon?

I should like to essay an explanation or two, lest the folks throw away their computers. Very probably the computers were inadequate to take care of the Hungarians who came to visit the Fair. It is said of Hungarians that if you precede one of them through a revolving door, he will still come out ahead of you. I have a good friend who is a movie producer from Hungary whose success can be attributed to his never forgetting his family's motto: "It is not enough to be a Hungarian."

It's either that or some two thousand kids sneaked through the fence some place along the line.

Alligator rustling

CHIEF BILL OSCEOLA of the Seminole Tribe has posted a fifty-dollar reward for the apprehension of alligator rustlers. An

Indian village with thatched huts arts and crafts center was burglarized and damaged and the alligators killed for their hides.

No Indians were around at the time as the village is held as a tourist attraction.

What hurt worst of all, the marauding miscreants took the television set.

Ma Joad knew

"GRAPES OF WRATH" Joads?

Thirty years after California met some of the dusted-out Okies with armed guards on her borders, the Okies look back on the first years as slim pickings. They had a love of owning land and most of them got a-holt of a few acres. A subdivision grew here and there and some of the Okies woke up to find their land had made them wealthy. Others opened service stations, car repair shops, and the women opened beauty shops, trained in hospitals to be nurses' aids, sent their children through college, and now the third generation are in large part teachers, engineers, and physicians.

Remember what Ma Joad said: "We are the people."

Open line for insomniacs

BETWEEN the hours of 1 and 5 o'clock in the morning, the disc jockeys are varying the tedium of their jobs by maintaining an open telephone line for listeners to call up and get things off their chests. You can hear the opinions and the experiences of fellow humans. You might tune in on a recipe for carrot pie or a dissertation on the superiority of living an encapsuled life by a member of the John Birch Society. A young girl wants to know where there is a home for unmarried mothers and a bewildered father wonders why his daughter left home. It beats the hell out of counting sheep.

Reviving the staff

THERE is nothing like modernizing and installing new equipment to renew the enthusiasm and efficiency of the staff. The sense of being valued enough to be given good tools to work with revives the human spirit and gets the work out.

Red-blooded boys

AT THE Woodside High School, not far from San Francisco, the cops arrested thirty of the students, charging them with the sale and possession of marijuana cigarettes.

The kids all came from the "best families" (read high-income for best) which prompted the mayor of Woodside, the Honorable Donald J. Graham, to make the sociological comment, "In a slum, it might be a habit. But here, it's just a novelty."

The kids were only out for kicks.

Our hidden slums

SLUMS are the most profitable of all income-producing properties. The crowded tenements return proportionately the highest rents for the space let. There are tenements in every one of our large cities built to accommodate at best forty families into which two hundred are jammed and crowded. And the upkeep on a slum dwelling is minimal.

The slum is institutionalized because it is also a socially approved method of segregation. The slums segregate not only the races but the poor. Keep the slum hidden, away from the business district and far from the neat residential areas, and the middle and upper middle classes do not have to face up to the prospect of their inhumanity.

In the North, the middle class never sees the slums. They are out of the way, in areas never normally traversed by nice liberals. The decent Northerner may step into an elevator and say "Good morning" to an operator who has just left a tenement crawling with rats and lice, but the operator is dressed spotlessly in his uniform and the evil he should present is hidden and invisible.

Street gangs

THERE were gangs on the Lower East Side of New York fifty years ago. Each street, in fact, had a gang. I remember the leader of the Orchard Street gang was absolutely fearless. Once he stood his ground alone, a solitary target for the rocks of the Allen Streeters when the rest of his companions had fled. He came back to his crowd with great scorn and contempt for them, uttering curses on their manhood. Eventually this fellow became a lawyer and a Tammany Hall district leader.

Barbershop talk

I HAVE never objected to talkative barbers. I always figure they do not know on whom they are picking because I can outtalk any barber who ever handled a clipper.

When they ask me who had the most hits as a Yankee I can always ask them what Yankee was also an All-American halfback. I know it's Earl Combs and they usually know it's Lou Gehrig but they can rarely identify two other All-Americans who made baseball their career (Eric Tipton and Sam Chapman).

Barbershop conversation is probably the last of the great American dialogue that started with Hamilton and Jefferson and was continued by Douglas and Lincoln, Woodrow Wilson and Henry Cabot Lodge, and John Kennedy and Richard Nixon.

The three stages of man

WHEN you are young; when you are middle-aged; and finally when people tell you how well you look.

Progress

ON the Lower East Side the high school students held a dance once a year. There were no formal gowns and the affair was all over at 10 o'clock. Mr. Herman Brown, who was in charge (he is still around, an employee of the New York Board of Education), always opened the dance with "The Star-Spangled Banner" and played it loud enough for everybody to hear. On dance night all the windows were open and you saw the people leaning on the windowsills or standing on the fire escapes to hear the music.

I have observed the four-times-a-year ball held at the fanciest high school here in Charlotte. It costs a little over two thousand dollars to decorate the auditorium. The kids have a special party of their own before the dance, and after the dance they go to another party previously arranged with yet a different band and in a different place—three places on dance night. I asked one of the boys and he told me it cost him fifty dollars for his date and this does not count the use of the family automobile and neither does it take into consideration the contributions made to the main event by parents.

A nearby girls' college announces it is embarking on a big expansion program. Great! Is it going to have more classrooms, more teachers, more books? No; but there'll be three new dorms . . . and a beauty shop in the student union.

The most precious thing

THE MOST precious thing in America is the college classroom.

The uninterrupted dialogue goes on in politics but it is often inhibited and sometimes sacrificed. The congressman who disapproves of the big budget still wants federal subsidies to his constituents so he supports Johnson. The conservative candidate who wants to be a senator often has to keep his mouth shut when he talks to union leaders.

No salesman tells the sales manager or the owner that the product is overpriced. He simply competes. Certainly the bank clerk doesn't tell the bank president about mortgage rates.

As far as the church goes, long ago the laymen took over from the Protestant clergy and the rabbinate. To a lesser degree this is true in many Catholic parishes, too. A minister may well serve on the town Recreation Commission, arranging tennis permits and Little League ball games, but there are whole areas of community activity he dare not invade and he knows it.

The press is free, admittedly, but it is still in many ways conditioned by regional considerations and by the politics of the owners. A publisher may tell his editors and reporters their personal opinions are their own but he will set policy for the paper.

That leaves the college classroom. Once the professor shuts that door, they take off. Nothing stands in their way. A college professor I know was discussing the "God Is Dead" controversy. "How many here believe in God?" he asked. Out of thirty-one students, eighteen put up their hands. Nothing happened to the other thirteen. The congressman would not dare not raise his hand, nor would the insurance salesman, nor even the editor.

Our institutions of higher education in this country carefully preserve this freedom of expression.

When Professor Altizer of Emory University, a school heavily endowed with Methodist money, reactivated this old controversy about God, there were some angry rumblings from alumni. Some of the alumni even muttered they would renege on pledges for the building fund. Emory University wouldn't even dignify these rumblings by replying.

Out of these classrooms perhaps come the young boys who parade with signs of protest as well as the young boys willing to spend two or three years in Africa as a Peace Corps Volunteer, or enlist in the Air Corps to fight in Southeast Asia. The uninterrupted dialogue of the classroom has given them all a sense of pride in America.

How to fool the sheriff

REVEREND EDWARD CAHILL, of the Pittsburgh Unitarian Church, was telling me about his experiences in Mississippi. His assignment was to bring assistance to the poverty-stricken Negro farmers who were camping out in deserted army barracks.

Cahill was carefully briefed. He put an expensive bag of golf clubs and all sorts of fishing tackle in the back seat of his car, ostentatiously displayed, and all over Mississippi the sheriffs smiled happily as they waved him on.

PART 4

The Golden Insurance Plan

Let Jews forgive Christians, too

I HAVE a suggestion to offer the Jewish leaders of the world. It is in the form of an invitation addressed to the Chief Rabbis of Israel, United Kingdom, France, Denmark, Argentina, as well as to the Rabbinical Councils of America, the B'nai B'rith, American Jewish Committee, and American Jewish Congress.

My plan is to call a Jewish Ecumenical Council in Jerusalem some time in 1967, for the purpose of issuing a Jewish Schema on the Christians.

The Catholics and many of the Protestant brotherhoods have recently issued the Christian Schema on the Jews. We have been absolved from personal responsibility in the crucifixion of Jesus.

Now it is our turn. I propose that we forgive the Christians for the Inquisition, the Crusades, the ghettoes, and the expulsions. I think we can also include forgiveness for the usurpation of property which continued unabated for one thousand, six hundred years, the worldwide discrimination; and we may also waive our annoyances at the barriers that guard country, city, and fraternal clubs.

The Christians have been nice. Now we can be nice. There is no reason for us to hold bitterness in our hearts because Crusader Godfrey of Bouillon drove the Jews of Jerusalem into the synagogue and set it on fire.

There is no reason in the world why our Christian neighbors today should be held responsible for the wholesale slaughter of the Jews in the cities on the Rhine by the Christians of the Second Crusade. Nor should they be held responsible for the murders perpetrated by Peter the Hermit and Peter of Cluny.

And why should we let the memory of the Inquisition haunt us? England's crime of expulsion and expropriation in the year 1290?

And there is every political reason these days to forgive the

Germans, Ukrainians, Hungarians, Croats, Poles, and Roumanians, the traditional anti-Semites. The Germans are even on our side in the Cold War against Communism.

As for the quotas in the medical schools and the colleges which had been used to control the influx of Jews, why there is no doubt they will disappear now that we are no longer guilty of the death of Jesus, and when the Christians read our own Schema of forgiveness.

For all this terrifying history, let us clear those Christians living today. The Jewish Schema on the Christians would not only express appreciation for the recent events at the Catholic Ecumenical Council, but would clear the air for brotherhood and remove our own memories of bitterness. I strongly urge the Jewish leaders to call this conference. It is the time for—love.

Negro morality

DURING THE question period after nearly every speech I make around the country, there is always a statement from the audience about the problems of the civil rights movement and "Negro crime." They block traffic, violate the laws of trespass, engage an entire police force to control their freedom rides, sit-ins, marches, and protests—and furthermore, the arrests of Negroes for crime is vastly out of proportion to their numbers.

I do not believe that Negroes should receive preferential treatment when arrested for crime or when their conduct is challenged by authorities. It is necessary, however, to make the point that crimes committed by Negroes are usually the crimes of the poor, easily recognizable as the crimes of the slum and the ghetto.

Negroes have never scuttled a ship or sunk one without warning; they never looted a city's treasury, padded construction costs of highway or courthouse, or watered the milk; they never got a kickback for drugs sold to our men in embattled Vietnam; they never dispossessed a tenant and put his bedstead out on the sidewalk; they never sold faulty wire or bullets to their government during a war, or rigged prices, or hired call-girls to influence purchasing agents, or conspired to establish phony bids for government contracts; they never cornered the shares of Northern Pacific, nor watered the stock of the Erie Railroad; they never locked out their employees or called the National Guard to protect scabs and fire on pickets; and in all the history of the United States there is no record of Negroes lynching a white man.

Now it could be argued that they did not commit any of these crimes because they had been successfully separated from the open society, and that if they had had the chance they would have done all of these things. . . .

Maybe. But at this point in our history no one can prove it.

The Commie Right and Christianity

"WHY DIDN'T she stay home?" That's what we heard many Southerners say, in commenting on the murder of Mrs. Viola Liuzzo by segregationists in Selma, Alabama. They said the same thing after the murder of Dr. Reeb, the Unitarian minister from Massachusetts.

Interesting how often these people of the Far Right employ the methods of the Commies. If a Russian wants to go from Moscow to Odessa he must get permission, and the first thing he must do in Odessa is report to the police station, tell them where he will stay, for how long, and for what purpose. It's worth repeating: The Far Right in America has no chance at all unless it uses the ideas and the methods of the Bolsheviks. This does not mean that the Far Right might not win. They have a good chance precisely because they use the tried-and-true methods of the Communists.

But I still think we can beat the Commie Right by democratic means, maybe even convict an individual here and there for proven excesses.

Do you have any idea how many black bodies, black half-bodies, black headless bodies, are rotting in the swamps of Louisiana, Alabama, Mississippi? The Negroes were smart to encourage the participation of the white clergy, and the white men and women freedom riders. Martin Luther King once told me, "They *look* for white bodies." He was right, of course.

About these people from "other" places being in Alabama "where they had no business being," that is what they said about St. Paul. Why don't you stay home in Palestine? And as a matter of fact, the Reebs and the teamster's wife from Detroit are the ones who made Christianity a universal religion. The brilliant Pope Hildebrand understood this: "Our missionaries must always be strangers to the people to whom they preach."

Without these "strangers" the Southerners would probably be worshipping Mithra, who had become very popular as a god in Britain until those "foreigners" came from the Mediterranean.

What's the point? After we are long gone, our great-grandchildren will be reading about all of this in the year 2035—big story will be about a man—Martin Luther King—who, in the process of saving the Negro race in America, may well have succeeded in making Christians of us all—Gentiles included.

La Dernière Classe

ANYONE WHO has ever studied French has read Alphonse Daudet's great short story, "La Dernière Classe." Probably it is one of the best short stories ever written. It is the story of a schoolboy who is always late but on this one particular morning gets no reprimand from his teacher. In fact, contrary to all expectation, the teacher is kind and gentle. He is kind and gentle because it is the last day he will teach these boys. At the close of the session, the boys see the spiked helmets of the German soldiers through their window. The Germans have won the war and the French provinces of Alsace and Lorraine have been ceded to them. Henceforth all lessons will be conducted in German. The teacher dismisses the students, but not before this one last lesson. He turns to the blackboard and writes, *Vive La France.*

I would like to write a short story and call it "La Dernière Classe." But its ending would be far happier and in many ways far more significant than Daudet's. It would be a story about the Charlotte Junior College (Negro branch) whose Commencement speaker I was at the graduation of its last class. The junior college with a new name, Central Piedmont Community College, was integrated at the next term.

The last graduating class of Charlotte Junior College (Negro branch) ends one of the sad eras in our history and turns a page that has brighter prospects not only for white and colored boys and girls but for Americans everywhere.

For despite what the newspapers call the "white backlash," despite the stall-ins and the riots, despite the votes George C. Wallace of Alabama wins, the American problem of inequality is diminished day by day and graduating class by graduating class.

Anti-Semitism

THERE IS always a question-and-answer period after the lecture. It goes with the territory, as the drummers used to say.

One of the questions is: "Why is there anti-Semitism?" It is followed by modifications, like, "Is there anything in Judaism which would of itself give rise to anti-Semitism?" and, "Is ill feeling toward Jews confined to Christian countries?"

Then I surprise my interrogator.

Sir, you are asking the wrong man that question. You are asking the *victim* to explain why he was assaulted on his way home from the poker game.

Right around the clock of the centuries, every minute of every hour, someone asks a Jew why he is disliked. This is a question which reverses the Anglo-Saxon concept of law. For this crime, it is the victim who is subjected to questioning and no one tries apprehending the criminal.

If a man hates me for no other reason than that I am a Jew— well, it's not what's wrong with *me*, it's what's wrong with *him*. Go ahead and ask *him*: "Why is there anti-Semitism?"

If we could isolate the cause we might effect a cure. But isolating any virus is not so simple.

We Jews have been contemporaneous with all of recorded history. This is a great burden.

The identity with all the social upheavals of mankind is an eternal burden. My fellow Jews who are today concerned about the professional anti-Semites who call them "Reds" should read the anti-Semitic literature between the years 1850 and 1920, which was filled with hatred of the Jews for having invented capitalism. Only fifty years ago, in the state of Georgia, Tom Watson, in his anti-Semitic campaign, accused the Jews of being the real power behind Wall Street.

Karl Marx, whose father converted the family to Lutheranism, was as much of an anti-Semite as Gerald L. K. Smith. He said the bourgeois Jews were the great obstacle in the path of the class revolution. Stalin came to the same conclusion. His pogrom started with charges against Jewish doctors of "cosmopolitanism," as good a synonym for "capitalism" as we have.

I'm not ready to say that anti-Semitism is incurable. Cancer is incurable because we do not yet know the cause; there may indeed be as many "causes" for cancer as there are for anti-Semitism. But science has made some great strides. If you detect cancer at an early stage you have a good chance of controlling it. Some cancers cannot be controlled even if you detect them early, but many do respond to early treatment. But anti-Semitism turns on factors not easily detected.

Two factors involved are (1) the condition of the economy and (2) the condition of the anti-Semite. It is extremely difficult to determine the needs, longings, and frustrations of each individual. There are those who hitch a ride on every anti-Semitic movement that comes along; their teeth hurt, they are sexually impotent or sexually discarded or neglected. The early Nazi movement was financed by wives and widows of industrial tycoons. But the main factor involves failure.

Marcel Proust writes that the Dreyfus case came as a great boon to the French bourgeoisie. "I'm not a mailman, I am an anti-Dreyfusard." In the same way the redneck and linthead Southerner sees the door of the aristocrat opened to him because of his attitude toward the Negro.

But anti-Semitism turns on a more important factor—the economic well-being of the Gentile. When the Gentile is in trouble the Jew catches hell.

The worst-off country in Europe in the nineteenth century and in the early twentieth century was Russia, which was the most brutally anti-Semitic.

Germany was industrialized and the governing groups of the time were not anti-Semitic.

Rebecca West writes that it was Edward VII who set the face of England toward philo-Semitism. Significantly, Britannia not only ruled the waves at that time but its empire and commerce had reached a zenith.

In Germany, the impoverished middle class and the sense of hopelessness and frustration it felt in the period of post-World War I inflation gave the Nazi Party its chance. The multitude of Germans who lost their savings through the nightmare of Prussian militarism and defeat were ready for the nightmare of anti-Semitism.

Primitive man went home to his family carrying the prize on his shoulders—a wild hog he had killed. After walking for miles he suddenly placed the animal on the shoulders of his son, who had accompanied him on the hunt. He was not yet able to associate his great sense of relief with the shifting of his burden. The Germans needed desperately to shift their terrible burden of misery. Once again—the Jew—it's not *our* fault that we lost the war—*nothing* is our fault.

Mussolini did not need demonology. He became dictator over a land which was the birthplace of Western culture. He had Caesar. He needed something close at hand, easily identifiable and perennially popular.

The low state of anti-Semitism in the United States today is due to the high condition of our economy. But there is yet another factor which is rather new in the history of this morbid phenomenon. It is the fantastic mobility of the American culture. Traditionally anti-Semitism represented the hatred of the agrarian-warrior class against the rootless "hustlers"— brokers, salesmen, agents, and businessmen, the people everlastingly *on the move*. Well, all America is on the move now and this has caused anti-Semitism to recede.

All the anti-Semitic writers of the nineteenth century expressed hatred of the Jew—because the Jew, they said, gave birth to the middle class. And they were international bankers. William Houston Chamberlain and Brooks Adams said it in almost the same words—the Jew helped destroy the world of priests, knights, peasants, and artisans by the invention of capitalism.

It is true that we have no control over the man who becomes an anti-Semite because his teeth hurt; but mobility, urbanization, and prosperity will continue to render that anti-Semite ineffectual if we continue to pray daily for the success and happiness of the Gentile world. The prosperity and good health of the Gentile majority is our best security.

The Golden Insurance Plan

ATTEMPTING to register to vote is as dangerous in Mississippi and Alabama as playing with nitroglycerine in North Carolina or New York. And while there are FBI agents scouring Mississippi and Alabama, they are apparently still looking for Communists and Soviet saboteurs since they take no notice of the local deputies who line up in brown uniforms and white crash helmets outside the registration places and proceed to crack the skulls of citizens who want to vote but are black, and that is precisely how it happened in Selma, Alabama.

There may be but one way to stop the bombings and the killings. It will have to be inventive, since neither Christianity nor law seems effective now. It comes to me that perhaps we should rely on capitalism.

Every civil rights worker or Negro in Mississippi and Alabama ought to sit right down and take out a term insurance policy for twenty-five thousand dollars. It is not expensive. Term insurance can be had for a period of one year which is adequate coverage in case of death. But the civil rights worker and Negro ought to make positive he takes out a term policy with no company but a Mississippi or an Alabama company. New York or Oregon won't do. If Alabama and Mississippi don't care about human life they are likely to care even less about insurance companies in other states.

But I am quite sure the home-grown insurance companies are near the hearts of folks in Jackson and Birmingham, Oxford and Selma.

The state insurance companies are underwriting the big buildings that have given cities in the South a skyline. They are building the shopping centers. They are issuing the accident and retirement plans for the new industry. It would not do to have them go broke and insurance directors are not going to sit by idly while their insured are being shot up, especially insureds on term policies. The insurance presidents will call for law and order. Hopefully, their voices and prestige will have influence. They may even be unanimous in their insistence that the murder rate drop. I propose that a fund be established—the *Golden Vertical Negro Insurance Fund*—to pay the premiums. We can raise the money in a jiffy. The moment a civil rights worker starts out for Mississippi or Alabama, he gets himself insured! Before the Negro family goes to church on Sunday, they sign up for the term policy for every member. The moment a Negro decides to register to vote he first gets himself insured. It is true that my plan would be a bonanza for the Alabama and Mississippi insurance companies, but they would begin to police this terror. I am convinced that they would put an end to the bombing and killing.

It is worth a try.

The story of LeRoy Jones

EVERY TIME I hear from my friend Dr. Frank Porter Graham, former president of the University of North Carolina, former United States Senator, and now of the United Nations Secretariat, I think of LeRoy Jones.

LeRoy Jones was a nineteen-year-old Negro student whom Senator Graham selected as an alternate for possible appointment to the West Point Military Academy. This was several years before the Supreme Court's decision declaring racial segregation in the public schools unconstitutional.

Senator Graham had conducted a series of written examinations and LeRoy Jones qualified as an alternate. Senator Graham did not know LeRoy Jones. He insisted that those taking the exam provide no background information, and numbers, instead of names, were used. The applicants remained anonymous.

When Senator Graham ran for reelection, the managers of his opponent, the late Senator Willis Smith, distributed hundreds of thousands of copies of LeRoy's picture (retouched to make the hair more "kinky"), under the caption, "This is what Senator Graham appointed to West Point."

This piece of propaganda was effective and this is what defeated Senator Graham. And it was a disastrous defeat, not so much for Frank Graham as for America and for many thousands of people around the world. It was an election to fill an unexpired term, so the victor in the race took his seat immediately. And they waited two extra days for Frank's defeat so they could pass the McCarran-Walter Immigration Act over President Truman's veto. Dr. Frank was the one Southerner who had voted against the bill originally. It was passed over the President's veto by one vote, the vote of the fellow who beat Dr.

Frank. And with the "help" of a Negro boy, the *most* innocent bystander of our times.

Dr. Frank is a little fellow. In his younger years he might have qualified as a jockey. But he is a great scrapper.

I'll tell you of an interesting event during that campaign. We all went over to Pineville, a small mill town not far from Charlotte. One of Senator Graham's most enthusiastic volunteer workers was a charming Southern lady, Mrs. Leitner Miller. Mrs. Miller went ahead of the party to ask the superintendent of the mill for permission to have Senator Graham shake hands with the workers as they came out of the plant. The superintendent of this Pineville plant of the Cone Mills was very abusive; he denied the permission, shouting such things as "nigger lovers," and "Reds." Mrs. Miller, of an old Southern family, was shocked. We knew there would be terrible trouble for that mill superintendent if Mr. Miller found out what had happened.

We called the mill owner, Caesar Cone, in Greensboro. Mr. Cone was deeply chagrined and by phone he ordered his superintendent to chase after us and apologize to both Mrs. Miller and Senator Graham.

Before finally leaving Pineville, we passed a group of men who kept shouting after us "nigger lovers." The leader of this group was an old resident of Pineville in the business of making loans to farmers. Senator Graham and the rest of us walked up to this man's office, the windows of which were plastered with blown-up pictures of LeRoy Jones, and these more heavily retouched than any of the others. The *banya* (as these farm-money-lenders are known in India), was a big fellow, but Senator Frank shook his finger in his face and said, "Mister, you are spreading lies about me." And as the *banya* got to his feet, Senator Frank let go way upward with a right to the *banya*'s jaw. To save the *banya* from further punishment Legette Blythe, famous author and Southern historian, a close friend of Dr. Frank, stepped between the contestants.

The "alternate" LeRoy Jones made a valiant try but missed qualifying for the formal appointment to West Point. I have no idea where he is today.

Things we didn't know about the Negro till now

AFTER the enactment of the segregation laws in the South about sixty years ago it was necessary to put every Negro child through a course in reading almost before he could walk. After he learned to say "mama" and "papa" he was taught to say "white" and "colored."

In later years a surprisingly large number of Negro mothers used a visual arts system—two blocks of wood, one marked WHITE and the other COLORED. The child was required to repeat those two words over and over again and the two panels were on the table during every feeding. Often the child was encouraged to play with them.

About once a week the mother gave a formal lesson. She held up the WHITE panel. "No—bad—don't go there—trouble— you'll be hurt—like this," and she usually gave the child a little slap on his hand to show what she meant. "When you see this" —and she held up COLORED—"go—no trouble—no hurt; remember, 'white' is bad—don't go there; 'colored' is good—go in there. It's all right."

By the time the Negro kid was five years old he could see those two words in his sleep. But he knew what he needed to know to move about in the outside world—and stay healthy.

The war the Nazis won

DR. HANNAH ARENDT's book, *Eichmann in Jerusalem*, has provoked a vast controversy since its publication three years ago. The noted sociologist had two principal themes: one was

that Eichmann represented "the banality of evil" and the other
that some Jewish leaders were cowardly and thus contributed
to their own fate and the fate of fellow Jews by "cooperating"
with the Nazis.

I am surprised that neither Dr. Arendt nor our own
diplomatic experts understand that the Nazis really waged two
separate wars—one against the Allies and one against the Jews.

The war against the Jews had its own general staff and an efficient bureaucracy to carry out the strategy. Between Novem-
ber, 1944, and March, 1945, in the matter of transport, the war
against the Jews had priority over the war against America,
England, and the Soviet.

The war against the Jews is the war the Nazis won.

Why did the Jews go to the gas chambers like "lambs to the
slaughter"? Why didn't they resist? Doesn't Dr. Arendt know?
Is it really possible to "fight back" against genocide? Why didn't
the five million kulaks—strong, sturdy peasant stock—run
from Stalin? Why didn't they resist?

The Bulgarians are known as fierce warriors. They didn't resist when the Turks slaughtered a half million of them in 1876.
The Turks stationed drummer boys around the town of
Harput to drown out the cries of thousands of men, women,
and children murdered during the ten days of indiscriminate
slaughter. But Dr. Arendt wanted Rabbi Leo Baeck to stand up
to all of this. She refers to the rabbi as a "Jewish fuehrer."

Now if a government official asks a rabbi for a list of his members, is he supposed to imagine it is for the purpose of wholesale
slaughter?

I remember talking with the actor Canada Lee, who had been
blacklisted during the McCarthy era. He told me that he had
knocked on one hundred doors in an attempt to fight back, but
it was no use.

"There's nothing I can do," he said; "there's nothing anybody
can do." This was not in Nazi Europe, it was in a café on West
Forty-ninth Street in New York City. And only a man's liveli-

hood was at stake. Just imagine what the terror can be when it concentrates on wholesale murder.

Why didn't the Nazis kill the Jewish woman Gemma Gluck? Why did they transfer her from one concentration camp to another? Why did they give her special medical attention? Her brother, Mayor Fiorello LaGuardia of New York, was an outspoken enemy of the Nazis.

On two occasions Secretary of State Cordell Hull had to apologize to the German Embassy for the attacks made upon the Nazi regime by Mayor LaGuardia. Yet the Nazis did not kill Gemma Gluck. To put it in almost childish terms I would say that the Nazis did not kill Gemma Gluck because *somebody* cared, *somebody* was watching them.

The Danes *cared* and they saved their Jewish population. The Italians said "no" even after Mussolini had formulated anti-Semitic laws. Dr. Arendt tells how General Mario Roatta sent word in 1942 that "it is incompatible with the honor of the Italian army" to deliver the Jews from the Italian-occupied territory of Yugoslavia to the German authorities. The Italians said "no" and the Jews were not slaughtered. In Germany, Austria, Hungary, Croatia, Poland, and Bohemia, Eichmann came along with a small cadre and the following morning a thousand applicants appeared out of the local population, saying, "Welcome, we'll show you how to kill Jews." But when the Bulgarians said "no," the Bulgarian Jews were saved. The Croatian Jews were killed but the Serbs living next door said "no" and the Serbian Jews were also saved.

What surprises me about Dr. Arendt is that the actions she condemns are the ones she described in her books as having worked wonders for the Jews for nearly a thousand years in a hostile Europe—total nonviolence, some bribery, and lots of Uncle Tomism. Jews had no reason in the world to think that it would not work again. Dr. Arendt, the author of the classic work on totalitarianism, instructed us in many of these matters and for her to have gone off into this intellectual wild blue yonder makes me very sad indeed.

Bogalusa story

EIGHTY-YEAR-OLDS follow the Negro marchers, shouting "Nigger."

Housewives hold their children on their shoulders, encouraging them to yell insults at the civil rights pickets.

Used-car dealers, undertakers, and other businessmen are beside themselves with rage against the "Communist conspiracy" which threatens to break down the caste system of racial segregation.

Why Bogalusa? Bogalusa, Louisiana.

But nothing explains the resistance of the segregationists of the South better than Bogalusa.

Bogalusa is less than fifty years old. It became a town when Goodyear and the great Southern Lumber Company and later, the Crown-Zellerbach Corporation, established plants there between 1906 and 1918.

There is absolutely no connection between Bogalusa and the "old plantation" society of the Confederate South. The Bogalusa defenders of Southern chivalry and the Southern way of life have no tie with the chandeliers, the crinolines, the dueling pistols.

History clearly indicates that there was less enthusiasm among the poor whites for the Confederates in 1865 than there is for racial segregation in Bogalusa in 1965.

How do you explain Bogalusa?

In 1896 the Supreme Court handed a deed of gift to the poor whites of the South. In those days the Federal Government was very popular. The deed of gift to the poor whites of the South said, "You are superior." And the poor whites in possession of this deed of gift, called Plessy v. Ferguson, thought it would last forever. They had no idea the Supreme Court was an Indian giver.

With that gift in their hands, the poor whites saw no need to hustle in order to achieve merit, because they had secured by

law what most men have to fight for all their lives to achieve—
self-esteem. The law said they were superior, and what else
does a man have to do?

Thus the poor white fears that the Negro stands between him
and social oblivion. Keeping the Negro segregated makes the
poor white a plantation owner and an aristocrat, retroactively.
This attitude gives him a big advantage over the poor white of
Confederate days. In 1865, less than twenty percent of the
Southerners owned more than one slave. And of those only a
handful owned more than ten slaves.

In 1965, however, the fellow working in the sawmill or trying
to sell a used car under the broiling summer sun of Bogalusa
creates for himself the happy illusion that he is standing beneath
the old magnolia, defending Southern womanhood, and listening to the soft singing of the darkies: "Swing low, sweet char-
iot . . ."

What they are really fighting for in Bogalusa is to keep alive
a pipe dream about a time and a condition that never really
existed.

John C. Calhoun and Lena Horne

OLD JOHN C. CALHOUN, the greatest apologist for the
slave culture of the South, looks down from a parapet in heaven
and sees an image of himself in the autobiography of that handsome and talented woman, Lena Horne.

Miss Horne, in writing about her grandmother, notes she was
the daughter of a slave and the white man who owned her. This
was in the John C. Calhoun family of South Carolina and Lena
Horne quotes her father as saying of this grandmother, "She
was the get of one of the lousiest s.o.b.'s in the South and she
was determined to rise above it."

Miss Horne puts pictures in the book and one of them is of
her grandmother's father. This picture shows a planter-type

Southern gentleman. He has a straggling sort of beard and mustache and a slight balding around the forehead. His hair is combed rather thickly down the side with a few stray hairs sticking out like elfin horns. He wears a white linen shirt and one of those black frock coats. His eyes stare ahead and are rather soulful. He probably was an elder in the Methodist or Baptist Church.

Anyway, it is hilarious to think of Mr. Calhoun seeing his picture in Lena Horne's book along with Cora Calhoun, Edwin Horne, Frank Horne, Lena Calhoun, and the unbelievably beauteous Lena herself.

I once asked a Southern senator about this development of the brown race in America. He said it never happened that way at all, just some sailors who came to Southern ports, ran clear out to the Mississippi River, made it with the Negro women, and then ran back to their ships before sailing time.

Not every Southern woman was naïve about what was going on around her. A century ago Mary Boykin Chestnut, wife of a plantation owner of Charleston, South Carolina, put these words in her diary.

> God forgive us, but ours is a monstrous system, a wrong and an iniquity! Like the patriarchs of old, our men live all in one house with their wives and their concubines; and the mulattoes one sees in every family partly resemble the white children. Any lady is ready to tell you who is the father of all the mulatto children in everybody's household but her own. Those, she seems to think, drop from the clouds.

Wilma Dykeman, the Southern novelist and reporter, records an incident that happened in Tennessee during a conference between a Negro civil rights group and white merchants. One of the white men said, "Well one thing, we're not going to have Negroes marrying our daughters." And a Negro replied, "Now wait a minute, mister. You mean Negroes aren't going to marry your wife's daughters. We've been marrying your daughters for a long time."

Sex and the stranger

THE English condemned the French in many ways for their sexual excesses. Syphilis was called the "French disease" although in Italy it was called the "Spanish disease." The Calvinists in Holland forbade their young women from learning French in school for fear French literature would corrupt them.

English, German, French, and American novelists always referred to a Jewish heroine as "voluptuous," although all the other heroines hopped from one bed into another bed, remaining just plain Irene, Sophie, or Brett, without the "voluptuous" business.

And of all these strangers the Negro, by his color, exercises the imagination most. On him the white man in the South pours out all the frustrations and fears and guilt that sex inspires.

This transfer of sexual anxiety into another is not solely restricted to racists. During the height of anti-Catholic feelings in the South, the native-born entertained every conceivable kind of radical notion about Catholics. Tom Watson weekly reported the bodies of children which had been disinterred from Catholic convents and monasteries. He described in clinical detail the licentious behavior of priests and nuns. In fact, all the pornography and obscenity in the American South for many decades centered on the Catholic convent and the despoliation of innocent Protestants therein.

When the French were feeling particularly anti-British during the Vichy regime, Pierre Laval usually referred to the English as a "race of flagellants."

This has passed. But the fears of the Negroes' sexuality are daily enforced and hardened. Dr. R. N. Hayling, a young colored dentist who helped lead the N.A.A.C.P. action in St. Augustine, Florida, was severely beaten with three others when a Ku Klux mob found them.

When the Klansmen thrust the men into the center of the conclave there was a hushed silence from the segregationists and then Dr. Hayling heard a woman scream, "Castrate 'em."

Poverty and riots

I AM distressed to read in many of the Anglo-Jewish publications that there was a definite anti-Semitic undertone to the unfortunate Negro riots in Los Angeles.

This is utter nonsense. A Negro anti-Semite, of which there are a few, is about as convincing as a Jewish white supremacist, of which there are also a few.

It is true that a good portion of the property wantonly destroyed by the careening mob was Jewish-owned. It is hard to credit that a mob, completely out of control, is selective enough to spare the Gentile store and raze the Jewish one. Indeed, the mob in Watts toward the end indiscriminately attacked both white and Negro property.

The rioters in Watts were nothing less than a lynch mob, and the object of their frenzy was property. It made no difference to whom it belonged.

The first white man to extend humanity to the Negroes after the Civil War was the Jewish peddler. He extended humanity in the form of credit. The Southern white Protestant did not extend credit until long after the New Deal helped propel the Negro toward the open society.

The Jewish merchant was the first white man in the South to let the Negro try on clothes he might want to buy. The white Protestant refused to let the Negro touch anything in the store. "Don't touch unless you buy" was the rule in the "uptown" stores.

This is not to insist the Jewish merchant and the Jewish peddler were heroes. The Jew of the 1880's saw, with that instinct for self-preservation, that the place where he could immediately thrive was in the slum, among the Negroes. And thrive he did

And sometimes the Jewish store exploited the Negroes of the ghetto.

Dick Gregory, the comedian who grew up in a St. Louis slum, said the exploitation was reciprocal. If the Jewish merchants charged more, some of the Negroes still evened it up by stealing.

So the slum dehumanized both merchant and customer for the same reason poverty dehumanizes everybody it touches. I have seen this happen myself and not only to Negroes, but to Jews and Irishmen and Italians and Poles.

The truly surprising thing is that we do not have riots every day in the week. Slum residents, virtually unemployable except in the service industries, see the shopkeepers come down from the nice Beverly Hills section or from the Long Island suburbs and one day, when that tension generated by hopelessness snaps, they will strike against the symbol of the rich world they see all around them but in which they never share.

To make of this anti-Semitism is not only fruitless but in a way cruel. Nothing should obscure our vision of why these things happen.

The convenient Armenian

IN A small community composed mainly of people of English, Irish, German, Dutch, and Polish descent, there is a man who stated during a discussion on prejudice that he is prejudiced against Armenians.

At first this struck me as being rather ridiculous; you would have to do quite a bit of investigating before you found an Armenian, and there must be instances where you just don't know whether someone is Armenian, Lebanese, or what.

On second thought, however, this seemed like an almost fool-proof method for people who have prejudices to give way to their feelings in a harmless manner. For instance, this man, living in a town where there are no Armenians, can blame all his troubles on the Armenians and yet never cause any real problem. Likewise, one person could be prejudiced against women who smoke cigars; another against Pennsylvania Dutch people who marry native Alaskans; and a third against Italian girls named Gertrude.

As Elbert Hubbard noted, "Fools are not born! They are graduated!"

Alien in perpetuity

NEITHER the Tories, the Liberals, or Labour has been forthright in discussing the proposed British restrictions on immigration.

Mr. Selwyn Lloyd put his foot in his mouth when he said, "Even with no new entrants, the numbers of immigrants here would grow because of their high birthrate."

The first reaction is to sit down and laugh. Mr. Lloyd has created a brand-new type of immigrant—a born immigrant.

What he does not say, what no one dares say, but what they all really mean, is the Negro.

What Mr. Lloyd implies is that if you are not a white Protestant Anglo-Saxon, you are forever alien, even unto the tenth generation.

Unclutch your fingers

IN THE SOUTH, the low-income white folks say "nigger." Aristocrats say "nigra." The word "Negro" is reserved for official statements and medical reports. "Darkie" is often an endearing term while "Negre" is a Louisiana Cajun word.

"Colored person" is patronizing.

Many Jews shudder at "Jew." After many years you begin to believe the charges made against you. Thus it's the rare individual who says, "I am a Jew." Instead folks say, "I happen to be of the Jewish faith."

The vast majority of people are full of tensions and fears and a sense of futility. They hope for higher self-esteem and to prove individual worth, but I hope the time comes when people of intelligence will say to themselves, "Look here, I intend to unclutch my fingers, relax, and go about my business."

I think the main thing is to eliminate self-contempt or self-hatred. If you love yourself thoroughly you will have enough to spare for others. If you hate yourself, well, you know the answer to that one.

Forecast for Washington

IN 1900, the Hon. George White of North Carolina was the last Negro member of Congress from the South. White supremacy was now in the ascendancy. Congressman White bade his Congressional colleagues good-by. His closing words were: "We'll be back some day," and indeed they will be, soon, and based solely on individual character, ambition, merit, and talent.

Dr. Charles Drew

CALIFORNIA is studying new material for school textbooks, among which is the story of Dr. Charles Drew, a Negro physician who developed the method of blood plasma transfusion that has saved numberless lives. Dr. Drew died in his forties, a sad loss to science. Dr. Drew was on a visit in the South and was the victim of an auto accident in which a big blood vessel was severed. He was refused admittance at the nearest hospital because of his race and died because he could not receive the help of the medical discovery which he had given to the world.

Integrating taxes

SOME OF the newspapermen in Atlanta tell me that the Negro senator Leroy Johnson is probably the most valuable member of the Georgia legislature today.

His most recent proposal is to repeal the law which provided for segregated tax lists in Georgia. He wants them integrated.

The section of the law which Senator Johnson wants repealed provides for the names of colored and white taxpayers to be listed separately on different colored slips.

There is more to this law than meets the eye. The main purpose was to be able to eliminate prospective Negro jurors because the jury lists are prepared from the tax digests.

Some day a humorist will list all the segregation laws enacted between 1900 and 1922 and after the struggle is over and people are more relaxed, Americans will pick up such a book and laugh themselves into hysteria.

Frederick Douglass's white wife

FREDERICK DOUGLASS, one of the great Negroes of our country, was severely criticized for marrying a white woman.

Douglass had been a fugitive slave out of Baltimore who, saving his wages up North, bought the freedom of his childhood sweetheart. She came North and they were married. Some years later she died, and Frederick Douglass took to himself another wife, this time a white woman.

There was a big hullaballoo from both sides. Some Negroes called him a traitor to his race; many whites heaped scorn and contempt on both Douglasses. To all of this Frederick Douglass replied in effect: "I don't see what they are troubled about. My first wife was the color of my mother. My second wife is the color of my father."

Frederick Douglass was welcomed by Lincoln at the White House and the essay he wrote about that meeting is not dated at all. Douglass wrote that in the presence of Lincoln, *he*, Douglass, was color-blind.

Good going!

Negro anti-Semitism

WHY SHOULD we segregate anti-Semites? If a colored man is an anti-Semite, let's put him down as one even though we may understand why, which we don't often in the case of white anti-Semites.

It was inevitable that the Negroes would produce some anti-Semites. In the fight to enter the white society, there were Negroes who would copy anti-Semites in the hope that these prejudices would make him more like a white man. The remarkable fact is that there are so few Negro anti-Semites.

Anti-Semitism is a constant of Western culture. Negroes participate in that culture.

To bring up Negro anti-Semitism anyway is irrelevant to the main issue. Whether some Negroes are or are not has nothing to do with whether all Negroes should or should not enjoy equality of opportunity in the voting booth, the school, in housing, in the job market and in public facilities.

Basically, the struggle for civil rights is not waged for the Negro. To be truthful about it, I do not care one way or another what a particular Negro thinks or whether or not he likes me; the civil rights movement is not *for* the Negro, it's *for* America. The concept of a second-class citizenship makes me nervous. Out with it! When I hear a member of a Jewish lecture audience ask me about Negro anti-Semitism I always think there's somebody who wants an *out* from this most noble commitment.

PART 5

Tarzan, Lolita, and Seventy-Six Trombones

The great irony of the atomic age

AT THE turn of the century a great power always dispatched a couple of cruisers and contingents of marines to put down incipient revolts or disorders in any of its colonies. Today, the great powers have stockpiles of bombs, three of which could wipe out whole populations and devastate hundreds of miles of countryside forever. But the great irony of the atomic age is that a few thousand students snake dancing in the streets represent the irrepressible. Hydrogen-bomb stockpiles ought to keep revolutionaries, radicals, and native patriots quiet, subdued, and amenable. Not so at all. A demonstration becomes a political force these bombs can obliterate but not control and the cruiser —a thousand students can laugh it out of the harbor. A cruiser cannot fight a bandit or guerrilla war.

We should not be too disturbed about the restlessness, the searching, the wave of demonstrations and protests. It was that old conservative Republican, Nicholas Murray Butler, who claimed that in the Garden of Eden, Adam stopped and said, "Eve, we are living in a period of transition."

Miscegenation

MISCEGENATION: people wrote of it as something slithery. To be "the product of miscegenation" sounded dreadful. I was greatly relieved when I found it merely meant everyone has a little Irish, or English, or German, or Slav, or Tartar, or Jewish in his or her background.

Take the Britons: the Hebrews had already written their poetry; the Greeks had already established the Academy, written their dramas, and created their architecture; the Romans had already built roads, dams, aqueducts; but the inhabitants of

the British Isles were still living by tribal law, many of them
painting their bodies blue and eating wild berries.

Then came the Roman legionaries teaching the British
maidens Latin phrases. From Antioch came the Jewish merchants, and eventually came the Jutes, Celts, Angles, Saxons,
Danes, Normans, Spaniards, and Illyrians. And everybody lived
and loved and the result was Shakespeare and Churchill.

The people on welfare

THE PEOPLE on welfare who get surplus commodities at
the warehouse here ask for turkey and canned peaches.

Turkey and canned peaches are the most sought-after packages at several other welfare warehouses I checked. The Commissioner of Welfare has confirmed this.

What surprises me is that too much of turkey and canned
peaches would eventually make a salami sandwich a luxury.

Television and civil rights

MASSCOMM, according to critic W. H. Ferry of the Ford
Fund for the Republic, is the collection of newspapers, radio,
magazines and television and *masscomm* "delights in the
shoddy." Ferry charges that *masscomm* is not only a synthetic
view of reality, but on many occasions a meretricious view. It
never shows people what is there. "The condition of the American Negro," Ferry writes, "would be a festering canker to this
day had the issue been left to *masscomm*."

Ah, let me disagree.

As a working newspaperman what could I have written to
tell the public, the President, and the Congress about the Negro which would have been as effective as the television news

broadcast showing the police dogs chasing Negroes? What would have been as effective as the televised picture of a burnt-out freedom riders' bus? When Roy Wilkins of the National Association for the Advancement of Colored People and A. Philip Randolph, the daddy of the Negro social revolution, thanked President John F. Kennedy for his civil rights proposals, Kennedy said, "The dogs of Alabama had as much to do with it as I did."

Television, unwittingly to be sure, was the decisive factor in the success of the Negro civil rights movement. Not only did it instruct whites about what the Negro was doing, it instructed Negroes about the way whites lived. The movies were never able to accomplish this. The movies are fantasies. The average Negro could not identify with Gloria Swanson, Clark Gable, or Gary Cooper, but he could identify with a fellow who smoked filter cigarettes and carried his sandwiches wrapped up in cellophane. He saw the tired salesman come home from the office to a home equipped with a washing machine and a dryer and a garage with two cars. He saw a family all clean and spic-and-span testing three kinds of toothpaste and worrying about the most effective deodorant. And he thought, This is the average American, and I live in a house on stilts in a dirty alley with no toilet and all they're worried about is deodorants. And the Negro said to himself, "I want *in*."

Just how importantly television figured in the civil rights movement will take years to determine. The televised picture of the bombed-out church in Birmingham with the tarpaulins covering the bodies of dead little girls did more in one single minute than a decade of agitation, debate, and lectures ever could.

The Reconstruction myth

WHEN the Selma demonstrators assembled below the Capitol in which Jefferson Davis took the oath of office as president of the Confederacy, Governor George C. Wallace took this occasion to remember the dark days of the Reconstruction, one of the most blatant myths ever foisted on the American intelligence. Said one, "The Reconstruction left the South devastated and the destiny of the white man was placed in the hands of ignorant and often brutal blacks, slaves who could neither read nor write. . . ."

But this is completely doctored history, brainwashing which unfortunately has been fostered by some of our most reputable historians.

The aftermath of any war leaves the loser prostrated. But it was the war which crippled the South, and not the Reconstruction. Jonathan Daniels, editor of the Raleigh *News and Observer*, a blood-of-the-blood and bone-of-the-bone Southerner, was the first man to expose the myth of the Reconstruction in his book several years ago, *Prince of Carpetbaggers*. In tracing the career of the Southerner Malcolm Littlefield, Daniels reveals how a large majority of greedy Southern boys also had their hands in the Reconstruction till.

And now we have another book exposing the myth. Henrietta Buckmaster, a Northerner, in her new book *Freedom Bound*, sets forth all the facts about the length of the Reconstruction. It lasted all of two years in North Carolina, four years in most of the other states of the Confederacy, and six years in South Carolina.

The lynchings, the Black Codes, the grandfather clauses, the segregation laws which followed the close of the Reconstruction period came not because the Negro legislators of the several states were bad, but because they were good. That is what outraged the white supremacists.

Negro legislators were obsessed with the idea of education. They appropriated money for schools and more schools. In fact, the day after the South successfully eliminated the Negro from political life, the first thing these states did was to cancel the school bond issues.

Not until the 1920's did the old Confederacy bestir itself to build schools for white children, let alone for the Negroes.

What happened to Knowland?

WHEN Ronald Reagan announced that he would run for Governor of California, the question popped into my hay-ed: "What happened to Bill Knowland?"

The Knowland interests produced the Oakland *Tribune* and a brief senatorship for Knowland, Junior. They screamed against Social Security, old-age pensions, unemployment insurance and TVA as socialistic. But after twenty-five years the *Tribune* is strangely silent. You would think by this time they could point to the ruins and say, "I told you so." But they are going along with the rest of the business people, quietly accepting the new subscriptions to the *Tribune* from thousands of people who pay for the paper out of Social Security, or old-age pensions, or unemployment insurance: which like the gentle rain from heaven falleth on the just and unjust alike blessing even the Knowlands.

They don't make ambassadors
like that anymore

WHEN, six months after the English colonies in America had declared their independence, it was known that Congress had sent the aged and illustrious Dr. Benjamin Franklin as envoy to France, there was a distinct feeling of relief among Europeans. Benjamin Franklin was the only American most of them had heard of. Even George Washington was little known. He was spoken of variously as Vasinton, Waginton, Vazhigton, and Vachintin by the best-informed Europeans.

Franklin's grandson, William Temple Franklin, aged sixteen, was his private secretary in Paris. (Later, John Quincy Adams, aged eleven, was to hold this post for his father.) When Voltaire visited Franklin, the American ambassador presented his grandson, asking for him a benediction. Replied Voltaire: "God and Liberty—the only benediction fit for a grandson of Franklin."

The main problem of Franklin's tenure was money—again and again he had to go, hat in hand, to Versailles to beg for loans for the young Continental Congress. To his friend John Adams he wrote:

> I have lately made a fresh and strong application for more money. I have not yet received an answer. I have, however, two of the Christian Graces, Faith and Hope; but my faith is only that of which the Apostle speaks, the evidence of things not seen. For in truth I do not see, at present, how many bills drawn at random on our ministers in France, Spain, and Holland are to be paid. . . . I shall, however, use my best endeavours to procure money for their honourable discharge . . . and if these endeavours fail, I shall be ready to break, run away, or go to Prison with you, as it shall please God.

Thomas Jefferson was chosen to succeed Franklin as minister to France. He wrote of this:

> The succession to Dr. Franklin at the Court of France was an excellent school of humility. On being presented to anyone as the Minister of America, the commonplace question used was, "C'est vous, monsieur, qui remplace le Docteur Franklin?" [It is you, sir, who replace Dr. Franklin?] I generally answered them, "No one can replace him, sir; I am only his successor."

It was Jefferson who arranged for flour from America to be sent to the starving French. That the people were starving, and that revolution was around the corner, he didn't realize, even as he made out the order for twenty-one thousand barrels of flour. It is said that no man was ever less an alarmist. "If a rumor reached him that three thousand people had fallen in the streets, he and his secretary would go to the spot, and, after minute enquiry, reduce the number to three."

Jefferson wrote to James Madison from Paris that "the French revolutionists regard Americans as a model for their imitation," and added, "Our authority has been treated like that of the Bible, open to explanation, but not to question."

Jefferson left France in 1789, flinging a garland over his shoulders: "I cannot leave this great and good country without expressing my sense of its preeminence of character among the nations of the earth. A more benevolent people I have never known, nor greater warmth and devotedness in their select friendships."

Six months later his successor, Gouverneur Morris, wrote in a rather different vein, "Gracious God, *what* a people!"

In June, 1792, the thirty-seven-year-old Morris was presented at Court. On the twentieth of that month the mob forced the gates of the palace and compelled the King to put on the red cap. "At that moment," recorded Morris, "the Constitution gave its last groan." He told Lafayette that "in six weeks all will be over," and his prediction was accurate. During the Reign of Terror that followed he was the only foreign minister who dared to remain at his post.

Morris was involved in a desperate and chivalrous plan to help the unfortunate Sovereign and his Queen to escape from Paris. When the plan failed because of the King's reluctance to leave until it was too late, Louis sent for the American and confessed his regret that he had not followed Morris's advice. He begged the young man to take charge of the royal papers and money. Morris did not take the papers, but he accepted the money, using it to hire and bribe those individuals obstructing the King's flight. Once again the plot failed, but this time those behind it were arrested. One plotter was executed, but by using the royal money liberally Morris was able to allow the others to escape. Four years later, Louis's daughter the Duchess d'Angoulême, then in exile in Austria, received from Morris a detailed account of his stewardship and a draft for what money remained—a hundred and forty-seven pounds.

Morris wrote home that to give a true picture of France he would have to "paint it like an Indian warrior—black and red."

Many times he would be seated quietly at dinner and hear by accident "that a friend was on his way to the place of execution," and have to sit still and wonder which of the guests dining with him would be next.

These men—Franklin, Jefferson, Morris—were among a select group of America's early ambassadors. There were James Monroe, appointed at the age of thirty-six, Charles Cotesworth Pinckney of South Carolina, Robert Livingston, John Jay, John Marshall, and Charles Francis Adams, who kept England from siding with the Confederacy in the Civil War and whose ambassadorial portrait was drawn so finely by his son in *The Education of Henry Adams*.

They just don't make ambassadors the way they used to.

The miracle of Africa

MOST ANTHROPOLOGISTS and sociologists believe societies emerge from violence. One tribe or sector gains ascendancy over the others and little by little establishes a rule of law. There are some exceptions to this.

Chief of the exceptions of course is the United States, which first established a government and a constitution and then turned to defend its integrity in a revolution. The other exception is Africa. Thirty-seven countries have achieved independence there without violence.

That is not, of course, to say there was no agitation. Indeed there was. But independence and government came without a war.

It is true that the Congo was wracked by mutiny and secessions upon its independence; it is also true that several of the African countries have suffered coups. But the point remains: Africa will one day be regarded as a political miracle.

That the majority of us do not so regard Africa now can be laid to the fact that very few of the independent nations are economically viable. They are dependent for aid upon their former metropoles, upon the United States and Communist Russia and Red China and to lesser degrees upon nations like Italy, Israel, and Yugoslavia. But make no mistake: they will be viable one day.

Every known mineral is in Africa. It has more arable land than the United States and Europe put together. It has water resources and water power beyond the wildest dreams of hydroelectric engineers. There is every chance that Africa will one day be an economic miracle, too.

Even more amazing is the fact that after three oppressive centuries of slavery, exploitation, and cruelty by white Europeans, black Africa did not align itself with any continental bloc on the basis of race. In fact, African political leaders are insistent on nonalignment.

There is every chance that this world can avoid a racial alignment. One of the reasons that the world has this chance is because America is the second largest colored country in the world. Only Nigeria has a larger Negro population.

In fact, the Bantus of South Africa and Rhodesia actively identify with the progress of the American Negro. Which should teach us that what progress we make here will influence for good or bad untold generations.

I found this argument unassailable during question periods of my speeches in Europe and Asia in 1960-1962. Invariably a group of Communist students would be in attendance and always the same question attempting to link the Nazi atrocities with the travail of the Negroes in the American South. I stopped them cold. The Nazi tyranny was initiated by, and carried out by, the Government. Hatred and murder were government policy. In the United States the Government stands for equity. The obstacles placed in the path of this equity are illegal, perpetrated by people who are breaking the law. You have lawbreakers here, we have lawbreakers there; but the Government will win because the United States has very deep roots in freedom and a very solid tradition based on the sacredness of a single human being.

The Negro golfers

NEGRO high school students here have a golf team and they played the upper-middle-class Myers Park High School golf team. And guess who won?

The Negroes won. The point of the story is that we owe a salute to the defeated golf team from the fancy Myers Park High School. Only seven years ago these kids heard all sorts of angry sounds from their elders about how the blood would flow if a Negro were admitted to their high school. Now they are not only classmates but engage in all sorts of competitive sports, with enthusiasm and fair play.

How much suffering and how much wealth went into these myths before they were finally smashed? No one will ever know.

The family in literature

THERE is a good case to be made that *The Way of All Flesh*, Samuel Butler's posthumous work, is the best novel in the English language. Butler's single book does not equal the output of Charles Dickens so it would be foolish to say Butler was the best novelist in the English language.

English novels are usually about the family. So are American novels.

Butler himself came from family, as we say, though he was not himself a family man. Certainly he was a misogynist. Literally he hated Regina, the mother in *The Way of All Flesh*.

In his personal life, Butler did manage a relationship of sorts with Miss Savage, a woman who encouraged and loved him but

who was crippled. Butler never thought about marrying her until she died. One of his friends consoled him with the advice
that Butler gave Miss Savage exactly what she expected him to
give, that if she had wanted marriage she would have mentioned
it.

By family, I mean the English novel often concerns itself with
the preservation of the family unit, with the preservation of the
home. Robinson Crusoe preserves a society as does Leopold
Bloom in *Ulysses*. At the end of *Ulysses*, Bloom is the master
of his home just as at the end of *The Way of All Flesh* Ernest
becomes his own master by succeeding to riches not derived
from his father's patrimony.

John Steinbeck wrote a great family novel in *The Grapes of
Wrath*. Grandpa Joad looks forward to squashing grapes on his
face, which is symbolic of the Kiddush, the basic religious ritual
of the Jewish family: "Blessed art thou, King of the Universe,
Who has given us the fruit of the vine." Throughout Steinbeck's novel, Ma Joad worries lest the family break up. Of course
the Joads do suffer disintegration but Ma Joad feels she won a
victory because the Okies are beginning to realize their communal strength—they are now *all* one big family.

All Jewish art, literature, and the theatre centered around
the family. Perhaps that is one of the reasons the English novel
deals with the family while the Russian novel deals with the
self. It is hardly a coincidence that the most popular of all
Shakespeare adaptations for the Jewish theatre was *King Lear*
—the story of a father who contends with good children and
bad children, the theme which runs through all Jewish literature.
Sholem Aleichem's Tevya is the archetypical Jewish hero, the
father forever concerned with marrying off his daughters.

Artemus Ward

"I HAVE already given two cousins to the war, and I stand
ready to sacrifice my wife's brother."

Don Quixote

I BELIEVE *Don Quixote* contains as many wise sayings as any book in the world except the Bible and Shakespeare:

"Who but a madman would mind what a madman says?"
"Diligence is the mother of good fortune."
"It is pleasant to govern though it be but a flock of sheep."
"Some people go out for wool and come home shorn."
"Letters without virtue are pearls upon a dunghill."
"Though habit and example do much, good sense is the foundation of good language."
"When they give you a heifer be ready with the rope."
"When good fortune knocks, make haste to let her in."
"Clothe me as you will, I shall be Sancho Panza still."

Cervantes told us what it takes to be an honest politician:

"Naked came I into this government and naked come I out of it."

And Cervantes knew all there is to be known about women:

"Between the yea and the nay of a woman, I would not undertake to thrust the point of a needle."

The news from suburbia

THERE WAS a time when several of the major American newspapers reported that the liner S.S. *Titanic* had struck an iceberg but all aboard had been saved. I do not think this could ever happen again. The press is not constrained to print unconfirmed rumors. Helicopters, airplanes, remote TV cameras, can tell an editor as much of the immediate truth as his columns can take.

The danger with the American press is that there are incidents it does not report at all. But understandably, newspapers have been habituated by war to withhold certain stories in the interests of national security.

It is obvious that the government scandals the press relishes are either those the courts or Congress itself have uncovered. This is not a blanket criticism, because it was a newspaperman who uncovered the price-fixing scandal some of the big companies indulged in, and a newspaperman uncovered the embezzlements of over a million dollars by the Illinois auditor some time back.

But in general much of the reporting in the papers is dull. Invariably the best reporters sooner or later become writers or syndicated columnists—or disappear into the public relations agencies and make even more money than writers and columnists.

Where the press is really behind in the news is precisely in those areas where we are growing fastest, namely, in the suburbs. The reporters there often know less about town affairs than the councilmen, but the councilmen have the defense they are amateurs.

Out in every higher status land, more ink is wasted on the news that one twelve-year-old has passed to another twelve-year-old two of his mother's sleeping pills than on the prospective tax rate. More space is wasted by the publication of anonymous letters worrying about teen-age dope addiction than is ever devoted to the need for police retirement benefits and to the problem of sixteen thousand of our teachers leaving the profession each year.

The movies

I STARTED at the beginning. I have been going to movies for fifty-five years. I watched Louise Fazenda and Bronco Billy Anderson and saw them succeeded by Rudolph Valentino and

Pola Negri and saw them succeeded by James Cagney and Jean Harlow and they, by Rock Hudson and Sophia Loren.

One of the truths I have learned through this lifelong experience is that movies were never meant to be edifying.

What the movies always guarantee is relaxation through anonymity. That is why the movie I saw last night, whatever it was, did not annoy me. Over my lifetime I have seen only one truly bad movie, and that was *The Five Little Peppers Grow Up*.

One of the fondest memories I have is that of the late Sir Cedric Hardwicke, of all people, that brilliant English actor, in a movie with the title *The Invisible Man Returns*. Why Sir Cedric Hardwicke was miscast I have no idea unless it was that Claude Raines had refused to return after inaugurating this improbable series. Sir Cedric spent the narrative chasing the Invisible Man and finally had him cornered with a loaded forty-five above a coal chute. He took careful aim with his automatic.

Up in the balcony, someone shouted, "For heaven's sake, don't shoot him. Shoot me."

Everybody laughed. And as we piled out of the movie when THE END flashed, the whole audience realized we had had a moment of enjoyment.

Nothing relaxes a man like a movie. Often, in the middle of the working day, I leave my desk and perambulate over to the Visulite Theatre up the street from my office. I do not look at the posters, don't even worry what's playing. When the cashier says, "The movie has already started, sir," I reply, "Don't worry, dearie, I'll catch on."

That's what the movies are for.

The French chef

THE FRENCH CHEF John F. Kennedy recruited for the White House tossed in his apron. He was gone—poof!

What this Frenchman did not realize in his utter dedication is that Americans are a nation bred on sandwiches. American football players grow to maturity on peanut butter and our astronauts have a long history of hamburgers.

The sandwich, after all, is the mark of the busy man. Whenever a publicity hack wants to impress the public with how hard his client works, one of the staple news releases is that the work schedule permits only the consumption of sandwiches at noon, at his desk.

I know I have found true culinary happiness by restricting myself to a diet of steak, roast beef, and Chinese food. Evenings hold no surprises for me, no anguish over fallen soufflés. A lettuce and tomato salad now and then gets me over the rickets.

Within the next two generations, I suspect much of our food will be distilled from chemicals. If the French chefs are in despair now, they will be on the brink of nervous collapse then.

Seventy-six trombones

AMERICANS LOVE band concerts like they love railroad trains. John Philip Sousa was a national institution long before any crooner or movie actor.

The band culture itself emanates from the Midwest. The reason is obvious. The big shows and productions could not play in the small towns and so the folks used the local band to express their love for both music and extravaganza. Iowa is without doubt the greatest band state in the Union. The state appropriates funds for bands. There is no begging for funds for this purpose in Iowa. And no selling of cookies from door to door. The state says if any high school, college, private, or civic institution organizes a band, the money is available for instruments and uniforms.

Texas and Florida lead in the South and Ohio in the Midwest, closely followed by Illinois, Indiana, and Michigan which is enhanced by the presence of Professor William D. Revelli at the University in Ann Arbor.

Think of the American communities which would never have known of Verdi, Brahms, or Rossini had it not been for the band arrangers! They adapted the great classics and it is a mistake to believe all bands simply play oompah. In the United States over one hundred music publishing houses publish one hundred and twenty-seven catalogues of band music which are disseminated to over thirty thousand bands.

Prominent in the band movement in addition to Professor Revelli is Karl King at Fort Dodge, you guessed it, Iowa, who played in the Sousa band. The dean of band music composers is Professor A. Austin Harding at the University of Illinois. And, of course, there is Meredith Willson, who expressed his love for the band with those seventy-six trombones.

The importance of Plutarch

AFTER FIFTY-FIVE years of uninterrupted reading I have come to these conclusions:

(1) If you start early enough (ten, preferably), it becomes a lifetime habit.

(2) Reading is a joy, not in the sense that it makes life easier, but that it makes life more interesting.

(3) From my experience and from my knowledge of at least six great writers, you must first be a reader in order to write. You learn to speak because you hear, and you learn to write because you read.

I read many books in the Settlement House library before I was twelve, but I look back upon one book as particularly important, *Plutarch's Lives of Illustrious Men*.

The importance of Plutarch, particularly if tackled at an early

age, is that it puts you squarely in the open field—you can run
at will in every direction, with nothing ever to stop you.

Julius Caesar, Cicero, Alexander, the stories are thrilling; and
if you have any blood at all it all makes you want to learn more.
And if in your Sunday school or religious class you are also reading the Bible, you have it made—getting an idea about what
made us in the Western world, its foundations, that is—Greece,
Rome, and Judea.

The high school

I'LL SAY our elementary schools are excellent—maybe
even wonderful—and our colleges and universities are doing
great work, but the high school is a problem, a rat race really
between the drive for a black-tie outfit for the dances and worrying night and day about the forthcoming college boards examinations.

After ten years of lecturing around the country, I see one
possible solution—the two-year community college for *every*
high school kid, automatically, to cool off this drive for status
("My son will go to Princeton"). If the kid is a genius this will
do him no harm—he'll loop-the-loop after those two years, but
it may save hundreds of thousands of other boys for good pro-
ductive lives outside the academic world instead of spending
their years worrying why they didn't get into Duke University.

The truth about editors

THERE IS no doubt something presumptuous about one
editor writing about the work of many editors. A catalogue of
what's wrong with the others is only going to stir things up and
get a lot of friends mad at you.

But one salient fact about the business of newspaper editing
needs plain talk, mainly because this fact victimizes all of us. I

think back to the time when the ordinary newsman, let alone the advertiser, could not get into the editor's office unless that editor pressed a button which released the latch on his door. That button was sacrosanct. Editors didn't fear the entry of an outraged partisan with a bullwhip as much as they feared any biased intrusion would throw them off the track of thought they were pursuing.

There were eras when no one reached a newspaper or magazine editor save through an intermediary. But everyone can reach an editor today. Today, the editors belong to the Kiwanis, to the Chamber of Commerce, to the Knights of Columbus and to the B'nai B'rith. They are sometimes fixtures at the fancy uptown luncheon club and they can often be found beside the pool or on the golf links or near the bar of the country club on weekends. They are everybody's buddy.

That does not mean editors necessarily pull their punches.

A large advertiser can get his wife's picture in the paper when she is elected president of the PTA Council; but he cannot keep his own picture out when the Federal Government indicts him for income tax evasion. Withal, there is no doubt that today editors largely reflect the attitudes of the Establishment.

In short, the editorial office has become secularized, just as the pulpit has become secularized. The analogy is exact. The editor who was inaccessible in 1912 was much like the clergyman who led his flock. But today, in churches and temples, the layman has taken over just as the Establishment has taken over editorial policy. The clergyman is reserved for delivering the invocation and benediction and the editor for summarizing the news of the day.

The vast majority of Southern editors knew that when the Supreme Court ruled school segregation unconstitutional, all segregation was forfeit, just as the vast majority of clergymen knew. Segregation was immoral and illegal. But only a handful of editors and clergymen spoke of this topic in the years between 1954 and 1962. Neither clergyman nor editor considered himself the watchdog of the community; both felt they were swallowed up by it.

The great performers

HERE ARE my candidates for the greatest performers of
our times:

MALE—Enrico Caruso; Charles Chaplin; George M. Cohan;
Harry Lauder; John Barrymore; Al Jolson; Maurice Chevalier;
Fred Astaire; John McCormack; Jack Dempsey; Babe Ruth;
Sammy Davis, Jr.

FEMALE—Ethel Barrymore; Geraldine Farrar; Lillian Rus-
sell; Helen Hayes; Gracie Fields; Bette Davis; Anna Pavlova;
Amelita Galli-Curci; Marian Anderson; Beatrice Lillie; Babe
Didrikson; Sophie Tucker.

The movie as an art

LOOKING over the entire history of the motion pictures
I could select five movies as great works of art:

*Intolerance; Citizen Kane; The Informer; Dr. Strangelove;
Bridge on the River Kwai.*

A buyer's prize

WERE IT not for the encyclopedias and the cookbooks
and the textbooks for the schools, publishing would be in a very
bad way. Fortunately for publishers, most of America's housewives like to pick up their dictionaries and reference books at
the supermarkets where they also receive trading stamps for
their devotion to literature.

It is the trade books that don't move—the novels, the biographies, the books about adventures under the polar cap—that gather dust on the bookstore shelves. And the publishers ought to wise up to this. They ought to reward the consistent book buyers with a National Book Buyers Award, like they reward the writers who publish books of merit.

Every year the publishers give awards to the best novel, the best piece of non-fiction, and the best volume of poetry. For a long time, no money went with these awards. Often publishers were disappointed when the award winner had forgotten to show up at the cocktail party at which the plaques were handed out. But now I believe a one-thousand-dollar honorarium goes with the plaques and the cocktail salon is crowded with hopeful writers who figure even if they don't win they can still belt a few of the hard stuff and cadge enough hors d'oeuvres to do for the night's dinner.

If the publishers gave a plaque and a check to the folks who bought books, they could crowd two or three cocktail salons and do the bookstores a big favor.

Most people get their hands on a book when Aunt Minnie sends them one for a Christmas present or when they borrow one from a friend who has, in turn, borrowed it, or when they take the time to frequent the local library. But how many people buy a book every month?

I do and have for many years. I have bought enough books so that casual visitors are led occasionally to ask deprecatingly, "Have you really read all of them?" To which I give Coleridge's answer: "Some of them twice."

Israel's press

NEW YORK with eight million people has five daily newspapers; Detroit, with nearly two million, has two dailies. Tel Aviv with the population of half a million has twenty-three dailies.

There are some good reasons behind this. The Tel Aviv papers represent (with the exception of the English language *Jerusalem Post*) the entire Israeli press. Israel is about the size of Massachusetts—with fewer than two and a half million people. This makes regional newspapers unnecessary. Every daily is a national paper.

Another reason is that only half of the newspapers are printed in Hebrew, while the other half are in a dozen different languages—French to Yiddish, Arabic to German, Hungarian to Polish. There is even a Bulgarian daily.

This, of course, reflects the basic nature of the country of comparatively recent immigrants, many of whom haven't yet learned Hebrew. For every Jew who lived in Israel on May 14, 1948, there are four today. This gives you some idea of the scope of "the gathering of exiles."

But how can two dozen daily newspapers exist in such a small market?

The answer is: they can't.

Among the dozen or more Hebrew papers, only three make money: one morning and two evening papers. The rest are subsidized by the political parties, ranging from *Hamodia*, financed by the ultra-orthodox, to *Kol Haam*, the official organ of the Communist Party.

The three newspapers which make money, *Haaretz, Yedioth Achronoth*, and *Maariv*, are politically independent and thrive on Free Enterprise.

While *Maariv*, the biggest newspaper in Israel, sells a hundred thousand copies a day, some of the dailies barely make the one-thousand mark. But they are still kept going, despite financial losses, because a political party in Israel isn't worth its slogans if it doesn't have a paper.

This creates a problem entirely different from that known in the American press. While most newspapers in the United States are influenced in varying degrees by the agencies, advertisers, and business, the influence in Israel is political.

Advertising pressure is practically unknown in Israel: the political party papers scarcely have any advertising, while the profitable independent newspapers depend more on street sales than on advertising revenue.

An analysis of *Maariv* shows that no newspaper of similar size in the world makes comparable efforts to provide accurate and timely information to its readers. No American newspaper with a circulation of one hundred thousand or even several times that would keep three of its staff members permanently abroad. *Maariv* has its own men in Paris, London, and New York.

More than half of *Maariv*'s front page and features are foreign material. This of course reflects not only the traditional Jewish cosmopolitanism, but also the outward-mindedness of a small country which depends in many ways on the daily doings of the giants abroad. And the giant that gets the widest coverage in the Israeli press is Uncle Sam.

Poets

ON OCTOBER 15, we salute National World Poetry Day. Just how we salute it, I shall have to leave to the imagination of the poets.

National Poetry Day has been with us since 1938. But aside from exercising the penmanship of a great many elected public servants who are usually in a quandary as to whom to send their official greetings, I doubt if the Day has put a penny in the pocket of any poet. If Congress felt kindly toward poets, it might make National Poetry Day a yearly moratorium in which all debts against poets are forgiven, providing the forgiven poet then gets himself into a useful business, say, like selling roofing materials or judging Baby Derbies in lower California.

It is true in America that some poets have made some money, or at least they have acted like men with mortgage-free homes. Robert Frost and Carl Sandburg did well enough; not as well, of course, as if they had gotten into the marine engineering dodge when the getting was good, but well enough to support their families and educate their children.

But there is a trick here. You have to live very long and have a secondary profession in order to make it as a poet.

Any American who can make it to a vigorous seventy-five can count on being called "the eminent writer and poet."

Of course, the American poet has freedom, unlike his Russian counterpart. We read where Russian poets bring upon themselves thunderous denunciations by the Soviet Presidium for their "misinterpretations." The reason the American poet has his freedom, however, is because no one bothers to read him. If they did, he might be in as much hot water as any Russian.

I have even known subversive poets who confided they wished they could attract the kind of audience the Russian poets do. There is something much more romantic about being shot in a cellar than by being strangled by neglect.

Uses of a newspaper

NOT TOO long ago I outlined briefly the subsidiary uses of the newspaper which included:

(1) insulating shoes with holes in their soles
(2) cleaning auto windshields
(3) lining dresser drawers
(4) lining garbage cans
(5) serving as a makeshift bag for coffee grounds
(6) wrapping fish
(7) attracting bees

My mail was heavy. Everybody responded. Of course, some of the folks wrote to say they used my newspaper to clean out garbage pails or to set fires with, but some of the folks volunteered more practical and kinder suggestions.

Nellie Lewis of Los Angeles described a very practical use of the newspaper. Years of experiences, she said, have taught her that nothing deters moths more than newsprint. Newsprint is better than mothballs or any manufactured spray. It is cheaper, too. The moths shy from newsprint and no housewife has to tolerate the pungent smell of mothballs or anything else.

Editor Tom Heffernan of Wilkes-Barre reminded me his Sunday *Independent* served an excellent purpose as a furniture and floor covering for folks about to paint the ceiling.

I had to be reminded too by a Bronx housewife that for generations city women have used newspaper to cover the floor after they've washed it. My mother always spread newspapers after she scrubbed the floor. In fact, it seemed to me my life was spent in an apartment covered by wall-to-wall newspapers with my mother constantly admonishing, "Don't walk on the floor!" We had to edge along the wall to get in and out.

A Mr. Fortune of Cliffside, North Carolina, said that thousands of tenant farmers wallpapered their homes with old newspaper. The tenants performed the papering themselves with a bundle of discarded Sunday editions and a can of shellac. A shack so insulated is well-insulated, or at least better insulated than one without newsprint along the walls. Mr. Fortune also said that in his section of the South, the highest tribute children paid their dead kittens and other pets was to wrap the deceased in colored funny papers for a dignified burial.

Tarzan and Lolita

I saw a movie called *Tarzan Goes to India.* If you like monkeys, elephants, and Sikhs this is the movie for you. For myself I prefer to wait for the Tarzan sagas bound to follow. *Tarzan Goes to the Stock Market* and *Tarzan Meets the Creature from the Pennsylvania Turnpike.*

One of the movies I did see here in North Carolina was *Lolita* which starred James Mason, Sue Lyons, and Peter Sellers. The art-theatre owner told me he did better business with *Lolita* than he did with the nudist-camp movie except, he added, the picture wasn't doing well in Kentucky or Tennessee since the folks there don't understand what the fuss was all about.

America and music

WHEN SEVENTY THOUSAND people turned out in New York's Central Park to hear the first of the New York Philharmonic's outdoor concerts it was front-page news in all the papers. The officials of the Philharmonic had been worried that perhaps too few music lovers would come to sit on the grass and listen to Beethoven's Ninth to justify the expense and the effort. They thought a thousand people would be a representative crowd.

Any American would have told them they were thinking to no purpose, those officials of the Philharmonic. Americans love good music the way an Italian city or a Bayreuth loves music. The only reason there are not a Philharmonic and five weeks of grand opera in every American city of one hundred thousand and over is not because they would lack customers, but because the music entrepreneurs are snobs and the cities lack both imagination and real estate.

The kindness of villains

IN HOLLYWOOD, the tough guys and the villains are preferred as friends and neighbors. There is no kinder person than Boris Karloff. Edward G. Robinson is a cultured gentleman of graciousness and charm. Before his passing, Bela Lugosi was a great favorite with the ladies. He presented every hatcheck girl, movie queen, or waitress a flacon of precious perfume. They all adored him.

Irish coffee

THE IRISH STEVEDORES would have scorned the concoction that passes for "Irish coffee" at many swank bars. Irish coffee is at its best at four o'clock of a cold wintry morning. The cup must be large, the cream warm and poured to a quarter of the cup. A generous shot of whiskey, the cup filled with fresh, strong hot coffee, and there you are, deciding how much sugar. Men have moved freight and have blasted mountains to one side on the fortification of real Irish coffee.

None of this whipped-cream, namby-pamby stuff for them. They would be surprised at what we call Irish coffee.

PART 6

From Bolsheviks to Birchers

Protest in the streets

WHILE most Americans pay lip service to the concept of civil rights, a large segment despises the Negro revolution. Sooner or later the more articulate ask: Why is it the Italians, the Poles, the Irish, or the Jews never needed a freedom ride, a sit-in protest, or a street demonstration? The Irish had it tough. Yet John Kennedy became President of the United States; the Hungarians, the Slavs, the Japanese—none of them stayed forever in the steel mills, coal mines, or the chicken farms. Why can't the Negroes do by themselves peacefully what these other groups did?

The argument is specious.

Because the poverty-stricken, the oppressed, and the exploited didn't march through the streets for civil rights does not mean the need for the protest was not there.

It is true in the past one hundred years there were no street demonstrations for civil rights, as such, but then no one had Social Security, workmen's compensation, or an eight-hour day; no bank was insured; no child was protected from exploitation; none of the factories had fire escapes. Someone won these victories by protesting "in the streets."

First things first.

When the reformers first asked for restricting the working day for children under fourteen, the legislators laughed them out of the chambers. The church ladies who went from office to office begging factory owners and managers to install fire escapes were called busybodies and were told the workers didn't want fire escapes.

The civil rights struggle is not wholly a Negro phenomenon. It seems so, but that is because the Negro was a sub-citizen at the precise time civil rights needed institutionalization.

Establishing civil rights by law is no sudden impulse, any more than one hundred years ago public education was an impulse. The need was always there. The institutionalization came at the moment men waited for, when their hopes could be realized. So "civil rights" has become identified as a Negro need but indeed civil rights is everyone's need. The former poverty-stricken immigrant groups are not active participants in the current civil rights movement for the simple reason that the country cut off immigration in 1920; the second- and third-generation immigrant groups are now part and parcel of the American middle class, or nearly so. They can afford to be spectators, although none of us should minimize the support which has come from some of these men and women.

More to the point, we should dismiss the myth that none of the other "minorities" protested. Indeed they did and won many a fight against injustice. Who can ever forget the Mayflower ladies who protested "in the streets" for women's suffrage? Others fought to better the workingman's wage and to establish some measure of dignity in the industrial jungle which saw women working twelve hours a day, subjected to a personal search when they left their machines to make certain none had stolen a piece of ribbon.

Those who think there were no protests forget the number of men and women who had their heads cracked on picket lines as they agitated for the right to band together to protect their interests. I can remember a teacher asking a boy in my classroom what his father did and without guile the answer came back, "My father is a striker." I remember a yearlong bakery strike. The bakers received thirty cents an hour for a ten-hour day plus two loaves of day-old bread.

Anyone who insists the Negro is the first American to agitate "in the streets," conveniently eliminates from history fifty years of labor war.

In Ludlow, Colorado, the streets ran red with the blood of pickets and in Harlan County, Kentucky, the guards shot down the strikers who left the mines. In the mill villages of the South, hundreds upon hundreds of men and women were daily dehumanized and none of them were Negroes or members of a minority; they were all southern white Anglo-Saxon Protest-estants.

Those who think the Negroes *invented* the protest "in the streets" forget the IWW, the Haymarket bombing, the assassination of the Governor of Idaho, the bombing of the Los Angeles *Times*, the Molly Maguires and the Pinkertons.

What is different about the Negro revolution is that the Negroes do not want to change any existing institutions; they want no new constitution, nor do they want to cut off the King's head nor storm the Bastille, nor throw the tea overboard; they want no changes rung, they simply want to participate in the institutions already established.

They choose to wage this revolution with the Christian ethic of nonviolence.

And it is this ethic, the despair of the segregationist, which won the battle.

The Southern liberals

THE NIGHT one of my Army sons returned, we had dinner with a group of our old friends in Charlotte and he looked over the ten or eleven of us and asked, "What are you people calling the organization this year?"

This tells much of the story of the liberals in the South. They are individual groups of ten, twenty, forty (in some Southern cities one hundred and fifty) people who rotate the name of their local organization from year to year in the hope of attracting new members and achieving some influence. Some of these groups started out as chapters of the ADA (Americans for Democratic Action), others worked as committees in support of the United Nations, or to fight "right-to-work" proposals, or to combat the arguments of veterans' groups and the D.A.R. in their opposition to fluoridation, but, in the main, nearly all these loosely organized clubs eventually directed their efforts toward winning supporters for the Supreme Court decision of May 17, 1954. Many of them became affiliated with the Southern Regional Council, supported by the Fund for the Republic. The Council provided the speakers and the literature, and in many cases paid the office rent and the salary of the secretary until the local organization became self-supporting.

When we speak of liberals in the South, therefore, we mean "liberal" on the race issue. I may be disputed on this; but, after all, we have been involved in a great social upheaval, the changing of an entire social order, and those who once considered themselves "liberal" in religious, political, or economic matters have, during the past ten years, voluntarily dropped the term like a hot potato, because in the South today "liberal" describes only the person with even a nominal sympathy for the Negro in his struggle for first-class citizenship.

Nevertheless, "liberal" must remain an ambiguous and ambivalent term. These are people in the eastern part of North Carolina, for instance, who revere the New Deal as they revere the Gospels. In fact there is still a strong residue of the Populism of the nineteenth century in much of the rural South. The cotton, tobacco, and peanut farmers and peach growers looked to William Jennings Bryan and then to Franklin D. Roosevelt as saviors. Yet it is precisely in these farm and rural sections where the strongest resistance rears against the Negro's struggle for civil rights. These champions of social legislation refuse to be called liberals or vote for liberals. However, in the industrial Piedmont, where I live, there has been a rather liberal viewpoint right from the beginning about race. But labor unions, TVA, and Medicare are anathemas. The farmer reveres Franklin D. Roosevelt and hates Martin Luther King, and the city businessman is indifferent to Martin Luther King and hates Walter Reuther.

The genuine liberal is therefore reduced to a state of schizoid shock. He must often contend against the economic liberal in the farm areas and side with the fiscal conservative in the industrial sections. Much of the genuine liberal's program must be dissipated and compromised, for no matter what, he cannot deny the Negro's advance and to help this advance he finds himself writing political pamphlets for fiscally conservative Republicans and shouting down social welfare, REA, and farm subsidy racists.

You can live, but they won't let you, my father used to say.

You will find this ambivalent situation in every Southern state.

Texas has the arch-conservative Dallas, and North Carolina has the arch-conservative Charlotte; but significantly Texas and the two Carolinas have more users of federal rural electrification than all of New England and New York and New Jersey combined.

Which suggests a word about Georgia, too. When Senator Richard B. Russell was the leader in the fight against the Civil Rights Act of 1964, he argued that such legislation encroached upon the sovereignty of his state. The voices of thousands of fellow Georgians echoed, "There's too much federal control." But the casual traveler through Georgia is struck by an amazing sight: Georgia has more new post offices than any state in the Union. At every crossroads there is a beautiful little building built in 1960 or 1961 or 1962 or 1963 or 1964. The traveler must say, "What wonderful senators are Richard B. Russell and Herman Talmadge, because no one gets all these new federal buildings, so many of them, without effective work by representatives in the Congress."

Amazingly, the local groups of liberals are composed of interchangeable people in each city. Going to such meetings in Norfolk, New Orleans, Savannah, Atlanta, Memphis, Dallas, and Orlando, one could make up the roster if not the individual names of the participants and certainly one could guess their station in life: two or three Protestant clergymen, usually Episcopalian or Presbyterian; a Roman Catholic priest; officials of the steel, textile, and garment workers unions; three or four Unitarians; three or four Quakers; two or three social workers, and two or three Jews. The Jews within these groups, I might add, are rarely part of the so-called "power structure"—established retail merchants, manufacturers—but more usually college professors, physicists, or perhaps a sales manager who represents a firm in New York, Philadelphia, or Chicago. In nearly all of these groups I have found one or two women from the local "power structure" whose wealth or social position was such as to make her unassailable and unafraid.

The clergymen come from the smaller churches where their personalities and long tenure have made them relatively secure. While they take no parishioners with them into the organization, still they can express themselves publicly and identify with the integration group.

There have been few, if any, martyrs among these liberals. The reason is that they have never really been looked upon as renegades, traitors to the South. The politician segregationists and even the red-necks recognized or thought they recognized no threat: "Oh, that's just a Jew talking," they would say, or "Oh, that's just a no-account preacher shooting his mouth off." The local liberals were more or less left alone and that is why they did eventually achieve considerable influence. They appeared before every school board and before every legislative body, and they wrote letters to the editors; many, many letters to the editors. Often their mere presence in the community was enough to have some effect. In my own city, for instance, the school board in 1955 listened to some harebrained proposal to defeat the edict of the Supreme Court. A member spoke up, "No, we better not, that Human Relations Council will have us spread all over the New York *Post* tomorrow morning." In another city the mayor addressed his City Council thus: "If we don't do something about the Negro hospital that bunch of do-gooders will have the N.A.A.C.P. down on our necks." However, if a member of the Establishment expresses himself for integration even at this late date, he is still in for trouble.

I think I can explain some of this by relating a personal experience. In the days when every legislature in the South was figuring out schemes to beat the Supreme Court decision of May 17, 1954, in North Carolina the legislature invented a gimmick called the Pearsall Plan. The legislators held perfunctory hearings pro and con.

Two of us spoke out forcefully against the proposed Pearsall

Plan, I and Dr. Maggs of the Law Department of Duke University, who attacked the Pearsall Plan on constitutional grounds. His talk was highly restrained. He rarely mentioned the word integration and he rarely mentioned the word Negro. He spoke as an authority on constitutional law. He said that the Pearsall Plan was a subterfuge. North Carolina was wasting its time in these maneuvers when it could proceed to begin working toward the inevitable. I discussed the terrible tragedy of eleven million Negroes living on the margin of our society and the tragedy it was for the United States, for Christianity, for North Carolina and the rest of the South to leave them there.

After the hearings we went to the Governor's office. Everyone was frothing at Dr. Maggs. I heard such words as "Red," "Commie," "renegade," whereas I, who had made a more emotional speech, was greeted with genuine fellowship. The Governor put his arms around me. I thought about this on the way home and it dawned on me, "Of course, that's the answer. Dr. Maggs is a 'renegade,' I am not. I am not only a Jew, but a Yankee Jew at that."

But it hasn't all been peace and quiet. The obscene letters keep coming, week after week, year after year. I hold today's letter in my hand. It is in red crayon. Did this fellow borrow a crayon from his little girl—print "Kill all the nigger-loving Jews," seal the letter, and walk to the mailbox to send it on its way? I wonder.

And the middle-of-the-night phone calls! They come at irregular periods, every night for two weeks, calls to each known member of the group, no calls for two or three months, followed by another short period of calls. Do these people hold meetings? Do they use maps? Does someone hand out the assignments—you call A, and you call B, and so forth? I wonder.

I had one lady who called me every time my name appeared in the papers. She was not obscene and she was not anonymous. She pleaded with me each time, "Mr. Golden, why are you doing this to us? The South has been so good to you, why do you take up for the Negroes?"

Finally, after eight or ten such calls across a six-month period,

I told the lady that I had decided to reveal a secret to her that I had never told anyone else. I said, "Madam, why shouldn't I take up for the Negroes? I am half-Negro."

The woman literally jumped for joy. I could almost see her at the other end of the telephone. I had confirmed everything in her mind and she was very happy and full of compassion. "Oh, Mr. Golden, now I understand, of course." And I gave her a bonus. I told her to be sure not to tell anybody else.

On Medicare

I DO not know of any institution in the United States of America today that is as humorless as the American Medical Association. They are angry. There hasn't been a single smile out of the whole sociological struggle against "socialized medicine" in the last twenty years.

There was a bit of humor which no one considered humorous, when the North Carolina Medical Association integrated. They said the Association would integrate "only for science" and not for social activities.

I have a better right to speak to doctors than television's Dr. Kildare. The Jews have a long history in medicine. It may surprise you to know that in the twelfth and thirteenth centuries the only doctors in Europe were Jews. In those days the doctor was looked upon as a threat to the Establishment. The church derived much of its power at the time from indulgences and prayer to cure the sick. Not only did medicine as we know it today develop because of Jewish persistence in the science, but the Arabs who held their torch on high for six centuries had originally been inoculated by Jewish physicians with learning. They met, the Jews and the Arabs in Alexandria, and the Arabs received private and personal instruction in medicine from the Jews.

It was this intellectual activity that communicated an impulse to all of Europe, even though the Jewish doctor was viewed with wonder, fear, and hatred. Way back in the thirteenth century you had from the hand of Isaac Ben Soleiman, an Egyptian Jew, a series of pamphlets with such titles as: "On Fevers," "On Medicine," "On Food," "On the Pulse," "On Philosophy," "On Melancholia," and his greatest of all works, "An Introduction to Logic." This from a doctor.

And what saved medicine for Europe really was the rise of Islam, for Islam was powerful in numbers and Islam's patronage of the Jewish physicians is what advanced the science. The first medical school was founded by a rabbi at Montpelier, France. The rabbinical seminary required study of medicine and thus a great rabbi, Rabbi Solomon Ben Isaac, better known in Hebrew literature and philosophy as Raschi, the initials of his name, wrote commentaries on the Bible and also a book of instructions for surgical operations. Just imagine that Raschi wrote the first pamphlet instructing surgeons how to perform a Caesarian section.

And the greatest of them all was Maimonides, recognized in time as the "Glory of the West and the Light of the East," second only to Moses. His name was Moses Ben Maimon. And to this day Jews have a phrase, "From Moses to Moses, there is no one like Moses." He was a doctor born in 1135 and he became personal physician to Saladin. He wrote books on medicine with titles such as *On Hemorrhoids, On Poisons and Antidotes, On Asthma, On the Preservation of Health, On the Bites of Venomous Animals, On Natural History,* and many others.

But the doctors of America will get over their sad faces. After Medicare the doctors will find that nothing really bad has happened except the lifting of a burden. It will be like the ingration of the movie houses and restaurants in Charlotte. It's as though it's always been that way.

The A.M.A. can no more stop the extension of Medicare than stop the flow of the Mississippi. This is a pattern of history. Mankind institutionalizes that which will help its survival. It institutionalized the military. It no longer took a chance on feudal barons maintaining armed men to protect the countryside. Later it institutionalized the police. It was too important to leave that to what we call "private initiative." And Horace Mann, over one hundred years ago, talked to us about the public schools. Only a few rich went to school in his day and so we institutionalized it and now we are attempting to educate the entire population of America.

And the people will institutionalize health because they have finally realized what it means to the increase in life expectancy. And eventually we will also institutionalize art.

That great creeping socialist Prince Otto von Bismarck institutionalized health with the first Medicare program and St. Augustine was the first to institutionalize art. He married Christianity to the arts and thus helped make Christianity a universal religion.

You missed it, Governor Scranton

I HOLD Governor William Scranton of Pennsylvania in deep affection. The Governor and I have been pen pals for years. I had occasion to write him recently when some of his fellow Republicans held a convention in North Carolina, heah:

DEAR BILL:
You owe President Johnson a vote of thanks, Governor. He called you governors to a Vietnam briefing on the very day you were to speak here at the North Carolina Republican Convention. You don't know how lucky you are. First off, when the chairman read your cancellation, the folks booed for a solid minute. When I asked why Republicans would boo a Republican governor, one delegate told me, "We're not booing Scranton, exactly. We're booing Johnson." But he had that gleam in his eye which betrayed he was getting in two licks for every catcall.

The delegates then proceeded to adopt some resolutions, the pain of which I thought of sparing you but then I realized you are a man who can take it. The resolutions were drawn by a group calling itself "The Committee to Preserve Constitutional Republicanism." Among those who would "unpreserve" Republicanism were Earl Warren, Nelson Rockefeller, Earl Warren, Thomas E. Dewey, and Earl Warren again.

A proposal to demand the Federal Government to send an ultimatum to Red China lost by an impressive margin. But the proposal for a Cuban blockade almost passed. And of course the delegates voted overwhelmingly to ask for a universal ban on Communist and Communist-front speakers who would subdue tar-heel college students with their rhetoric.

This out of the way, the delegates really got to work on a resolution which called for a constitutional amendment to override the Supreme Court's "one-man, one-vote" decision. And on civil rights these Republicans were masterly. To help the two fellows running for Congress in the rural, white-supremacy districts, the delegates passed a resolution castigating the Federal Government for going "too fast" on "so-called civil rights." For the fellows contending in the Piedmont with its large Negro voting blocs, the delegates passed another clause condemning the Democrats who "haven't done enough for civil rights." But then, Bill, you may not understand that there are many Southern politicians who firmly believe the United States Government is an alien power and that Washington is in some insidious place like Asia or Hong Kong.

Yes, Southern liberals will have to wait a little while longer. Most of us looked forward hopefully to the emergence of a strong Republican Party in the South. Such a party would help us clear out of the Democratic Party those typical politicians whose principles and policies are to the right of Louis XIV. Southern conservatives have had it both ways for too long. They have their cake and eat it, too. Apparently they'll still get fat. The way things look now, Bill, the Republican Party is trying to out-Southern the Southern Democrats. It will not work.

Jewish and Polish lawyers

I HAVE told before how Charlie Murphy and the Tammany sachems were selecting the judiciary slate and how one of their nominees for a judgeship was a Jew who had forgotten about the meeting.

"We'll have to wait until tomorrow," said one of the lieutenants.

"It has to be tonight," said Murphy.

Murphy walked to the rostrum and when all the delegates quieted, asked, "Is there a Jewish lawyer in the house?"

One fellow put up his hand and Murphy said, "You're the Democratic nominee for Municipal Court Justice," and that fellow served thirty years. With distinction.

Now, not so long ago in Connecticut, the congressman-at-large, Mr. Kowalski, contended with Abraham Ribicoff for the senatorial nomination. Traditionally, the congressman-at-large in the Nutmeg State is a Pole, but Mr. Kowalski raised such a fuss that the State Democratic chairman doubted whether the delegates would support him again.

This chairman also addressed the convention with the question, "Is there a Polish lawyer in the house?" and a young lawyer named Grabowski said, "I'm a Polish lawyer. What do you want me to translate?"

"Translate?" said the chairman. "You're the nominee."

Mr. Grabowski has proved an admirable representative ever since.

The Bolshevik revolution

IN FEBRUARY of 1917, the Russian people revolted against the Czar. They won their fight and established a parliamentary government copying Western models. The first premier was Alexander Kerensky. In October, the Bolsheviks under Lenin and Trotsky staged a coup. With bayonets, they dismissed the parliament and Kerensky and started to consolidate their power.

Alexander Kerensky has lived in America for many years since that coup. He is today a visiting trustee professor at Mills College in Oakland, California. Kerensky has outlived his Czar,

Woodrow Wilson, Lloyd George, Lenin, Trotsky, and Stalin. Good for him.

Not too long ago, Mr. Kerensky gave out in a newspaper interview that he hoped President Lyndon B. Johnson would sit down with Soviet Premier Kosygin in personal consultation.

I thought of Mr. Kerensky recently while listening to one of the major evangelists in the anti-Communist crusade business. This fellow told an audience of two thousand, five hundred people that nine men and nine men alone made the Russian revolution. And two thousand, five hundred people nod obediently at this demagogue and look suspiciously around themselves wondering which nine in the audience would dare make an American Communist revolution.

The even more respectable Professor Sidney Hook in his book, *The Hero in History*, says one man has made the Russian revolution, Vladimir Lenin.

In 1917, when the democrats had seized power, Kerensky promised the Russians land reform and representative government. He also promised to continue the war. The Germans shipped Lenin across Europe in a sealed railway car to the Finland Station because he had promised to quit the Allies and make a separate peace.

Lenin succeeded to power but not because he was a solitary genius nor because he had eight other solitary geniuses to help him. He succeeded because millions, literally millions, of Russians had been sent to Siberia during the previous one hundred years. He succeeded because priests like Father Gapon had led protest marches, and were shot down by the Cossacks.

Above all, he succeeded because the Russians never had a constitution under a pane of glass in a museum, because there was no Liberty Bell in an Independence Hall. He succeeded because though there were Russians who talked about freedom and liberty like Kerensky there were no symbols by which other Russians could make plain what this talk meant. There had been no Jefferson, John Locke, Roger Williams, and Magna Carta.

At last count, I believe there are one hundred and thirty-six professionals in the anti-Communist crusade business, men who make their living by pointing out the menace of the fatal nine among us. If ever we were to have a revolution, part of the casual chain would be those one hundred and thirty-six professional scarers. Fortunately for us, our Kerenskys all live at home.

The war in Vietnam

I CANNOT help but sympathize with the President's policy in Vietnam. It is unthinkable to pull out, as many of my friends suggest. Perhaps we shouldn't be there, but we are there and in a fight.

What some of my friends ask is that Johnson become famous as the "pull-out President," "the abandoner." He does not deserve this, but that would be his fate. Which brings me to an area of our foreign policy which has rarely been explored:

Our foreign policy today grows not only from external realities but from internal fears. No one is immune from the libelous charge that he is "soft on Communism." Every intelligent layman and certainly every elected official knows how easy it is for a minor demagogue to exploit this gnawing fear.

Not long ago I read a review by a competent critic of a performance of the Bolshoi Ballet. This particular critic prefaced his piece with a ringing denunciation of Communism and I knew he was paving the way for an ecstatic review of the dancers.

Former Senator Barry Goldwater supports President Johnson's policy in Vietnam. But the President, says Senator Goldwater, is not going far enough. Goldwater, out of office, is a primary exponent of the "let's drop the other shoe" school of American foreign policy.

President Johnson not only has trouble with this school, the Far Right, but also with the Far Left, members of his own coalition. The Left wanted the Nazis and the Fascists beaten; the Right wanted us to concentrate on the Far East. The "we lost

China" boys (who apparently thought this nation of one-sixth of the human race was *ours* to lose) achieved a dominant position in determining some of the calculations of our international posture. They said losing China was proof of subversion and if we lose anything else, why that must be subversion, too.

If Lyndon Johnson pulls out of Vietnam as the Left asks him to do, the next President of the United States would not be Hans Morgenthau but Barry Goldwater or a reasonable facsimile thereof. Overnight, the Birchers would recruit four million new members, and Billy James Hargis would sing loud and clear.

These are the facts of life. Fear has created some myths as they involve China. After the Napoleonic Wars, England adopted a policy of keeping Russia out of Europe. We are all paying the price for that policy today. But our policy of trying to keep China out of the world is an even more catastrophic policy. Think of the price mankind may be called upon to pay for that!

Perhaps China is bent on the war of suicide. But she has made no move against those two islands hugging her shore, two enemy islands not as close to her as Cuba is to us, but almost as close as Staten Island is to Greater New York.

So what else is new?

Karl Marx's tomb

SOME CUBAN exiles tried to blow up Karl Marx's tomb in Highgate Cemetery, London.

Whoever, besides Castro, may be responsible for their exile, it is not that stone marker above the grave of Karl Marx.

In fact, it is not even the ideas of Karl Marx that brought Castro into power, nor Mao Tse-tung, nor Stalin and his successors. A year after the Russian revolution they threw Karl

Marx overboard and established a self-perpetuating totalitarian state.

As for the philosophy of Karl Marx himself, the testament *Das Kapital* was written for an early Victorian era and has about as much relevance to the world today as the maps of the thirteenth century which called the Atlantic the sea of darkness. Even the "class war" idea which was still discussed fifty years after Marx died has been laid to rest. Marx had no idea what a short jump it is from a near-starvation diet to the hairdresser, the electric icebox, and the bridge game.

Of course Castro speaks for six hours at a stretch calling the name of Karl Marx a hundred times, and this would shock the daylights out of the old German-Jewish-turned-Lutheran economist. He thought the agricultural nations such as Russia and China (and Cuba) would be the last people on earth to embrace Communism. The revolution, he thought, would come among the industrial workers, who would one day "lose their chains." But Marx did not envision lipstick, Social Security, workmen's compensation, pension funds, and the sale of ten million new automobiles every year to the proletariat.

The Russians have his picture on the wall and so do the Chinese and the Cubans, and the picture serves to fool the people into thinking the regime has substance rather than a statism interested in perpetuating itself.

And those pictures of Karl Marx in Russia, China, and Cuba are a big help to the Far Right in the West. In South Africa, for instance, they prosecute people who oppose apartheid under a law called "suppression of Communism." So Karl Marx not only serves Castro but also makes a contribution to the maintenance of racial segregation in South Africa.

Poor Marx, a stubborn old man, does not know that our own Far Right can ruin a man by calling him "Marxist" if a man so "accused" lacks the money and the guts to sue.

If Karl Marx knew all of this the Cuban exiles wouldn't have to blow up his tombstone, he'd get up and knock it down himself.

White vote becomes a threat

OVER IN our 50th state—Hawaii—the political leaders are beginning to worry about the growing white vote—the "new Caucasian vote" as they call it.

In 1960, one of six voters was white. Mainlanders emigrating in recent years have increased that figure.

County Chairman Kimura says, "These whites have become voters and will be a factor in our elections."

Hawaiian political parties, Democratic and Republican, have found a challenge—whites.

Will they vote as a bloc?

Victory for 14-B

SENATOR SAM ERVIN of North Carolina declared his proudest moment in the United States Senate was helping defeat the Johnson Administration's proposal to repeal Section 14-B of the Taft-Hartley Law. Section 14-B allows any state laws which are in essence anti-union laws.

The Orwellian idea that peace means war, and hate means love, applies here; no union means freedom.

Freedom to do what? The worker is told what he will be paid, how long he will work, when he must report, when leave, and when eat lunch. He is told when and where he can smoke; on assembly lines he may even be compelled to regulate his natural functions with the production schedule.

Up to the time of the Civil Rights Acts of 1964 and 1965, particularly up to the time of John F. Kennedy's directive on equal employment opportunity, the big fear in the minds of the industrial workers of the South was that Negroes would be working beside them if the union won a contract. It is interesting to note this fear is abating bit by bit. Negroes are hired to do white men's jobs because segregated plants risk losing their government contracts, and with the entry of the Southern Negro into industry, the interest in unionization is growing. But that is why the resistance to the union shop is also becoming more intense.

In the two Carolinas there are close to half a million cotton mill workers. Less than fifty thousand of these are in organized plants.

The Textile Workers Union, AFL-CIO, was at a standstill until Kennedy promulgated the directive on equal employment.

In the twelve years following the passage of Taft-Hartley, the union was able to win but fifty-six elections, and in only twenty of those was the union able to establish any sort of continuing relationship.

The old beat-'em-up, hose-'em-down techniques of strikebreaking have disappeared. More genteel practices have succeeded them. The employer now has an office of highly trained intelligent public relations people. The most effective among these are several clergymen, most notably the Rev. Dr. George Heaton, formerly of the Myers Park Baptist Church. These clergymen and other public relations people use the high road and their approach is based on philosophy and decency. At the same time, the propaganda machine is in operation; propaganda is circulated through rumors, letters, news stories, advertisements, and speeches.

Sometimes the whole community organizes on behalf of anti-union activity. Labor espionage is rife. Union sympathizers are fired. Injunctions follow injunctions. Finally the employer closes down the plant or merges the plant, or moves the plant.

Few organizing campaigns can survive the carefully planned gambits.

I often wonder how many editors in the Carolinas have read the reports of what goes on at these labor hearings: the charges, the evidence, the witnesses. Much of the testimony is based on the myth that Southern workers are an independent bunch of people. "The independent white Anglo-Saxons are not union material," wrote one Southern editor. "They don't want to be organized." Which is utter nonsense. The Southern members of the Typographical and Carpenters unions are white Anglo-Saxons. Try monkeying with their unions.

After the successful filibuster against repeal of 14-B, Senators Ervin and Dirksen each spoke of the "victory for freedom." It struck a familiar note. Many years ago Senator Jim Watson of Indiana fought a bill which would have prohibited children under fourteen years of age working more than eight hours in any day or more than six days a week. Senator Watson said he was trying to achieve a victory for freedom.

Birchers in Charlotte

THOMAS J. DAVIS, Eastern public relations director of the John Birch Society, came to Charlotte drumming up conservative trade.

In North Carolina, the Birchers hope for seven thousand members in 1966. "But we have quite a distance to go to reach this," he conceded.

At the meeting held here not a single citizen of any prestige attended, just the rag-tag group of people who are "fighting Communism" because they hate one, two, or all of the following: fluoridation, Negroes, government spending, Jews, President Johnson, foreigners, civil rights, the Beatles, the sexually adjusted, people who speak a foreign language, the United Nations, and/or the people who are under five feet, ten and a half inches tall.

When the Charlotte *Observer* reporter asked Mr. Davis about membership, the Birch public relations director answered, "As Mr. Welch says humorously, about sixty percent Protestant, forty percent Catholic, and one percent Jewish, which he admits adds up to 101 percent, but that means we have very few Jews. . . ."

Very humorous, but far from original. It was almost the identical sentence used by an early Nazi leader, Gregor Strasser, 'way back in the late 1920's. It is a mating call.

What is obscene?

THE STORY or picture of a man and woman making love is not obscene.

What is obscene is the picture of that fellow in full Ku-Klux Klan regalia running for public office in Charlotte.

What is obscene is the sound of hundreds of white Southerners shouting that most famous four-letter word at Catholic nuns marching with the Negroes.

Whatever is dehumanizing, is obscene. Whatever attempts to shatter self-respect and hold others in contempt, is obscene.

What is truly pornographic is the evidence documented in a recent report of the Southern Regional Council of Atlanta, Georgia. In 19 pages of fine print the organization documents cases throughout the South—Negro families who are paying a heavy price when their children are moved into white schools. For example:

> Men and women who were already desperately poor were evicted from sharecroppers' cabins or tenant farms. Many without the training for good jobs lost the meager jobs they had held for years. Some were beaten and shot at. Others saw their children abused and imprisoned.

What is far more obscene than the picture of a naked woman, is the notice of the Veterans Affairs agency that it has approved legislation to name a U. S. Veterans Administration hospital after the late Congressman John E. Rankin of Mississippi.

What can possibly be more obscene than that?

Changing sides

LET US consider two of the most notable reversals in the political history of our country.

The first of these occurred when the conservatives and the liberals changed sides on states' rights.

From the earliest beginnings of our country to the Civil War, the liberals championed states' rights while the conservatives championed a strong central government. Interestingly enough, two Republican presidents, Abraham Lincoln and Theodore Roosevelt, asserted the Federal Government's complete sovereignty in matters concerning individual civil and political rights and in matters pertaining to interstate commerce, which is to say nearly all of American life.

It should come as no surprise to students that the whole idea of states' rights was still a liberal concept right up to the time of Franklin D. Roosevelt's first term in 1932, when the economic machinery of the state governments collapsed, and each of the forty-eight states found itself helpless.

The great reversal between liberals and conservatives took place then. Before Franklin D. Roosevelt, the conservatives were in favor of a strong central government, believing the United States Supreme Court the most sacred institution on earth (as do the liberals today, incidentally). Before F.D.R., liberals called the Supreme Court the "Bulwark of Privilege." The New Deal President himself said the Court was "nine old men."

With the enactment of a whole program of social legislation by the Federal Government the liberals and the conservatives switched sides, almost overnight.

This inspired another great reversal.

For the first seventy-five years of America's development from a rural-agricultural civilization to an urban-industrial society, the liberals fought against "the status quo."

Henry George, William Jennings Bryan, the Populists, Eugene V. Debs, the Socialists, Edward Bellamy, Jack London, the labor unions, the Farmer-Labor Party, Clarence Darrow, all spoke out against the status quo, which they described variously as "vested interests," "Wall Street," "entrenched wealth," "the money trust," "the international bankers." During those seventy-five years, the White House, the Supreme Court, business and wealth dedicated themselves to a strong central government.

The liberals were outside looking in, but now we are on the inside. We liberals are the status quo boys (and there have never been such ardent status quo boys in all the history of our country).

The conservatives are the ones who want in; it is they who speak out against the all-too-powerful Federal Government, curse the Supreme Court, urge impeaching Earl Warren.

"What Does the Liberal Want?" The answer is—nothing. The liberal wants nothing, except that maintenance of status quo. This maintenance requires constant vigilance, implementation, improvement, and expansion. At the moment, therefore, we status quo boys would like to see:

1. A broad program of federal aid to education
2. Medical and hospital insurance for the entire American population, every man, woman, and child
3. A federal Fair Employment Practices Act
4. "Right to Work" laws repealed

Up to Goldwater's nomination, the Republicans avoided the mistake of the Whigs, they did not contend irrevocably against the inevitable and their strength was not in their fight against the liberal measures but in their acceptance of the Federal Reserve System, the eight-hour day, controlled freight rates, Social Security, the minimum wage, the National Labor Relations Board, TVA, farm subsidies, old age pensions, and the rest.

Now the Far Right has indicated its intention, if not of eliminating this vast social legislation, of at least reducing it and certainly stopping its expansion.

Political wisdom indicates that Robert F. Kennedy will probably emerge as the leader of the liberal forces in the United States. (I said this in a speech at the Amalgamated Homes during R.F.K.'s campaign for the Senate, and fellow liberals laughed up their sleeves.) The Far Right has its leaders. The moderates—Case of New Jersey, Romney of Michigan, Lindsay of New York, Kuchel of California, Scranton of Pennsylvania—have already become entrenched because of the Goldwater debacle. Robert F. Kennedy is the best politician around today and he will work for dynamic liberalism if indeed his goal is the Presidency.

Matzo balls in space

HASSEIN HEIKAL, editor of the influential Cairo daily, *Al Ahram*, warns his readers that the Israelis will soon be able to produce an atomic bomb.

Which reminds me of an incident involving the late Irish playwright Brendan Behan, who once told a Canadian audience: "Israel will send a couple of matzo balls around the moon before you Canadians succeed in sending a spaceship there."

I have been assured on good authority that neither the Egyptians nor the Canadians have any cause for worry. Israel is making no atom bomb and has no intention of sending matzo balls around the moon. They need all the matzo balls they can make for next Passover, with God's help.

The United Nations

NEXT TO the founding of the United States of America the greatest political event of human history is the founding of the United Nations. I doubt seriously whether life would be worth living anymore without it.

Question from the chair

SOME TIME AGO, meetings of the League of Women Voters in Atlanta, Georgia, were being broken up by the Minute-women, an auxiliary of the John Birch Society.

These infiltrators were trained for their job. They took the floor and harangued the audience and shouted arguments, and the members, unaccustomed to these Communist methods, seemed helpless until they developed a system of their own. When one of these Minutewomen rose to speak, the chairlady banged the gavel and said, "First tell us if you are a Communist." The Minutewoman began to tremble and splutter, "Why the very idea," but the chairlady kept at it and said, "This is how the Communists do it and we just wonder whether or not you are a Communist." The woman kept this up, demanding to know whether the heckler was a Communist and that's the only sentence she heard, "Tell us if you are a Communist."

The League of Women Voters has not been bothered since.

How not to win an election

IN THE last days of the campaign the candidate marks the days off on a little calendar. Like the Count of Monte Cristo, he counts the hours to the moment of his deliverance.

The pressure has been severe, mostly the deep concern lest anyone be offended among the dozens of fraternal, business, labor, social, religious, racial, and ethnic groups in the country. The candidate always praises the clergy, and eats the foods of ethnic identity, the blintzes in one neighborhood, chittlins, perhaps, in another.

George Bernard Shaw ran but once for public office. He stood, as the English say, for the London County Council in 1914 and was overwhelmingly defeated.

Here is how Shaw campaigned: he told an audience he was an atheist, just to get off on the right foot. To another group he said he was a teetotaler and that if it were left to him, he would make everybody drink a half bottle of rum at one sitting to cure them of the addiction for John Barleycorn. In another speech, apropos of nothing at all, he criticized the Roman Catholic Church, all the time confiding to the voters that he himself was an idealist of the purest water.

The trustworthy citizen

EXAMINE CLOSELY William Buckley's editorials in the *National Review* and examine just as closely the literature distributed by the John Birch Society. Then read the pamphlets distributed to their "schools" by Rev. Billy Hargis and Dr. Fred Schwartz. One basic theme is impressive—that the reformed Communist is the most trustworthy American patriot of our times.

Alabama's governors

GOVERNOR GEORGE WALLACE of Alabama, prevented by law from running for another term, put his wife into the gubernatorial race. Lurleen may win. In a joint announcement of her candidacy, the Wallaces promised that they would *both* act as governor—two-in-one, like the shoe polish. In Alabama *bedfellows make strange politics.*

How to die laughing

READ THE editorials in the Southern press and literally you will die laughing.

Take the Supreme Court as an example. The Southern papers are suddenly blessing the dissenters. The dissenters are those Justices who recently read contrary opinions when the Court struck down Virginia's state-applied poll tax. The Southerners waxed enthusiastic over John Marshall Harlan's dissent. Said the Justice: "Property and poll tax qualifications, very simply, are not in accord with current egalitarian notions of how a modern democracy should be organized. It is of course entirely fitting that legislatures should modify the law to reflect such changes in modern attitudes."

All the editors call Harlan a "liberal." They love dissenting liberals.

But these same editors poured venom against these justices, four in number, who dissented in the majority opinion which upheld Ralph Ginzburg's conviction for pornography. "It is frightening to think how close was this decision to uphold morality," said one of the Southern sheets.

It reminds me of the Southern newspaper which blasted the Government for its social legislation, ". . . which undermines the moral fiber of our people" on the editorial page while on page one they demanded to know in a big headline: "Why haven't we received our local anti-poverty funds?"

PART 7

Of Popes and Presidents

Excalibur

WHEN Mordred revolted, King Arthur was sorely wounded. He asked Sir Bedivere to take his sword Excalibur to the sea and throw it into the waters. Twice Bedivere went and twice refused to throw away the valuable sword, telling Arthur each time he had given the sword to the sea. But Arthur told him he lied and finally true to his trust, Bedivere hurled the sword into the sea and a hand rose above the waves to catch it and shake it. Then Bedivere took the bleeding Arthur to a barge on which sat many ladies clothed in black, among them Arthur's sister, Queen Morgan le Fay. Arthur told Bedivere the barge would take him to Avalon and there he would recover from his wound and come back to help England when she needed him.

In the mid-twentieth century Excalibur became fingers gesturing V for Victory and Arthur smoked black cigars and saved England and all of Western civilization.

Long life to Harry Truman

I WAS amused to read that Alabama's sheriff, Jim Clark, sent a message of congratulations to former President Harry Truman. Harry Truman called Martin Luther King a "troublemaker" and that pleased Sheriff Clark mightily.

What is amusing about the telegram is the memory of how all the Sheriff Clarks of the South used to feel about Harry Truman. I remember how they wanted to cut his heart out because he integrated the armed forces, how they put up a Presidential candidate of their own in an attempt to give the 1948 election to Thomas E. Dewey. Their hatred of Harry S. Truman was vast and profound.

As far as I am concerned, President Harry Truman is entitled to say anything he wants to say; everything he says is interesting; may he live to one hundred twenty, like Moses. Mr. Truman will never have to apologize to anyone for his civil rights record. Add up the scores of all the Presidents and Harry Truman will be pretty near the top.

Facing a campaign to win the White House for his own term, he ordered an end to racial segregation in the armed services. With the nominating convention but a few months away, Harry Truman sent an eight-point civil rights program to the Congress which had the Jim Clarks frothing at the mouth. I listened to the Charlotte leader of the Democratic Party shout, "To hell with the head of the ticket! Just concentrate on sending our congressman back to Washington."

Harry Truman comes from a Confederate background. Yet that background did not prevent him from discharging his duties as a senator, a Vice-President, and a President. He was a President of both whites and Negroes, the only major politician to respond favorably to a telegram from the National Association for the Advancement of Colored People, which was soliciting his views on the FEPC.

Truman was one of the most amazing political personalities in history. He followed into office an aristocrat who wore a Navy cape, was a senior warden of the Hyde Park Episcopal Church and a descendant of Mayflower stock, and who had revolutionized the Presidency. The folks were appalled to see Truman suddenly standing in Roosevelt's shoes. The liberals were particularly distressed. Some of the Americans for Democratic Action even suggested it would be wiser to run Dwight D. Eisenhower for the Presidency on the Democratic ticket. After all, Harry Truman wore his polo shirt outside his pants.

But of course they were all wrong. Truman belongs with Jefferson. Both were professional politicians, who, in the tradition of the Anglo-American world, have always provided the best government. They were both suspect about the little things, although a close reading of history will embarrass one more about Jefferson than Truman. But in the big things, each was a giant. Jefferson had been President of the United States and had written the Declaration of Independence and had purchased the Louisiana Territory. But on his tombstone he wanted inscribed *Author of the Virginia Statute for Religious Freedom.*

Mr. Truman will be remembered in history as the author of the Marshall Plan and the Point Four program which rehabilitated Western civilization after the Nazis and the Fascists had almost totally destroyed it.

And the historian will one day record the milestones in the struggle of the Negro for equality as a citizen, and the historian will have to begin with the creation of the first Committee on Civil Rights by President Truman 'way back there in 1946.

Let Mr. Truman take his walks in the morning with the attending reporters, tapping out with his cane whatever he damn pleases, and may he go from strength to strength.

David Ben-Gurion and Isaiah

THERE IS a subtle difference between making history and creating situations for the sake of history. For many years, David Ben-Gurion was making history. He was, along with the late Chaim Weizmann, the founder of a Jewish homeland. Then in 1948 he became the creator of the modern Jewish State. And in 1956 in the Sinai campaign he preserved Israel. All this was history in the making: deeds which put Ben-Gurion in the front rank of the great statesmen of our time. It also put him into the Jewish pantheon shoulder-to-shoulder with Moses, King David, and King Solomon.

But since he retired—formally at least—Ben-Gurion has not been satisfied to be in the company of kings. With his terrific sense for things Biblical, he wants to join the ranks of Prophets, with Isaiah and Amos. And like all Prophets he is searching for "the truth." With the same single-minded devotion that inspired

him when the Jewish State was only a dream, Ben-Gurion has
walked through the streets of Jerusalem like Nathan of old demanding "the truth." But following the pattern of all the
Prophets, this quest for truth has led Ben-Gurion into troubled
waters. The stand he took on the so-called "Lavon Affair"
turned his people against him and they repudiated him. He was
left alone because the Israelis don't want "affairs." They do not
care so much for the intangible truth as they care for uncom-
plicated everyday lives like the rest of mankind.

But Ben-Gurion can take heart. The old Prophets of the
Bible were repudiated too. Ben-Gurion can take inspiration
from their tragic fate because, through their search for
truth, they achieved immortality.

Timing is as much an integral part of good statesmanship as
any of its other attributes. Ben-Gurion was once a master of the
art. He proclaimed the State of Israel in May, 1948, at the only
time the international constellation made it possible—in a century. He led his armies in the Sinai campaign at a time when the
Russians were busy with the Hungarian revolution and the
French and British were interested in crushing Nasser. He
basically accented the nationalistic policies which he had once
repudiated and he embraced the ideas of his enemies at a time
when those policies seemed to be in the Israeli interest.

One can only hope that Ben-Gurion will relax. He has earned
the fruits of great age and great achievements. His place in history is secure. And the Israelis yearn to love and admire him
again. They will forgive him very quickly; the big question is—
will he forgive them?

I am sure Isaiah would take it well.

John Quincy Adams

My DEEP interest in the sixth president of the United
States, John Quincy Adams, is based on the fact that he was an

acknowledged authority on the works of William Shakespeare. Many years ago I read several of his essays on the plays.

In his political career, Adams was more interesting. A staunch Federalist (loosely equivalent to the Republican Party), his policy was for the expansion of the power of the Federal Government.

The plantation society feared that President Adams's attempt to expand federal power would lead to the abolition of slavery. Defeated by Jackson in his bid for reelection in 1828, President Adams retired to his home in Massachusetts to write. But in 1831 he ran for Congress and served eight successive terms. He publicly opposed slavery and once suggested that slavery might be abolished by military authority.

While he served as Secretary of State in Monroe's Administration Mr. Adams acquired Florida from Spain and urged the President to formulate a policy against interference of the European powers in the Western Hemisphere. This became the Monroe Doctrine which established an unwritten alliance with England which has existed to this day. Mr. Adams saw that the Monroe Doctrine could be effective only if we "married ourselves to the British fleet."

The silent retirement

NOTHING IS sadder than the closing of an important daily. And almost as sad is the news that a paper is on strike.

Contrary to the propaganda, there is still no substitute for the printed word. The human story is not immediately consumed in that frightening maw of what they call "communications media," and which sounds like some sort of a Greek tragedy, anyway. In a newspaper it lingers a while, becomes a clipping, might even be pasted into a book. It's a human story —it's important. "It was in Tuesday's paper," the friend writes, and here it is Saturday and I am reading it with deep interest.

Were it not for the 1964 Detroit strike I would have received a few clippings from the Detroit *News* telling of the retirement of the old "Commentator," columnist W. K. Kelsey. Perhaps four or five people in Detroit who knew that Kelsey and I were friends would have mailed the item on to me in North Carolina.

It is sad enough for a newspaper strike to come during an interesting Presidential campaign, but it is equally sad for a man to retire after half a century on a newspaper and not have that clipping, "Kelsey Retires . . . First Joined *News* staff in 1907. . . ."

Kelsey now lives in Toledo, writes lots of letters, cultivates a garden, and his kids are still crazy about him.

David Dubinsky and his accent

WHEN THE objective historian writes of Jews in the United States, one of the central figures will be David Dubinsky, retired president of the International Ladies Garment Workers Union.

Mr. Dubinsky recently retired at the age of seventy-four. He is the last of the war-horses who guided labor from tenement and sweatshop to the suburb and duplex. Dubinsky did more than that. His particular field was the ready-to-wear garment industry, which even thirty years ago was an industrial jungle so you can imagine what it was like in 1910.

I remember as a boy whole tenements were filled with families working for contractors around the clock. It was not uncommon for a family of five—a mother, a father, two sisters, and a brother—to work collectively for a grand total of seventeen dollars a week.

Mr. Dubinsky took over the International Ladies Garment Workers Union at a time when it was bankrupt, and with several locals infiltrated with Communists. Within a decade, however, Dubinsky made the ILGWU one of the great unions in America. After his first two years he turned an organization with forty thousand members and $750,000 in debt into a union of two hundred thousand members with a $500,000 surplus. And in the process, he eliminated the Communists. He did this at a time when it meant putting one's own life on the line, when there were no senatorial investigations, no help from the press or from the "uptown" conservatives, many of whom called Dubinsky a "Red baiter." In fact, the Communists used to sing a ditty condemning Dubinsky, but Dubinsky beat them song and all:

> The Cloakmakers' union
>   is a no good union
> It's a company union for the bosses.
> The right-wing cloakmakers
>   and the socialist fakers
> Are making by the workers double crosses
>
> The Hillquits, Dubinskys, and Thomases
>   are making by the workers the promises
> They preach socialism,
>   but practice fascism
> To preserve capitalism
>   for the bosses.

Today the ILGWU has over four hundred thousand members with millions of dollars in its welfare fund. The union provides pensions, college scholarships, homes for the aged, and vacation grounds. These are institutions which confirm David Dubinsky's faith in America's mobility.

Some years ago, the late Ed Murrow asked me to find out why David Dubinsky ducked him all the time. Murrow wanted Dubinsky on his *Person-to-Person* show, then at the height of its popularity.

I asked Dubinsky about this in the quiet of his office. He brooded momentarily and made a confession which was quite a thing for this proud, self-confident man to make. He said, "Harry, I am worried about the heavy Yiddish accent with twenty million Americans watching and listening."

I told him his fear was a serious mistake, that his Yiddish accent would add to his charm, and would be wonderful evidence of America's greatness. It would prove that an immigrant Dubinsky could achieve so tremendous a success for himself and for a million of his fellow citizens. I told him the United States Government should show that film all over the world.

Of popes and presidents

POPE JOHN XXIII was an eighty-year-old cardinal elected to the Papacy so the College of Cardinals could choose a new pope at leisure. But this amazing man, John, opened all the windows. In the three years of his reign, he reversed the process of fifteen or sixteen centuries. When he died, Protestants and Jews also mourned.

Pope Paul VI has proceeded more cautiously and more conservatively. One should say honestly, more cagily. He left the windows open and he is opening all the doors as well. He is implementing the program John first proposed. Pope Paul is doing the heavy work. He labors under a handicap. The age will remain the Age of John XXIII. History may well record that John was one of the five great men of the twentieth century.

A similar parallel obtains here in America. The parallel is between John F. Kennedy's Administration and Lyndon B. Johnson's. If a disinterested observer drew up a balance sheet of accomplishment, Johnson would clearly lead.

Johnson did the heavy work. But the charisma still attaches to Kennedy as the charisma of the Christian world still attaches to Pope John.

President Kennedy presented a certain intelligent optimism to the American public. He had a toughness and a quality of mind lacking in Johnson. But he was not half the politician. Yet the age was initiated by Kennedy and so will probably remain.

Johnson is a Southerner who supports civil rights, a millionaire who initiated a war against poverty, an insular man who wants desperately to see the United Nations succeed.

Pope Paul VI has kissed the ring of the Greek Orthodox archbishop. When an Episcopalian bishop grabbed Paul's hands and kissed his ring, Paul returned the reverence. The Schema on religious liberty promulgated by Paul is one of the most visionary documents to have issued from Christian fellowships in the last ten centuries.

I do neither Lyndon B. Johnson nor Pope Paul dishonor when I say that Kennedy's finest accomplishment was Johnson and that John's finest accomplishment was Paul.

Senator Thruston B. Morton

THAT INTERESTING Republican, Senator Thruston B. Morton, of Kentucky, delivered an important speech recently— a speech not without its humor. Senator Morton said most of the conservative Republicans in his state agree with whatever attacks he mounts against the President's domestic proposals but these same Republicans always caution, "Don't make an issue of this until we get the contract for the atomic energy plant."

This ambivalence puzzles the senator.

Motives haven't changed much. My father told me that in the middle years of the nineteenth century, any European city would elect a mayor who could guarantee to keep the regiment posted in the town. Everybody campaigned on the platform of knowing someone on the General Staff. A regiment posted to a town meant prosperity and when a regiment was posted elsewhere, mayors immediately lost office. But before his constituency diselected the mayor, a committee of citizens, always dressed in frock coats and high hats, called upon the colonel and ascertained if indeed the new orders called for a transfer.

Bernard Berenson

BERNARD BERENSON, the twentieth century's greatest art connoisseur and one of the most cultivated men of our times, left the Jewish faith and became a Roman Catholic at the age of forty. A half century later, at the age of eighty-nine, Mr. Berenson wrote this in his diary:

How easy and warm the atmosphere between born Jews like Isaiah Berlin, Namier [Sir Lewis Namier, English historian], myself, and Bela Horowitz, when we drop the mask of being goyim and return to Yiddish reminiscences, and Yiddish stories and witticisms! After all, it has been an effort (no matter how unaware) to act as if one were a mere Englishman and reposing to return to "Mother's cooking." The great majority of us who can enjoy this return are of Russian origin, and to some small extent descendants of the first generation. I doubt whether Sephardim enjoy it or many of German extraction, and probably no Anglo-Saxons of third generation. For them their Jewishness counts as little as Catholicism to Catholics in matters political, indeed even less, and yet a Catholic can count as wholly, unquestionably English or American, while I doubt whether in either community a Jew ever ceases being a stranger.

Sol Hurok the immigrant

I WONDER whether the late Pat McCarran and the late Francis Walter, the two politicians who authored the anti-immigration bill of the 1950's, had ever heard of Sol Hurok? Hurok is an immigrant. He is also the greatest impresario in the world. Also, he belongs on any list of the ten most valuable Americans of the twentieth century.

These thoughts came to me at a banquet honoring Hurok's

accomplishments at the famous Players Club in New York in March of 1966. The contralto Marian Anderson and the pianist Artur Rubinstein were among the guests.

Rubinstein said he had enjoyed great popularity in Europe when he first came to America. But he could never quite make it here. The Steinway Piano ads on the programs always read, "The Steinway is the piano of Rachmaninoff, Paderewski, and Hoffman." Even after the critics acclaimed him the ads never said, ". . . and Rubinstein." It saddened him. So he returned to Europe but Hurok followed him. Hurok gave him lots of money and lots of encouragement and Rubinstein came back, this time to his full share of success, to this very day.

Marian Anderson told us her road was rockier. We all knew what this great Negro singer meant. But Hurok was the first to know the power and beauty of that voice and would not sacrifice it. He told all the concert managers where he booked his famous ballet, "Take her or no ballet." And they took her.

What Sol Hurok did for America was literally take it by the scruff of the neck and toss it into the concert hall—which made life wider, more beautiful, and more profound for millions.

I asked Hurok about some of his most interesting experiences.

The most memorable evening of his life, said Hurok, was one night in his hotel suite in Paris with some of his artists: "Nellie Melba and Chaliapin sang, Ysaye was on the violin and Massenet played the piano."

Once, he said, Chaliapin was at a party at the Fifth Avenue mansion of banker Otto H. Kahn. Chaliapin spoke no English, so Kahn told Hurok to ask Chaliapin to entertain the guests with a song. Hurok relayed the message in Russian. Chaliapin replied in Russian and Kahn asked Hurok what he had said. Hurok replied, "Chaliapin says only birds sing for nothing."

"Indecisive" Adlai Stevenson

IN BOTH his campaigns for the Presidency, Adlai Stevenson had to listen to critics calling him "indecisive." I remember several cartoons which portrayed him as Hamlet. "The man can't make up his mind," some said.

This criticism echoed again when President-elect John F. Kennedy offered Governor Stevenson the post of Ambassador to the United Nations.

Kennedy made the offer in Palm Beach. Almost every morning the President-elect appeared on the steps of the Kennedy resort home and announced to the press that he had a new Cabinet member to introduce. One morning Kennedy introduced Governor Luther Hodges as the new Secretary of Commerce; later Orville Freeman as Secretary of Agriculture; and a day or two after that, Dean Rusk as the Secretary of State. Governor Stevenson had visited him a day or two later and Mr. Kennedy told the newsman he had offered him the Ambassadorship to the United Nations. The President-elect then said that Governor Stevenson would make a final decision shortly.

The critics slapped their thighs in glee. They said, "We knew it all along. Everybody else accepts immediately but Adlai has to think about it."

Adlai Stevenson, however, had every reason for delaying his decision. He explained to the President-elect privately that he had a personal problem. He pointed out to Mr. Kennedy that as the senior partner of his law firm he secured most of the clients while the other partners did most of the work and it would be unfair to these men to have him abruptly cut off the relationship. These men, said Stevenson, had joined him at his request and in several instances had left behind them highly important associations.

A week later Stevenson had a call from President-elect Kennedy. Kennedy said he had the solution. Newton Minow, one of the partners, was particularly suited to become the chairman of the Federal Communications Commission; by training and intellect Willard Wirtz, another partner, would make an excellent Undersecretary of Labor; and William McCormick Blair, the third associate, would represent the United States handsomely in a diplomatic post.

Forthwith Stevenson said he would be proud to become the

United States Ambassador to the United Nations. He also said later that he regretted he had but one law firm to give up for his country.

To paraphrase Winston Churchill, "Some indecision! Some Hamlet!"

PART 8

America Is Not What's Wrong With the World

America is not what's wrong
with the world

I HAVE crossed this continent more than twenty times, east and west, north and south, and I never cease to wonder about the Idea itself, the Idea of America. The Idea is mobility.

We are, to use an old figure of speech, a nation on wheels. We are not only constantly visiting distant places, but, as we move from one neighborhood to another, we are also moving from one income to another, one position in life to another.

The dissenters who fled from England first generated this idea of American mobility—the movement toward religious and political freedom, and then the movement toward what the Greeks called the good life. The pioneers of the Conestoga wagons enlarged upon it. And many of us, barely speaking English, contributed our mite, too.

An uncle of ours came to America in 1898. For the first five years he peddled suspenders which he hung about his shoulders. On rainy days, he stationed himself on a busy street intersection and sold umbrellas.

By 1905 he had saved enough money to gamble on opening a little shop in which he sold piece goods. He prospered. He never, of course, became what is called a merchant prince, but he was able to see both his sons through college. In 1919 the fellow was able to move his family from the ghetto to an apartment on Riverside Drive on the West Side of New York City, overlooking the mighty Hudson River and the majestic New Jersey Palisades.

Within a single generation, the immigrant had moved from a village in eastern Europe, where life differed very little from the way life was lived in the fifteenth century, into the middle of the American twentieth century. He who had arrived in the ship's steerage now said good morning to a neighbor whose ancestors had arrived in America on the *Mayflower* three centuries before.

R.F.K. aftermath

SENATOR ROBERT F. KENNEDY needs me to defend him like he needs another ten shares of AT&T. The critical pieces from James Baldwin, Norman Mailer, Gore Vidal, and many others including Pat Anderson who worked with Bobby keep piling up. Yet Bobby survives. His survival gets easier and easier because all these literary fellows make one monotonous charge —that Bobby is a guerrilla fighter, that he is ruthless.

There are fellows who worked with Robert Kennedy and who haven't written articles and the majority of them say exactly as I do, "I love him like a brother."

In each of my speeches in his behalf during the Keating campaign, there was always one question raised about how ruthless Bobby Kennedy was. After several experiments I found the answer to this gambit: "His wife and eight children don't think he's ruthless."

Bobby Kennedy and I had been in almost constant communication for three years about the civil rights struggle. I had no idea of participating in a campaign in New York. The "carpetbag" issue was hot enough without a Tar Heel intruding. But Bobby was terribly worried about the "Jewish vote" in New York. He told me, "The vast majority are Democrats; if the Democrats vote for me, I'm in—but I do not believe I can overcome wholesale defections."

Senator Keating had refused to endorse Barry Goldwater, his party's Presidential candidate, and made no attack on the National Administration, which was politic, considering those dozen or more "Johnson and Keating" Committees in the Jewish districts.

Abe Fineberg, the philanthropist, Max Schuster, the publisher, and David Dubinsky, the labor leader, said the Democrats needed all the help they could get. So I volunteered, on one condition: there must be no remuneration and I was to pay my own expenses.

As one who has worked in the civil rights movement for over twenty years, I was fascinated by the work of Attorney General Robert Kennedy. What made the new Attorney General so effective was that until he assumed his Cabinet post, he had no idea of the dimensions the social revolution of the American Negro had assumed. As Attorney General, Robert Kennedy encountered wrongs he could hardly believe existed in our time. Whenever he had to talk with Governors Ross Barnett and George Wallace, or Southern peace officers or sheriffs, Bobby kept asking, "But don't you know this is wrong?"

These old professional Confederates hadn't the faintest idea what he was talking about.

But it was this ruthless naïveté that produced amazing results.

That foxy old senator James Eastland of Mississippi knew something was in the wind when he asked Burke Marshall, up for confirmation as head of the Civil Rights Division, "Will you solicit complaints?" Southerners had learned to fight each of the civil rights proposals with all their might. Though often they faltered when the pressures of human decency and justice came to bear, they knew they held a trump card. Despite the decisions of the Vinson Court in the Sweatt and McLaurin cases; the Warren Court in Brown v. Board of Education, Topeka; despite the Civil Rights Acts of 1957 and 1960, the segregationists still held the Negro at bay. Their strategy was simple: "It is the law of the case," they said, "not the law of the land.

"They'll have to sue us county by county, school by school, voting-registrar by voting-registrar; they'll have to sue us for each and every Negro."

The Eisenhower Administration, which put civil rights in the lawbooks, initiated but ten cases in two and a half years, two on the Administration's last day, January 19, 1961; six were against registrars, four against individuals. None were brought in Mississippi or Alabama. During a parallel two and a half years the

Kennedy Administration initiated over sixty cases; fifty-four of them in the Deep South. They *did* fight Negro by Negro, registrar by registrar, school by school. For the first time in seventy years, thousands of Negroes were signing their names to formal complaints and affidavits. President John F. Kennedy had given his brother the order: *"Get the road maps and go."* They went.

True, Jim Crow dies hard but Bobby Kennedy, Burke Marshall, Nicholas Katzenbach, John Doar, and their corps of lawyers and investigators gave it the blow from which it could never recover. They unscrambled the eggs. They did it in less than four years.

I had every reason for supporting Robert Kennedy for Senator. I sent a personal letter to my six thousand subscribers in New York State. Soon my bookkeeper sent me clusters of little red cards: "These people refuse to renew because of your support of Robert Kennedy." I received a hundred more angry letters from civic leaders and rabbis, some of them my devoted personal friends. "How ungrateful can you be working against this wonderful man, Kenneth Keating, our best friend in Washington, the most effective friend of Israel?" they said.

I discussed all of this with Bobby at breakfast one morning at the Hotel Carlyle. This young Irishman sounded like a rabbinical student who had just spent a year listening to Horace Kallen and Maurice Samuel.

"I can understand it," Kennedy said. "There's still a deep scar for what the Church did to the Jews—it goes back to the Middle Ages. My brother was up against the same thing, but Jack's advantage in New York was that his opponent was Nixon and the Jews could not take Nixon. My opponent, on the other hand, is a man greatly admired and, from what I have seen, greatly beloved by the Jewish people. Furthermore, the Jews, since the days of the Cossacks, look with suspicion on the investigator and that's all I've ever really been so far, an investigator and a cop."

On another occasion I asked him why his candidacy aroused such opposition from intellectuals like Baldwin, Vidal, Mailer,

I. F. Stone, and other people who have been in the forefront of
the civil rights movement. Bobby replied: "There's only one
explanation I can give—many intellectuals resented Jack right
up to the time he was taken from us. They have transferred that
resentment to a more acceptable target—me. Maybe I'm wrong
but that's all I can make of it . . . fellows like Alexander
Bickel, knowledgeable men, have pointed to the Jimmy Hoffa
thing and I suspect that's where the 'ruthless' comes in. What
they conveniently forget is that the Morals Board of the AFL-
CIO drummed Hoffa out of organized labor on less than half
of what our Senate Committee and later the Department of
Justice uncovered."

When I asked him a question about his father, Bobby said,
"I think the cynics have deliberately withheld the fact that my
father tipped the balance in favor of Lend Lease before the Senate Foreign Relations Committee. The America Firsters there-
after called him worse names than any the liberals have ever had
for him." I never brought up Joseph Kennedy again. Bobby has
that old-fashioned devotion young sons used to have for their
fathers.

Once the campaign really got under way, I made several trips
to New York to tape radio broadcasts (three in Yiddish and six
of them in English, of all things) and to appear on a television
program, all sponsored by Bobby. On October 21, I canceled
several lectures to go to New York to speak to Jewish audiences.
The Liberal Party and David Dubinsky provided a limousine
and Walter Kirschenbaum, on his off hours as an official in the
License Bureau, volunteered as chauffeur.

Kennedy's plurality was amazing. Bobby ran less than 15 percent behind President Johnson in those districts which had
given us so much concern. President Johnson was campaigning
the heavily populated Jewish districts Kennedy was campaigning against Keating, a man with great decency and high prestige.

If the election had been held on October 15, Senator Keating
would have swept these New York City districts.

But the senator made a mistake during the last two weeks of the campaign. Bobby Kennedy and his supporters were quick to take advantage of it. By October 24, it was clear that Keating had overplayed the Israel issue. The Jews had become embarrassed by this pleading to their special interest. I communicated this to Bobby. Paul Screvane, president of the New York City Council and a Kennedy adviser, had also sensed it. He said, "Let's keep our fingers crossed." On October 29 at P.S. 95 in the Bronx, before a large audience of working people, I tried it out. I did not mention the words "Jew," "Israel," or "Nasser," but spoke only of Kennedy's hope to help liberalize the immigration laws and support a strong Federal Aid to Education Bill. The response was gratifying. We were on our way.

Senator Keating went right on and some of his supporters now compounded the blunder. The Citizens for Keating Headquarters at 521 Fifth Avenue distributed a poster, NASSER FOR KENNEDY which they quickly withdrew for another version, NASSER AGAINST KEATING. Mr. Herbert Brownell, Keating's manager, told a reporter, "It's factual." Knowing of the growing embarrassment of the Jewish voters, we literally jumped for joy. It had its effect also on the non-Jewish voters: "Why is he always talking about Nasser?" asked the Irish, the Italians, the Puerto Ricans, and the plain ordinary Protestants.

At an outdoor rally sponsored by the members of the International Ladies Garment Workers Union everybody spoke for Bobby Kennedy, including Dubinsky, Bob Wagner, and Hubert Humphrey, who held up the "Nasser for Kennedy" circular and shouted, "If you see any of these circulars, here's what to do with them," and Senator Humphrey tore it up in a million pieces and threw it into the air. The next day the *Jewish-Day-Morning Journal* and the *Jewish Daily Forward* came out for Bobby Kennedy.

There was still a hurdle—the Keating challenges to Bobby for a debate. Luckily Bobby Kennedy's liaison in these negotiations was this same fascinating Italian, Paul Screvane. The idea was not to debate on television but to lose as little ground as possible in the denial. Bobby Kennedy and Paul Screvane pulled it off. This was wise, as the California campaign between Salinger and Murphy proved. A highly aware Pierre Salinger debated on TV with an opponent who had spent forty years of his life before the cameras.

Bobby Kennedy said, "Why enter a fight where the most you can do is break even? Mr. Keating looks like everybody's grandfather, he's a beautiful man. On TV he will read what *The New York Times* and the *Reporter* said about him and then this ruthless young Irishman will talk about the amendments Mr. Keating voted on, and where will this get me? Let's get him on radio." Keating challenged these tactics. But the main test was yet to come. He bought one hour of prime television time on NBC, and dared Kennedy to appear.

It was a serious moment in the campaign and Bobby called for a full discussion. He was in Great Neck, resting after a strenuous day. There were ten of us at headquarters, each with a telephone receiver. Kennedy talked to each of us three times— asking an opinion on whether to go. Soon Ed Guthman, the press officer, shouted, "It's now the Hawks and Doves. Let's see how it turns out." The leading Hawks turned out to be Arthur Schlesinger and I who argued, "This is it, Bobby, you must go this time." The Doves were led by Paul Screvane, who kept repeating two words—"absolutely no." When it came around to me the second time, I repeated, "This is one time you must go, Bobby."

Kennedy said, "Harry, you've got white hair, you debate Keating." When it got around for the third time to Schlesinger, who repeated the argument, Bobby said, "Art, that's why I'm the candidate and not you."

Screvane and Bobby prevailed. The former Attorney General finally said, "No—let's get the helicopter and go make a speech some place—on Long Island, maybe. What I lose because I don't go is nothing compared with what I will lose if I go. Let's keep trying to get the fellow on the radio."

Luck was on our side. Four days before the election, Barry Gray, who conducts a popular radio program in New York, invited Bobby for a midnight interview. Amazingly, Senator Keating took the bait, demanding equal time. We came well prepared. Seated around Bobby were five assistants with ideas, clippings, and speeches. Senator Keating read what *The New York Times*, the *Reporter*, and the *Nation* said about him and Bobby asked, "Do you think it's something *special* for a New York senator to be for civil rights and for all those other liberal measures? I'd like to enumerate now your votes when you were a conservative congressman representing a conservative constituency."

It was a devastating argument, embarrassingly so, for most of us including Bobby were genuinely sorry that our opponent Keating was really such a nice guy.

When I hear the charge of "ruthless" made against Bobby, I always think back to our first meeting. The senator was then counsel to the McClellan Committee and we were both on the Jack Paar program. As we left the studio he asked me to have supper with him.

"Where would you like to go?" I asked.

He whispered, "I'd like to go to Lindy's Restaurant." He had the look in his eye that used to delight Nathan Detroit when he met a sucker from out of town.

We went to Lindy's and I excused myself. I made a telephone call to Ralph G., a retired hotel clerk. On several previous occasions he had performed the chore when I had some of my Southern friends up to New York.

We ordered. Bobby had a steak and two glasses of milk, and soon along came Ralph who gave me a big nonchalant hello, and whom I introduced to Bobby as the brother of the late Nicely-Nicely.

The eyes of the soon-to-be Attorney General of the United States almost popped in delight as Ralph gave us the best Damon Runyon talk I've heard since I myself was a hotel clerk on Broadway in the early 1930's.

My birthday parties

I'VE HAD two birthday parties. One on May 6, 1961, and the other on May 8, 1965.

In the spring of 1961 I went on a speaking tour for the United States Eighth Army in Korea and Japan. They assigned an officer to me to facilitate arrangements at each post. After a month together the escort major and I became friends and I happened to mention to him about my birthday. We were back at headquarters in Seoul May 6 and we went on to dinner as usual. The dining room was decorated, the orchestra played "Happy Birthday," and there was a long table of officers who rose and applauded when I entered.

At the head of the table was General Magruder, Commander in Chief of the United Nations Forces, Far East. There was a birthday cake and General Magruder said that Special Services had reported to him that at each of the Army posts I had attracted a bigger crowd than Jayne Mansfield, who had been there a month before.

The Orthodox Jews did not go in for birthday parties. We avoided the mention of years, dates, months—in effect, numbers, because there is a kind of finality about a number, a milestone which the Evil Eye would pounce upon as a cue for mischief.

The census takers had a difficult time with the Orthodox Jewish mothers at the turn of the century. "How old is your son Harry?"

Do you think your mother would tell him? Not on your life! However, she knew that something had to be done, and so she said, "My son Harry was born a year before Aunt Miriam came to America." The census takers were wise to all of this and arrived at the required information after a bit of research.

And so I came well prepared at the big birthday party on May 8. May 6 (1903) is really my birthday but I was speaking at Fisk University that day, so the party was postponed to May 8. The leading citizens of Charlotte were there; the editors, city officials, the clergy representing all the religions and denominations, including both rabbis of Charlotte.

Former Governor Terry Sanford made the speech. Hal Tribble, editor of the Asheville *Citizen-Times*, was the toastmaster and I closed the proceedings saying, "What greater glory can come to a man than the knowledge that his work has been useful and that he has earned the esteem of his neighbors?"

Many heartwarming telegrams and letters came from friends including President Lyndon Johnson, Vice-President Hubert Humphrey, Carl Sandburg, Senator Phil Hart, three members of the Kennedy family, Ambassador Adlai Stevenson, Dr. Martin Luther King, Dr. Frank P. Graham, Ralph McGill, Roy Wilkins, Bill Baggs, Julian Scheer, and I'm sorry about those whose names I have omitted but who are just as dear to me.

But I wish to assure my readers that I came well prepared against the Evil Eye. At home I left all the glasses upside down; I wore a red necktie, and after each encomium at the festivities I repeated under my breath the necessary Yiddish words my mother had taught me to cancel out the words of praise.

The elusive seasons

ONE OF the continuing events that fill an editor's life is the recurrent change of seasons. An editorial writer in New York can discuss the chirping of the birds in Central Park and presto, he's completed a day's work. A newspaperman in San Diego can point out the marlin are running again off the coast and this is the harbinger of spring.

But the syndicated columnist has to live in a vacuum. When he writes about the birds chirping in one area of the country, he little wots but that in another the real blizzards are on their way and the cows have to be brought into the very house itself.

When the dogwood blooms in Charlotte, North Carolina,

Hartford, Connecticut, is still paying overtime to the snow plowers.

What I am getting at is that the change in seasons in no way helps the columnist who has thirty or fifty or one hundred outlets. He has to stick to his Bible lessons or his letters from anguished teen-agers or his jokes with nary a break for celebrating nature.

Personally, I am an indoors man. I believe fresh air does more damage to a man's stomach than all the cigarettes he's ever smoked. If someone wants to call me Mr. Central Heating, I shall accept the title with gratitude and sincerity.

When I go out on lecture trips I am invariably met by decent, well-meaning people who can only be called town boosters. They want to show me the azaleas or the snow fences or the waterfalls, to which efforts I reply I am a student of ideas. By ideas, of course, I refer to a comfortable hotel room with ice, bourbon, water, and a chicken salad sandwich to reinforce me for my forthcoming appearance.

The Cursillos in Christianity

I SHARED the platform at the Cursillos in Christianity with the Rev. Dennis J. Gaeney whose parish is at Fort Wayne, Indiana, and was privileged to listen to a most remarkable speech.

I cannot help using the word "remarkable" about a Roman Catholic priest who delivers an address to assembled clergy and laymen with the same ideas Martin Luther King would use at a Southern Christian Leadership Conference, and Walter Reuther would express at a meeting of the United Automobile Workers.

We're not quite used to it, those of us who held fast to the stereotype of a monolithic society, aloof, rigid, and, you'll pardon me if I say, reactionary.

And I might add that the Catholics themselves expressed

some surprise. Many of them are not yet used to the idea of their priests not only exchanging views with Protestant clergymen and rabbis, but seeking support for Medicare.

All of this is a reversal of the "closed door" notion of Catholicism with which the Irish contemporaries of mine grew up. Before the reign of Pope John it was indeed different.

This remarkable Father Gaeney said as much to the assembled clergy and laymen. The time when a Catholic fulfilled his duties by making the Stations of the Cross and handling his rosary is gone.

Faith requires more today. Father Gaeney said it involves a total commitment to the problems of the life around us.

And this too was remarkable. I finished my speech and Father Robert Keller called upon the assemblage for a song. I had to lower my head as I saw nuns, priests, and laymen holding hands and swaying as they sang:

> "He's got Harry Golden in His hands,
> He's got Harry Golden in His hands,
> He's got the whole world in His hands."

It didn't last a thousand years

I WROTE an article for *Pardon*, of Frankfurt, a national humor magazine in Germany. They sent me all sorts of documents to fill out to prove that I pay taxes in the United States, otherwise their law requires they deduct twenty-five percent of my check for German taxes.

I decided not to fill out any of the documents because it would help my morale to know that I was contributing twenty-five percent of my money to the Fourth Reich!

Which reminds me of the time I was in Germany for *Life* magazine. I stayed at the Hilton Hotel in Berlin and every morning *Life* sent a big limousine for me, and the doorman, about six and a half feet tall, in full uniform, escorted me to the car.

As he opened the door for me I said, "It didn't last a thousand years, did it?" I said the same thing every morning for four weeks. Imagine that! And every morning the tall, uniformed doorman opened the door, saluted, and said "*Jawohl.*" Every morning the same thing! The ceremony never bored me.

The Arab contribution to Israel

WHEN Israel proclaimed its independence from the steps of the Tel Aviv Museum, an appropriate place for a history-conscious people, only extreme optimists gave it a chance. Those who held out little hope neglected to take into account what the Arabs did for Israel.

As soon as the Israelis proclaimed their independence seven Arab states declared war and simultaneously attacked. The Jewish population of six hundred and fifty thousand not only fought back and repulsed the Arab attacks but defeated these armies.

Future historians will point to the war of the Arabs and the Israelis as one of the great moments in human history not only for the remaining few of the Nazi death camps but for the whole world.

The Arabs, who tried to crush Israel, instead helped her. First of all, the Arab chieftains ordered all their subjects to leave Palestine immediately so as not to interfere with Arab military operations. The chieftains promised the Arabs would go back to Palestine as soon as they had chased the Israelis into the Mediterranean Sea. Thus the Arab refugee problem was created when the Israelis refused to be pushed.

Initially, the Israelis were faced with the problem of integrating more than a million immigrants from seventy different countries, all with different backgrounds and different cultures, into one nation. The idea of their Jewishness was all that kept them together. It would have been impossible to weld a nation out of such diverse peoples in a short time unless a war had made it imperative. The sense of urgency and alarm occasioned by the war facilitated this process. Israelis were successful because they were threatened by annihilation.

Lastly the huge advance of the Israeli economy was due to Arab pressures. When Israel became independent, its agriculture was primitive. In the absence of war, the Israelis would undoubtedly have depended upon the produce of the Arab farmers, who could have provided the Israeli population six times over. Suddenly there were no farmers and the borders were sealed as well. The Israelis were forced to develop a highly efficient agriculture to feed their armies and their population. They were so successful that in visiting the new states of Africa before you see your first lion or giraffe you will meet two Israelis advising the new government how to irrigate land and what crops to grow.

Israelis say their history is under the command of General Ein Brirra, which in Hebrew translates as General No Alternative.

Farewell to royalty

WE CAN presume now that the French Revolution is an unqualified success. I say this because Parliament got mad at the expenses incurred by Princess Margaret and Lord Snowden on their trip through the fleshpots of America.

But the handwriting was on the wall. England was the last refuge for royalty up until 1936 when Parliament decided Edward had better not marry a commoner and an American commoner at that, and an American commoner who had been divorced, Mrs. Wallis Warfield Simpson.

Being a lifelong monarchist, I personally believed the visit was a success, and I am sorry to see these negative opinions.

The Princess and her husband were here for only so many

days which meant only so many parties which meant only so many guests could be invited.

I was myself in Hollywood at the time the Princess and her photographer husband toured the fabled American dreamland and a major American movie studio tendered them a reception. A good friend of mine was at this same studio churning out a movie script, and had the studio heads invited him he would have been delighted. Instead they sent him a memo which read: "As you know, Princess Margaret will be with us tomorrow." He told me his heart leaped at this news. The next sentence went on in no uncertain terms: "Would you mind surrendering your parking space?" His heart leaped down. Had there been a Bastille, he would have stormed it. He did storm his producer's parking space the next morning at 6 A.M. and it did his revolutionary heart good to see one brown Rolls Royce circle endlessly in search of a vacant space from which to unload its already loaded passengers.

On New York

ALL TOLD, I have published ten books and I have read every review about every one of them. The words I cherish most were written by an editor on *The New York Times* who said I was one of the few New Yorkers who had left the city but who never ceased to sing its praises.

I think of myself as a man who loves New York and am pleased that I have made others think of me that way, too. I think as fondly of New York as other men think of their first love or best mistress—which is to say, I think of it constantly. Unlike the other men, however, I can repair to New York and re-invigorate the springs of memory and pleasure.

Men are, for the most part, what their hometowns make them. I was made by New York.

New York starts where Tokyo, London, Paris, and Rome leave off, and I have been to all of them—several times. New

York is the center of the New World and its destiny has always been to exceed the old. This has been true even from its earliest beginnings. Looking over the Hudson River once Alexander Hamilton prophesied that a great city would grow on its shore. Hamilton, if my memory serves, was looking at the Jersey side but I think that makes little difference. He knew it was going to be big. You can find a small town ten minutes over the George Washington Bridge on the Jersey side. But it is at the mouth of the Hudson that the one truly big town of the world lies.

New York is not only eight million people working and living every day, it is also twenty-eight million young people all over America yearning to come to the big town one day. Many of them will make it, too. That is what makes New York more than so much steel and concrete. It is built and nourished by the hopes of young people everywhere.

Now it is true not everyone wants to live in New York, just as it is true not everyone can live in it. I think the only time the hometown New Yorkers are uncharitable is when they tease the fellow on a convention who says, "New York is a wonderful place to visit but I wouldn't want to live there."

I have always believed it wrong to abuse this fellow. After all, why should he want to live in New York? His home, his livelihood, and his family are in Greenwood, South Carolina, or Terre Haute, Indiana, or Union Point, Georgia. New York is the place he has chosen to visit, in itself a great compliment, and he has even wondered about whether he could adjust to life in the town. New Yorkers should treat him with respect and affection. For at least a single moment he has weighed his roots, his wife and children, his job and his memories with what New York City offers.

The "retired" are working

THE TWO sons have been helping to run the business, a highly successful business. The father is now sixty-five or sixty-six, or sixty-seven, and the two sons and their wives keep telling him, "Papa, why don't you take it easy? There's plenty of money. Why don't you and Mama go to Miami and get a house?" Or they say, "Why not go to California? No rain, no winter, no snow. You've got a lot of friends there. Uncle Fred has been out there for four years and he loves it."

Papa and Mama finally give in, the lawyers draw up the papers, and off they go to Miami (or Los Angeles). They buy a house or a cooperative; plush, luxurious, and Papa begins to act the retired gentleman.

The first few months are not too bad. They listen to the auctioneers, visit the merchants, and take in all the "entertainment" they can handle—up to 10:30 P.M. But pretty soon Papa begins to visit the manufacturers, the fellows he had dealt with when he was in action, and first thing you know the retired man is beginning to give advice to others—how to do things better.

In the middle of the second year, Papa gives up retirement.

I haven't counted them, of course, but there are at least one hundred new businesses in Miami alone started by fellows in "retirement," fellows who just couldn't quite make it. Invariably the retired man goes into the same business that he had in the North. "I'll show my sons that at sixty-eight I'm still a better man than they are," is the attitude.

It is an important story and deserves closer study and survey.

Easier to make than to give away

I ONCE spent a whole day visiting with the late Billy Rose. A fabulous little man. He did it all within about thirty years. From the ghetto of New York where his parents paid eleven dollars a month rent, Billy now lived in one of the great mansions on Fifth Avenue. He had a private stock-ticker in one of the rooms in charge of an elderly auditor wearing a leather apron like in the countinghouses of the Middle Ages.

Billy Rose left some thirty million dollars, every penny of it made honestly in accordance with all the rules. His talent was in the ability to take immediate advantage of every money-making opportunity that presented itself. His genius was to guess right every time.

But alas something went wrong with Billy's genius in the division of his estate. His will is being contested and Billy himself remains unburied till a court decides the issues.

Was it Rockefeller, or Harriman, or Carnegie, who said, "Much easier to make it than to give it away?"

Dreams, bankers, and cookbooks

ONE OF the modern fairy tales is the big deal. It is one of the most romantic of fairy tales. And men recite it over and over. It sustains them.

I remember the times I hadn't two nickels to rub together and after expatiating on a couple of big deals, I would walk home estimating that no later than August I would have to hire a Brink's truck to tote my money each week.

In the middle of the Depression I remember a big deal that enraptured a whole table of fellows playing three-handed pinochle. The game took place in the Hotel Markwell where I was the night clerk and in the course of the game we began talking about the bank on the corner which had just failed.

"The trouble with the bank," I said, "was it owned too much vacant property."

"Well, you know," said one of the players, "it might not be a bad idea to put in a bid for those assets now."

"How're we going to develop them?"

"We don't develop them. We turn them all into parking lots. One of the things New York's gotta have in the future is parking lots."

"Say, that's good thinking. Figure twenty parking lots holding a hundred cars apiece at a buck a day, not a bad take at all."

We put down our cards and I did the arithmetic and so help

me it wasn't a bad take at that. To buy the bank, of course, meant some settlement with the depositors but we might get away with a dime on the dollar. We didn't think we'd need more than a quarter of a million for that and say roughly another quarter of a million for the assets themselves. The bank owned stock, sure enough, and we might even be able to cash it in. We filled dozens of napkins with figures before we went back to the game, each of us now an officer in the First New York Corporation. I forgot to mention: the stakes in the game were cigarettes.

Not too long ago, I had a fruitful discussion with an editor in one of the more reputable of Madison Avenue's restaurants. About the time we started on the third bourbon, he said to me, "You know what would be a good idea? The Harry Golden Jewish Cookbook."

"It's an original title," I answered. "I never heard of a book like that."

"You know the Fanny Farmer Cook Book has sold two million, four hundred thousand copies and that's just about Gentile food," my host volunteered.

"Sure," I said, ordering another bourbon, "it would be a lovely gift. You could sell a deluxe edition at ten dollars."

"A good meal is always in style and so is a good cookbook."

"We'd have to hurry to get it out before the Jewish holidays," I said.

"Those are just the mechanics," he said. "Don't worry about them. Just worry about the recipes."

"What recipes?" I asked.

"The recipes we're going to put in the cookbook."

"And where am I going to get the recipes?"

"Don't you cook at home? Every time you cook something, write it down."

"I don't cook at home," I said. "I eat out. I eat at Johnny's Oriental Restaurant or at the Epicurean, or buy the delicatessen from Leo up the street."

He ordered another drink. "Another idea shot," he sighed.

"If it wasn't for those restaurants that took my credit cards," I said, "we would have been on easy street."

The near-conquest of Kannapolis

THE NAÏVE FELLOW of the Kannapolis Junior Chamber of Commerce who invited me to deliver the speech at an annual banquet deserves a twenty-one-gun salute. I may be doing him an injustice in calling him naïve. He may very well be a man of great courage.

Kannapolis, North Carolina, is the last American barony, a city of nearly thirty thousand owned and run by the last American marquis, Charles A. Cannon, who makes most of our sheets, pillowcases, towels, and blankets. Kannapolis is the largest unincorporated city in the world. And I've written much about this benevolent monarchy less than twenty miles north of Charlotte.

When the invitation came, I could hardly believe my eyes. It would be like Charlie Cannon visiting the offices of the Textile Union and asking for a contract!

Several letters went back and forth and everything was fine for January 28 and then it came—a letter telling me the Jaycees appreciated my acceptance but had to cancel the arrangements. And, said this hearty soul, please, please, please, acknowledge this letter (that you ain't gonna come).

My brother Max and baseball

HAS ANY baseball team ever commanded the loyalty the New York Giants commanded?

No.

Has any ball team ever rewarded that loyalty as the Giants did in 1951 when they came from thirteen games behind in August to win the pennant in a play-off with the Dodgers? Is there anything in sports ever to equal Bobby Thomson's home run in the last of the ninth?

No.

The Brooklyn Dodgers had the support of the world. They were the Bums, the perennial underdog, the daffiness boys. The fans came to see a Brooklyn Dodger steal second with a team-mate holding the base. And they loved the Brooklyns for it.

The Yankees in the days when Babe Ruth batted third in-troduced thousands of people to the game. They came to see the Babe hit a home run. The folks came from the farms and bayous to see Babe Ruth. Then for years, the Yankees supported half the teams in the American League. The folks began to hate the perennial winner and they came out by the thousands to see the Yankees lose. Which they didn't.

The New York Mets are remarkable for a collection of guys, few of whom are young enough or talented enough to play base-ball. People watch them anyway. Maybe the fans like the pizzas they serve at Shea Stadium.

But no team ever owned the quiet affection and loyalty which the New York Giants had in the days of McGraw, Doyle, Mathewson, Marquard, Red Murray, and Chief Meyers. And later with Frankie Frisch, Art Neff, Mel Ott, and Leo Durocher.

Even the Giants transplanted to San Francisco still have their share of fans in New York. My brother Max, lo and behold, all these years with the Metropolitan Life Insurance Company, hangs on their every statistic. Last summer Max came to my room in the Algonquin Hotel to meet my son, Richard, who was buying an expensive insurance policy. Max was in the proc-ess of writing the policy when Richard, to make casual conver-sation, said, "It looks like the Dodgers are in this year."

"Wait a minute," said Max, putting aside his pen and, I thought, maybe his commission. "I give you Koufax. That's all I give you. Koufax. Don't tell me Marichal isn't as good as Drysdale. Don't tell me that. Now, who you got on first? You got McCovey? No, you haven't got McCovey. Have you got Willie Mays in center field? No, you haven't got Willie Mays in center field. I don't even give you shortstop. Have you got a Cepeda? No, you haven't got a Cepeda."

Later I heard them talking and Max, still insistent, was ex-plaining, "No, no. It was the bottom of the ninth. The score was four to one. Then we scored a run and knocked Newcombe out of the box . . ."

"Why are you rooting for the Giants," I asked, "when they play baseball out in San Francisco?"

"When Mays is gone," he said, "when Marichal is gone, then I'll maybe root for the Mets."

"Are you going to sell me this policy, Uncle Max," Richard asked, "or do you want to tell me who you have on the bench? Because I don't care who you have on the bench. You haven't got a Koufax, a Drysdale or an Osteen in rotation and you don't have a Perranoski in the bullpen."

Happy birthday, Hartford *Courant*

THE *Courant* is the morning paper in Hartford, Connecticut. It is now over two hundred years old. It is the American newspaper with the longest history of continuous publishing.

Right after my book *Only in America* was published I was invited to Hartford to deliver two lectures. In the course of this visit I met a young reporter from the *Courant* who drove me around town to see the sights.

Mark Twain's house still stands in Hartford and as we passed it this young fellow told me the years Twain had lived in the house and what he had written there. He also told me that every noon Twain would dress himself up and go downtown and have luncheon at the Heublein Hotel. Twain presided over what was an early round table.

One of the daily guests at this table, said my informant, was Charles Dudley Warner, I believe, who was the associate editor of the *Courant*. In the process of making conversation, my young reporter said that it was really Charles Dudley Warner who remarked that *everybody talks about the weather but no one does anything about it.* Twain quoted this remark and it has been forever attributed to him.

It was all interesting enough and I went about the business

of making my speech. But not long after that, I had occasion to write a column about Mark Twain. In the course of this column I remembered the story and somehow it seemed appropriate so I included it.

At the time, my syndicated column appeared in the Sunday *Courant*. The editors there sent me a marvelous letter in which they said, "Congratulations, Harry Golden. We are so glad we subscribe to your column. Not only is it an excellent column but you have at last revealed the truth about Charles Dudley Warner and Mark Twain, a thesis which we here hold in high regard. Would you please tell us where you unearthed this fact for we would like to put it on the front page? What are your sources?"

It was a chore to write them a letter explaining that my sources happened to be the Hartford *Courant* itself. I forbade mentioning the name of the enthusiastic reporter who simply repeated what he heard his editor insist.

The *Courant* and I have blundered on, each our separate ways. I suspect they will last another two hundred years because they do not report their own gossip.

Lady editors are after me

THERE'S only one thing worse than a couple of widows with literary aspirations after you and that's to have the lady editors come crashing down. Like cats they come down with four feet.

A charming lady of *McCall's* got hold of me first. She wanted to know my opinions about dieting. Would I write a short piece for her? But when people ask me about dieting I immediately put them down as either facetious or jealous.

I assured you, however, I am not a smart-aleck. In all sincerity I believe that whatever they say about overweight is unfortunately true.

No one can exaggerate the danger. A year or so ago we had a

forty-eighth reunion of the graduating class of 8-B—P.S.20 on the Lower East Side. There were twenty-six of us out of the class of thirty-eight who had graduated in 1917. Sad to relate all the fat fellows were gone. I was the only hefty one still around.

I console myself with what I believe is a scientific fact, that long life is contingent upon having been lucky enough to have picked long-lived parents and grandparents, keeping the weight down, and unclutching your fingers on a life without tension and laughing at pressures. I'm afraid I'll have to take my chances on two of those three.

I may be wrong but I think it was Ring Lardner who said, "The years skip along easily, it is the days that are tough."

Yet if a man my age can avoid getting in trouble with a woman and/or the Internal Revenue Department, he has a good chance of doing the rest of his time in reasonable comfort, barring, of course, cancer, arthritis, or a prostate operation.

1312 Elizabeth Avenue

My home and office at 1312 Elizabeth Avenue has served as a sort of terminal-underground railroad for the freedom riders. Those freedom riders who sped to Albany, Georgia, stopped here at all hours of the night and stopped here again on their return.

One day I had the Methodist ministers, the next the rabbis, and on another the young fellows. They come in pairs and individually. I gave the young boys a meal and the older folks, the clergymen, a complimentary subscription to the *Carolina Israelite*.

PART 9

The Jewish City

The Jews at Christmas

I THINK a more profitable pastime than this annual debate, "Should the Jews celebrate Christmas?" would be a project to get the Christians to observe Hannukah too. Thus we would have a whole "fortnight" as the British say, and our Christian neighbors would find our Hannukah as spiritually uplifting as we find their Christmas joyous.

We reflect the culture, mores, habits of the surrounding society—and Christmas, a national holiday, is as much part of our national life as Sunday, for instance, which is also based on Christian theology.

The first time I heard of Christmas was on the Lower East Side of New York. My mother, an extremely pious woman, went out of her way to get me a Christmas present for my teacher, Miss Peck, in the first grade of P.S. 20. I recall that my mother made no special thing out of this. It was all matter-of-fact, "Give it to her for her holiday." Which suggests the idea that if you are absolutely secure in your own faith, you can be respectful and nonchalant about the faith of others. Nothing will happen to you, except good, as my mother always said.

Many who write to me take exception to this idea.

But the whole question, "Should Jews celebrate Christmas?" reminds me of a story. The bartender signals the boss. "Is Jim here good for a drink?"

The boss asks, "Has he had it?"

The bartender replies, "Yes."

The boss says, "Sure, Jim is good for a drink."

I've been up and down this continent and I know. I've seen the Christmas trees and the kids have shown me their Christmas presents and the boys and girls have written me about what they will do when they are home for the Christmas holidays.

The best letter I received was from a lady who said that her son, Donald, came to the table and said, "Mama, what are you going to buy me for Christmas?"

The mother answered, "You've had your Hannukah presents. We do not celebrate Christmas, that's for the Christians."

Donald said, "Harry Golden says it's all right to celebrate Christmas."

"If Harry Golden says it's all right to celebrate Christmas," she said, "let *him* buy you a Christmas present."

An old-fashioned wedding

IRVING BERLIN is one of the few men in our civilization who deserves to "smell the flowers" while he is alive. Let us salute him for having passed his seventy-eighth birthday on May 11.

I once asked Irving what he considers his greatest song. He said he thinks of his work in terms of key songs, each of the key songs which resulted in a whole string of other songs.

And these key songs, he told me, were "Alexander's Ragtime Band"; out of which came another dozen or so popular tunes, and which incidentally ushered in the period of "gloriana" for Tin Pan Alley. Another key song was "A Pretty Girl Is Like a Melody," which set Mr. Berlin's brain to work on dozens of other tunes for great musical shows and revues; "Remember," which Mr. Berlin wrote during the days of his courtship of the society belle Ellin Mackay, resulted in more songs. And "Cheek to Cheek," part of that delightful movie *Top Hat*, was a key composition. The popular song was no longer a separate segment of the musical production, with the curtain down. It was Irving Berlin who integrated the song into the action as in opera.

I discussed all of this with Mr. Berlin before the fabulous songs "White Christmas," "This Is the Army, Mr. Jones," and the classic, "There's No Business Like Show Business," which I am sure Mr. Berlin would now add to his list of key songs.

The most popular key song of all was "God Bless America," the earnings from which Mr. Berlin presented to the Boy Scouts of America.

A few years ago I went down to the Bowery to look at the Pelham Café where Irving Berlin started as a singing waiter. The saloon was owned by a fellow named Mike Salter, a Rumanian Jew, whose bartender was Nick Schenck, later to become one of the wealthy motion picture moguls. While working as a singing waiter Mr. Berlin wrote his first song, "Marie, from Sunny Italy."

> On the shores of Italy,
> There my sweetheart waits for me.

The above from memory. I am sure I will miss a word here and there if I recreate all the verses, but I will gladly sing them for you any time we are within hearing.

By now the story is old but it's worth repeating. Irving Berlin was Israel Baline. And he was born in Russia, on May 11, 1888. His father, Moses Baline, was a rabbi and cantor. His mother was Leah Lipkin Baline. The family came to America in 1892. Two of the six children remained in Europe, a married daughter and an older son. The family settled on the Lower East Side and at the age of fourteen, young Irving ran away from home— four blocks away to the Bowery where his fabulous career began.

And now Irving has had a new success, a revival of *Annie Get Your Gun*. How could he, at seventy-eight, improve on a 20-year-old show that was already the best he had written? A new song, "An Old-Fashioned Wedding"! I saw the show in mid-June and I was not prepared for what happened. After some forty years of theatre-going I can only recall four or five similar audience responses to a single number: Caruso, after a *La donna è mobile*; Jolson, one night at the Winter Garden; Galli-Curci at the Hippodrome; and the Rain-in-Spain number of *My Fair Lady*. Said Irving Berlin: "It's good to know you can reach up to find it and it's still there."

We've had some great ones—Dick Rodgers, Rudolph Friml, Vincent Youmans, and those who have passed on, George Gershwin, Jerome Kern, and Cole Porter. All have, at one time or another, saluted Irving Berlin as the greatest of them all.

The Jewish city

I REMEMBER when the slightly anti-Semitic Gloomy Dean Inge was on his way back to England and he made a sneering remark about New York being "a Jewish city." Immediately all the Jewish organizations produced the old apologetics.

New York City is indeed the eighth wonder of the world and the greatest Jewish city since King Solomon reigned in Jerusalem.

Of course, the white, Protestant, Anglo-Saxons own it. Make no mistake about this. And this is no more than right. They were here first, they are in the vast majority, and they've had many centuries of experience with the feudal system, the development of the mercantile age, and creation of the industrial revolution. The white, Protestant, Anglo-Saxons of New York are smart enough to allow ample shavings for the others—Irish, Jews, Italians, Poles, and all the rest. But the white, Protestant, Anglo-Saxons can pull the plug any time they want to, and stop the entire process. All they have to do is call in the loans and the party is over for the Irish, the Jews, the Italians, the Poles, and the rest. When I say the white, Protestant, Anglo-Saxons own New York I refer to the stuff that counts. The insurance companies, which do indeed *have all the money*; the big banks, United States Steel, Allied Chemical and Dye Corporation, J. P. Morgan, Guarantee Trust; the New York Stock Exchange; Chrysler, Ford, General Motors, Du Pont, Eastern Airlines, United, TWA, Pan Am, New York Central, Pennsylvania Railroad, Delaware, Lackawanna and Western, IBM, General Dynamics, Eastman, Pitney-Bowes, the steel mills, the new space industries, the chemical factories. But they leave a bit of the manufacturing, retailing, and real estate to the rest of the folks, so they, the WASPS can feel free to go home to Westchester County, to the New Jersey coast, to the Hudson Valley, to Connecticut, to the Berkshires, or even to the Pocono Mountains in Pennsylvania—and they go home every evening.

Once in a while the white, Protestant, Anglo-Saxons are disturbed. Annoyed. There's a noise in the street; they look out the window, someone says, "The Jews are having a parade." Or, "It's St. Patrick's." Or, "It's a strike," or a "sit-in." But the white, Protestant, Anglo-Saxons go home at five o'clock and sometimes they have to push through the crowd. They say, "I hope I don't miss that 5:15." Sometimes they miss it. They have to stand at the bar in Grand Central Station and take the 6:10.

The Irish and the Italians *run* the city. Tammany Hall, the ward captains, the precinct managers, and they fill the offices of the Municipal Building. Irishmen and Italians—court clerks, bailiffs, policemen, investigators, and so forth.

But it is a Jewish city. The attitudes, the culture, the art, the theatre, the stores, the styles, the music, the concerts, the writers, the television, the producers, the directors, the artists, most of the architecture and the *chutzpah* (imagination and guts).

But it wasn't easy. First it was Walter Damrosch who tried hard to entice the little children to the symphony hall. Sol Hurok had it tougher.

But it was mostly in the social sciences. When the Jews came to New York, then New Amsterdam, the contract which they signed provided that Jews must not participate in public charity. The Jews took this to heart. Out of the ghettoes of eastern Europe they came to New York with less than an average of fifteen dollars per person, and established self-help societies which have become the models for the entire civilized world.

It is hardly a coincidence that the New Deal fellows like Harry Hopkins had their training on the Lower East Side of New York and so did Frances Perkins and the late Senator Herbert Lehman, Eleanor Roosevelt, and most of the others. The self-help organizations developed into what all Americans now recognize as the Community Chest or the United Appeal.

We owe much to the Jewish pioneers in New York, men and women whose names we will never know, who paraded with placards demanding an eight-hour day for women and fire escapes for factories.

The real big money is in the hands of the Protestants, the politics is controlled by the Irish and the Italians, but New York is nevertheless a Jewish city because the attitudes, the ideas, and the creativity are distinctly Jewish. All of this makes for the proudest accomplishment of the Jewish people since the destruction of the Temple of Solomon in the year A.D. 70.

King Faisal in New York

SOME OF the Southern editors seemed to be deeply concerned that New York's Mayor John Lindsay and New York's Governor Nelson Rockefeller canceled scheduled receptions and dinners in honor of Saudi Arabia's King Faisal. The Charlotte *Observer*, for example, said, "New York officialdom was too jumpy." And I sat in absolute fascination at the last sentence of this editorial: *"But today we can be fairly certain that Lindsay and Rockefeller didn't do us any good with the Arabs as they sought to ingratiate themselves with Jewish voters."*

Of course Lindsay and Rockefeller sought to "ingratiate" themselves! Since the days of Jefferson and Hamilton this noble land of ours has been a politically oriented society and amazingly—it works!

Suppose some foreigner had said that the Presbyterians are enemies of his people and the next day Mayor Brookshire of Charlotte (one-third Presbyterian), was officiating at a public dinner in that foreigner's honor!

So what else is new?

I have never questioned the right of the Roman Catholics to use their voting influence to prevent the passage of birth control legislation in New York, Connecticut, and Massachusetts for the past century. The Methodist Board of Temperance used its political influence to bring Prohibition to America; and the Southern Baptists prevented President Truman from appoint-

ing an Ambassador to the Vatican. And what about the Southerners themselves? For seventy-five years the Southern white
Protestant Anglo-Saxons have voted as a bloc to maintain racial
solidarity.

I salute them all because it is part of our great political system that enables the Negroes now to use *their* voting influence
to achieve civil rights. And it is precisely this which enabled
one-third of the population of the largest city in America to use
its influence to say to a foreigner, "You are a guest of the
United States, sir, you can't insult American citizens and get
away with it."

And, by the way, what is this worry about getting "in good"
with the Arabs? The Arabs have an ultra-simple foreign policy
which can be summarized as: "You've got to understand us:
we're hysterical."

Basically our national game, baseball, is a symbol of our
politically oriented society; three strikes and you are out—for
everybody. It is not three strikes for one and only two strikes
for someone else.

Enterprise in the Congo

THE CHRISTIAN missionaries in Luluabourg, one of the
thriving metropolises in the Congo, were having a hard time of
it. They had set up a bookstore to accommodate the religious
impulses of their Congolese brethren. The Congolese were
spending money all right, but they were buying colorful book
markers, sturdy Bible lecterns, hymnals, everything except the
Gospels, which the missionaries specifically wanted them to
have.

Then they hired Abe Pinhas, a refugee Jew.

He wasn't manager of the bookstore too long before he was
demanding missionary Glen Murray order some more copies of
the Gospel of St. John, a slender edition, with one side printed
in French, one side printed in Tchiluba. Abe Pinhas had ex-

hausted ten thousand copies of the book! Murray couldn't believe it.

Abe took the missionary over to the bookstore and sure enough the storage room was empty of the Gospel. All were gone but a few vagrant copies.

"How did you do it?" asked the delighted Murray.

"Simple," explained Abe. He took the missionary upstairs. A long line of customers waited. They bought the same bookmarks and hymnals and Abe took their francs, handed them their merchandise, and passed along with it the copies of the Gospel of St. John. That was their change.

Irish history

Up in Montreal, City Councilman Frank Hanley created quite a stir in a speech before the Balfour lodge of B'nai B'rith.

A transcript of Councilor Hanley's remarks includes this statement: "I am Irish, ladies and gentlemen, yet I have never sent a dollar to help build that impoverished country." Mr. Hanley's main point was that it is wrong for Canadian (or American) Jews to send money to Israel (United Jewish Appeal, Bonds of Israel). Said the Councilor, "I would much rather use that dollar to improve the lot of a needy person in Montreal."

The only important question impresses itself at once. Do individual members of the Jewish community neglect their local charitable and humane responsibilities? Based on fairly competent evidence at hand in every city, town, and hamlet in the United States, the answer would be a resounding NO. Indeed, the Jews often go overboard to "give" to communal and purely Christian causes.

I am not entirely unfamiliar with the Canadian communities, and I am willing to stake my argument on the contention that the same condition obtains there.

But Mr. Hanley knows nothing of modern Irish history. "I have never sent a dollar to help build Ireland," says he, to which I say, "Up Sligo, and the back of me hand to ye." As a matter of fact the Irish of Boston and New York had as much to do with the establishment of the Irish Free State as the Easter Rebellion itself. De Valera has often acknowledged this. Indeed I remember the fund-raising campaigns all over New York, and please note, Mr. Hanley, when a Jewish businessman contributes a thousand dollars to the United Jewish Appeal it is a bit of cigarette ash compared to what the Irish-American women gave to Ireland. I saw them with these very eyes, by the hundreds, and they threw pennies, nickels, and dimes, often a wedding ring, into a big Irish flag, and these women, bless them, with their husbands earning all of seventeen dollars a week for a sixty-hour week in 1914-1917.

And the Irish in their efforts on behalf of a Free Ireland had a tremendous advantage over the American Jews who wanted to help the new State of Israel. For one thing the Irish had already achieved full status within the American open society and it was possible for a prominent group of Irishmen headed by Judge Jeremiah T. Mahoney to berate the President of the United States for "not bringing home a Free Ireland from Versailles."

The American Irish were almost completely uninhibited. William Hale Thompson, Mayor of Chicago, won the Irish vote of his city by promising to punch King George V in the nose. And the Irish Mayor of New York, Mr. Hylan, was a bit flustered by the visit of the Prince of Wales, now the Duke of Windsor. Diplomatic protocol required Hylan to accept the Prince's invitation for lunch on the battleship Renown to return the Prince's visit to City Hall. Old Hylan added up the Irish vote in New York and told the royal visitor: "Prince, I never eat lunch."

Another advantage the Irish had was that there was no Cold War with all its problems of keeping the Arabs and their oil out of Communist hands, with all the political inhibitions and heartaches this policy implies.

But why does Mr. Hanley think there should be different rules for the Jews? The Poles in America tithed for a Free Poland in the days of the Czars; the Czechs literally created the Czech Republic in Pittsburgh, Pennsylvania; the Swedes in the Northwest toast the Swedish king once a year; the American-Dutch have tulip festivals in Michigan and Delaware; and in my state of North Carolina they have the bagpipe-playing contests.

In the late 1920's I used to drink with an Irishman who always raised his glass and said, "Here's to Ireland and my going there and kissing the Blarney Stone some day." How nice if I could have said then, "I hope to visit the Holy Land and see the tomb of Rachel."

There are Scotsmen whose families have been away from Scotland for three centuries. Yet when the Black Watch parades in Madison Square, these folks dress up in kilts and cheer like hell. They are quite sure they have a separate identity and quite proud of it.

Why should it be different for me? The answer is, it shouldn't and it isn't. The only ones who insist there is a difference are the American chapter of "the trembling tribes of Israel."

Indeed America's own Mr. Jefferson said, "A man should have two countries, his own and France." Mr. Jefferson, speaking for himself, was stating a philosophical truth of what makes the civilized man. To America (Canada) we owe our political loyalty and citizen's obligations, and to Israel (or France, or Scotland, or Ireland, or Poland, or Sweden, or England) we owe a sentimental affection, our help in time of need. We are all, culturally, like the salmon that always swim upstream—to the place of their earliest beginnings.

Note: They used to paint a green strip down New York's Fifth Avenue every year on St. Patrick's Day. Let us hope that one day they'll begin the custom of painting a blue-and-white stripe in honor of Israel's anniversary.

Father Divine

FATHER DIVINE, the God on land, sea and in the air, has been called to meet the God in the sky. Well before 1920 he had launched his religious movement and by the 1930's he had recruited thousands, both black and white, who worshiped him as the Messiah.

He did not quite rival in popularity Daddy Grace's movement in the South, but he was a legitimate rival. Had it occurred to Father Divine to build one Negro hospital, he might have won hegemony over the Negro religious movement. It did occur to Daddy Grace.

Father Divine has long since been in eclipse. So was Daddy Grace before his death. They were in eclipse for three reasons.

The first of these was that they were not genuinely Negro leaders. Both Grace and Divine were supported by the white Establishment. In every Southern town, the appearance of Daddy Grace was accompanied by a police escort. In their zeal, these two were keeping the Negroes in their place, as segregationists are so fond of putting it.

Indeed, both Daddy Grace and Father Divine ran segregationist movements, although it is true Divine recruited special white angels—for what purpose the reader will have to hazard a guess.

Daddy Grace and Father Divine fell by the wayside when the Negroes took over their own leadership and demanded their constitutionally guaranteed rights.

Before the civil rights movement, Marcus Garvey was a serious, if misguided, Negro leader. Garvey urged a Back-to-Africa movement which gained tremendous impetus in the 1920's. But Garvey missed out on an important consideration. The Negro in America does not subscribe unless the movement is identifiably Christian and Garvey's wasn't. He ran the Back-to-Africa movement much as his white brethren ran their fraternities, with an awful lot of mumbo-jumbo.

The true dignity came from Negroes who were college-educated, tough, smart and—Christian.

Jewish humor

I REREAD the Introduction I wrote for that excellent book, *Royte Pomerantzen,* edited by the late Dr. Immanuel Olsvanger and published by Schocken Books in New York.

In nearly all the collections of such stories there are no jokes about honeymoons—Jews did not have honeymoons. There are no jokes about maternity suits, or homosexuals; but plenty of jokes about women. The predominant figures in Jewish humor remain the same: the *schnorrer* (panhandler), the *gvir* (rich man), the *poyer* (peasant), the *poretz* (feudal baron), and of course the *balagoola* (ignoramus) and the *schlemiel* (sad sack).

Steve Allen has written that one of the requirements of the humorist is to be Jewish. Mr. Allen was exaggerating, of course, but he was making a point. The historian Ernest Renan, who was not particularly friendly, wrote, "When you write of Jews, write of their humor."

There have been three waves of Jewish immigration to the United States—Spanish Jews from Spain, Portugal, England, and Holland in colonial times, a much larger immigration of German Jews from 1848 to 1870, and finally a great wave of immigrants between 1880 and 1920 from eastern Europe. And since the 1880's, much of the American humor has been either spoken by Jewish performers or written by Jews for non-Jewish performers.

Why?

In the eleventh century the Jews were placed in ghettoes as punishment. The early anti-Semites had no idea they were giving the Jews a one-thousand-year seminar in living in the industrial age of the twentieth century. The Jew was an urban man before there was a word for it.

In the ghettoes of Europe the Jews developed a sense of humor as protection against the hostile society. But in America there was political and economic freedom and so the one great challenge in this ghetto was to *get out*. And the Jews prepared for the challenge, as always, with humor. Looking back upon it, it is still to me the wonder of wonders that laughter always rocked the Lower East Side of New York. Times were hard. But people laughed. So it does not seem strange at all that for the next two generations all America was entertained by Jewish comedians or "*Komikers*" as we called them. Jews learned to laugh at dire fate because they have an intimate relationship with dire fate.

I personally figured out for instance the reason for Dr. Arnold Toynbee's hostility. He found the pattern of the rise and fall of forty or fifty civilizations—beginning, rise, fall, silence; beginning, rise fall, silence. When he came to the Jews he found—beginning, rise fall; rise, fall; rise, fall; and rise; and he didn't know what to do with that. It just didn't fit.

The fact that it doesn't fit has made countless people angry, and the history has been sad, but the Jews always saw the humor in it. True Jewish humor is not dialect humor of the type, say, forwarded by Gallagher and Shean which was funny enough. Jewish humor is that deeply pessimistic irony born of centuries in Europe. Jewish humor was an attempt to mitigate despair, poverty, and terror.

Tevye, the dairyman, one of Sholom Aleichem's most famous figures, remarks, "With God's help, I'll starve to death." Tevye is the typical *schlemiel*, a word which, with countless other Yiddish expressions like "*kibbitzer*," "*chutzpah*," and "*mishigas*," has made its way into the American idiom.

A schlemiel is a sad sack. The proverb says, "When a schlemiel kills a chicken, it walks; when he winds a clock, it stops; when he falls on his back, he breaks his nose."

The sad sack, of course, is universal. The Jewish sad sack is probably a little more articulate about his fate because Jews often think of themselves as the collective schlemiels of mankind. Schlemiels, with a difference. They are much like the people who live at the base of the volcano, Mt. Etna, in Italy. The volcano rumbles and they move away. Then the eruption comes, pouring fire and lava all over the valley. The moment everything cools off the same people come back to the same place and build their homes on the same spot. And in two thousand years they've done it ten thousand times.

The Cuban exiles

I SALUTE the Cuban refugees! And I am proud of my country, which says, "Come one, come all, the aged, the sick, the decrepit, the destitute, and we will give you rest—we will send our planes for you without cost, and we will give each of you one hundred dollars a month until you are able to care for yourself."

Truly one of the most noble acts of humanitarianism in all history.

But I cannot help remembering the camp at Oswego, New York, where they stored a few Jewish refugees who had escaped with their lives from Hitler.

I cannot help remembering the story of the S.S. *St. Louis* with eight hundred Jews who had escaped from Hitler. And the ship stopped at seven ports pleading for a helping hand.

All sorts of delegations went down to see President Franklin D. Roosevelt—nothing doing. Don't you know we have a quota? The *St. Louis* finally sailed back to the Nazis, and five of the refugees committed suicide by jumping into the ocean. But the Dutch intercepted the ship and said, "Come here, maybe you can still save yourselves." Hitler and Eichmann caught up with them in Holland a few months later.

That is why I proposed a Jewish Ecumenical Council to formulate a Jewish Schema on the Christians. The time has come for love.

Atheist evangelists

IT HAS always seemed to me that the fellow who grabs you by the lapels and demands you do not believe in God goes far beyond the absurdities of the tent evangelist who says a couple of cold beers will get you into the eternal fires.

By all that is fair and just, the Deists have given us the best government and the best humanitarianism. The true rationalism belongs to the fellow who believes what he wants to, who can shake hands with the tent evangelist and the atheist, and go about his business relaxed and unafraid.

Years ago, on the Lower East Side of New York, I remember outside a synagogue a group of atheist evangelists who stood along the sidewalk laughing and offering us tickets to an atheist meeting where we could enjoy pork and beans. They promised us we would have a better time there than in the synagogue.

They should live so long.

"God Is Dead"

Is IT possible to get rid of the Jewish God and retain the Jewish Jesus?

At Emory University in Atlanta, Dr. Thomas J. J. Altizer has created some spirited discussion over his lecture, "God Is Dead."

I came to the conclusion long ago that there is considerable difference between a freethinker and one who thinks freely— one whose main hope is to chase God out of heaven by force.

The question to ask Dr. Altizer is whose god is dead? Hundreds of gods have died since the days of our father Abraham. These were Baal and Anat, Isis and Ishtar, Tammuz and

Mithra, Demeter, Kore and Adonis, to say nothing of Jupiter himself.

Yet those responsible for the great social and political reforms, those who gave us the best government, and those who were the great defenders of human freedom, have been the Deists. An uninterrupted noble dynasty—Spinoza, Montaigne, Locke, Grotius, John Stuart Mill, Henry George, Washington, Jefferson, Lincoln, the two Roosevelts, Churchill.

No one should wonder why "God Is Dead" is essentially a Protestant movement. The Protestant Church of the South does not yet realize the price it will have to pay for having backed away from one of the crucial moral issues of our time—racial segregation. The courts, not the church, resolved this moral dilemma and the church now must question itself. But it is not as bad as it looks. Christianity will survive even God's "death" and it may not come to that. It may not come to that because the Negroes themselves, in using Christianity as a weapon in their fight for social justice, gave their fellow Christians hope and proof that Christianity still has its uses.

PART 10

More Complaints and Free Advice

Flying saucers

THERE ARE people among us who say they see unidentified objects, commonly called "flying saucers." Their agitation
parallels the agitation that embarrassed us after World War I
that there were those who spoke to the dead.

As a matter of fact, about as many people spoke to the dead
in 1922 as see flying saucers in 1966. I was in on that speaking-
with-the-dead business, at its highest level.

The reason I walked away from the "agitation" forty-odd
years ago was that the dead could never bring themselves to
talk to Woodrow Wilson or to David Lloyd George or to the
Tiger of France, Clemenceau. The dead were content to talk to
a housewife in Kalispell, Montana, and to two adolescent girls
in Boston, Massachusetts. (So many of these things originate in
Boston.) I finally grew suspicious of the "phenomena" because
apparently none of the dead could speak Yiddish. I have had
thousands of relatives who passed into the great beyond, none
of whom could speak anything but Yiddish, and I wondered
why Henry James of Harvard "came through" to me but not a
single relative from my native Galitzia, a Polish province of the
Austro-Hungarian Empire.

I can't help but feel the same way about the flying saucers.
They only spin over great and peaceful towns like Double Oaks,
Louisiana, or Dexter, Michigan. Their existence is always cor-
roborated by a deputy sheriff on a swing shift who happened
to have a camera handy.

Let us make the fantastic assumption that there is an intel-
ligence so developed as to adapt itself to our atmosphere. Why
do they want to show off in Dexter Township, Michigan, or
Double Oaks, Louisiana? What's wrong with City Hall Park,
New York, or Pennsylvania Avenue itself, with Lincoln,
Washington, Jefferson, and the White House?

Another parallel of the Unidentified Flying Objects of the
1960's with the spiritual seance of the 1920's is this need some

of the folks have of hanging onto their story through thick and thin. I learned enough about the subject to conduct a spiritual seance of my own one day at Midland Beach where a group of us had taken a bungalow for the summer. When I realized that some of my friends—Columbia and Fordham men—were taking it seriously, I revealed the trick, showed them how it was done. Do you think that satisfied the true believers? Not on your life. One fellow, an outstanding law student at Columbia, said that I didn't really understand my own power.

Today when the Administration, the Air Force, and the leading scientists reduce "flying saucer" reports to absolutely nothing, the true believers say, "Aw, they don't want to tell us the truth."

There was a philosophy professor once who told his class, "I want you all to study the griffin who is now perched on the chandelier. (The griffin was an animal with the face of a horse and the wings of an eagle.) The class immediately began its scrutiny. They were disappointed.

"Ah," said the professor, "you can't see the griffin because he's invisible."

Which is the great logical truth: *no one can disprove that which does not exist.*

The dead can speak, but never in our language, and there are flying saucers, but not in our world.

On dieting

ONE OF the American phenomena which I have sedulously avoided is the diet. I find it easy to avoid dieting. All one has to do is avoid scales. I weigh myself only when I see a penny scale that also dispenses my fortune. I read my fortune but never my weight. Since my fortune has never been explicitly realized, I see no reason to trust the figures the gauge arbitrarily selects.

It would be a happier society if everyone in it turned to a discussion of his penny fortune rather than to what he does or does not eat. Some men and women take to dieting as other men and women take to barbiturates. There are ladies who describe to me their banana diets and men who writhe with agony as they recount the torment of every meal of either spinach or dry toast. I could understand it if the ladies wanted to play tennis and the gents wanted to make the New York professional Giants football team. But I think they want to diet so they will have a staple for their conversational gambits.

Once upon a time it was considered chic to be fat. Look at the portraits of all the Flemish burgomeisters. Look at the handsome divas and tenors who gloried in their avoirdupois. The days of Caruso and Tetrazzini were the gala days of grand opera.

It was a foolish escapade to trust someone as lean as Cassius. Do men diet because they want romance? Of course not. George Orwell remarked no fat man who could convince a woman he loved her ever had any trouble. Do women diet to hold the love of men? Of course not! They diet because their friend is dieting or because they want to wear clothes and look like the women in the ads, a dubious ambition to say the least, and I might add, an ambition impossible of fulfillment.

The most valuable commodity in the old country was sugar. Unbeknownst to most Americans, sugar is very good for you. The old folks used it on Easter and Christmas and at weddings but there wasn't enough to go around. My mother once told me that the poor in her village had a folk tale about sugar which involved only the emperor. It was a vision of Kaiser Franz Josef drinking tea and before him suspended from the ceiling was a huge sugar loaf which he could lick to his heart's content. Now at dinner tables fellows put sugar in their coffee as though they were doing everybody a big favor.

Once upon a time, writes A. J. Leibling in his book *Between Meals*, seduction was preceded by an eleven-course meal. Today, with the folks chewing dry toast and gulping chemicals, their only indiscretions occur when they sneak a hot corned-beef-on-rye and guiltily lie to themselves about it.

Nelson Rockefeller's future

NELSON ROCKEFELLER's divorce set off a moral chain reaction of such proportions that the Governor, one of our best men in public life, has decided not to seek the Presidential nomination as the Republican candidate in 1968. The divorce hurt him when he campaigned for the nomination in 1964, particularly in New England, California, and the Midwest.

Americans, in the main, are hypocritical about divorce. They much prefer their sex secret, out in the barn or behind locked hotel doors. That someone would resort to the courts and a legal process to end a marital and therefore sexual situation outrages them. But then Americans by and large do not really have a favorable view about marriage, always contracting it on the basis of romantic love only to find later to their distress that marriage is just that if it is anything—a contract.

His divorce did not particularly hurt Adlai Stevenson. The Stevenson boys were grown and Mrs. Stevenson had a career of her own, as a leader in cultural affairs in Chicago, one of the sponsors of *Poetry* magazine. Her image was not that of Mrs. Nelson Rockefeller, a wife who lost her husband to a younger woman. Besides, Governor Stevenson did not remarry. And this is what really irks the folks, happiness—the remarriage to a younger, perhaps handsomer woman. This, and not the divorce, is the key to the situation.

Eleanor Holm and Bobo Rockefeller, who won divorce-settlement riches from the late Billy Rose and Winthrop Rockefeller, respectively, gave us the whole story. Each of these charming girls said about the same thing: "He wants another woman, so let him pay."

It was a different story with King Edward VIII, who abdicated the English throne for "the woman I love." Hypocrisy played no part in this. The British pay eight million dollars a year for royalty, their symbol of unity and tradition; and eight million dollars is a healthy hunk of cash. They are entitled to their money's worth. I did not think the British were snobs when they refused to elevate Mrs. Simpson to the throne. While she is a charming, vivacious, well-bred, and beautiful woman, she wasn't the average Briton's idea of a Queen.

That Christmas the kids in London sang:

> Hark! the herald angels sing
> Mrs. Simpson stole our king.

Only Henry VIII got away with it. Nelson Rockefeller and the Duke of Windsor, however, did not have his power. Hank did not worry about public opinion. When Henry wanted a divorce from Katherine in order to marry Anne Boleyn he cooked up a reason which, though meretricious, won out. Katherine had been married to Henry's older brother, who died of consumption before he could ascend the throne. Henry claimed she lied when she married him. She had sworn that the marriage to Arthur, Henry's brother, had never been consummated. Henry produced a lady-in-waiting who swore to the contrary. When he went ahead with the divorce, the Pope excommunicated the English king, Henry established the Church of England, and Protestantism was on its way.

It was rather hard not to believe Katherine but Henry had the power and Wolsey, the Cardinal, lost out. When Wolsey, under house arrest, looked out of the window and saw Anne Boleyn walking to her coronation, he gasped, "There's the weight that pulled me down."

When they got away with things in those days, they got away with a lot.

The road to safety

CONGRESS for the first time is seriously debating laws requiring more automobile safety devices, but what can we do about the tragic pointless deaths on our highways except keep adding them up? Though we invent safety device after device from seat belts through nonshattering glass through roll-over cars, the incidence of crippling injuries keeps increasing.

And the reason is speed. Human reflexes are fast but at seventy miles an hour they are a second too slow. Do not tell me that installing governors in cars will ruin the economy. In most states it is a law that when the school bus stops, all cars must stop, in the left lane and the right, until the bus starts up again. Despite this law, our economy still prospers. All this law has done is save the lives of schoolchildren.

Now supposing no car could exceed the speed of forty-five miles an hour? A salesman on his way to a customer would probably spend an extra ten minutes driving but he would live to be seventy-four instead of dying in a crash at thirty-eight. He would spend an additional thirty-six years consuming our gross national product.

Confusion in the office

ALL OFFICES, no matter what product they supervise, service they dispense, or sales they chart, have their awesome moments of confusion. These are the moments when all the executives wish they had been hoboes and all the ladies domestics.

The very worst of all these moments comes when the boss tells his secretaries that the office is so rushed it would be a great help if they would go to lunch at separate times. The look of dismay these two girls exchange is indeed pitiful. No two secretaries can figure when they'll eat lunch unless they can go out to lunch together. Telling them they will have to eat at separate hours is like consigning them to starvation rations or cutting their salaries.

I have found however that this is often a self-defeating ultimatum. More time is lost between two women plotting individual lunch hours than is gained by having someone manning the telephone while they are both gone.

Another bitter confusion that afflicts the working girls is the collect telephone call. There are only a few reasons why people call collect. Either they have no money or they want some.

The last collect call I had came from a good friend who had been arrested in Pocatello, Idaho, for making an illegal U-turn. The judge there wouldn't accept his check or his credit card. He was in dire straits but if he expected AT&T to shoot him through to a savior, he was mistaken.

"Who's calling? Well, we don't know anyone in Pocatello. No, we don't know anyone on the Pocatello police force either. You sure you've got the right number?" After some intercommunication confusion between caller, operator, and secretary comes the information that Mr. Golden's on another call right now. It would be better to call back in half an hour. My advice to anyone arrested in Pocatello for making an illegal turn is that if the cop at the desk won't lend you the money for the pay booth, pull your time—it's quicker.

Perhaps the most confusing of all is the office love affair. An office love affair even confuses the boss unless he himself is, shall we say, intimately involved.

What everyone wonders about is the young man: are his intentions honorable? The second the young girl flashes that ring, all doubt is banished and the staff says to itself, "Well, we knew it all the time." But it strikes me that as soon as that young lady flashes the engagement ring we have to ask ourselves: were her intentions honorable?

Southern cooking

No PHENOMENON is more overrated in this world than Southern cooking. Southerners in self-defense should desist from ever using the phrase. But I suspect they will not. I suspect

they will take umbrage at my remarks and reach for the old dueling pistols.

During the long fight for the integration of public facilities
the Southern senators were aghast at the prospect of Negroes
entering the white Anglo-Saxon restaurants which are mostly
owned by Greeks from Sparta, Chinese from Hong Kong, Jews
from Brooklyn, and hotel syndicates from Boston and Chicago.

Take Southern fried chicken! I loved it as a real delicacy when
I dined on it at a place called the Dixie Inn in Tarrytown, New
York. It was indeed a beautiful restaurant, jutting over a pier
on the majestic Hudson River a few miles south of the baronial
estate of John D. Rockefeller.

In the South, the only fried chicken I ever saw is fried
in hot gasoline, although the cheaper drive-ins use crankcase oil.
It is nothing but a hurry-up job. The chef, so called, throws a
hunk of pink chicken into a skillet of boiling axle grease and
out it comes a few minutes later, ready for anyone who has a
stomach lined with oak.

Thank heaven, as a Jew, I don't eat pork. Even the pork-eating
Anglo-Saxon Protestants tell me the pork they get at pork
emporiums isn't fit to eat and is a disgrace to the noble pig.

Not only is the pork unappetizing but the restaurant itself
abets indigestion with its name. There's the "Chicken in the
Rough," "The Cackle Farms," and "The Pig." Literally, there
is a restaurant in my city called "The Pig."

All of the above are Bar-B-Que places. Whatever Bar-B-Que
is.

Since this is an objective report I should confess I have eaten
authentic Southern cooking. I have gone to private homes
where four or five tables are set up for Sunday dinners and are
usually run by two or three respectable Southern women, the
bone-of-the-bone, blood-of-the-blood denizens of the old South.
The dining room is electric with the grace and politeness of the
old plantation days.

The table groans, as they say. Seven or eight different dishes
constitute the main course.

But the ham swims in axle grease and big, flaccid chunks of fat bacon attack the fork which tries to pick out two string beans. No Southerner has yet learned the secret of boiling corn on the cob.

I will attest that many Southerners agree with me wholeheartedly. That is why in every Southern city there's a long line of Confederates in front of the Jewish delicatessen waiting to buy frozen knishes, pickled herring, and what Southerners like to call Jewish rye bread.

Cure for loneliness

I HAVE discovered a sure cure for loneliness. It is hard to understand why some people complain about being lonesome, expecially with the television set to intrude on their lives and with good books to read, but for those who are still a little lonely, here goes:

Buy a thermometer. Just a plain old unfancy thermometer. There is something magic about a thermometer. You can go out and get a good one, or the city's oldest ice and coal company may give you one mounted on wood. Either way, the thermometer suddenly becomes the big thing in your life.

No sooner do you hang it on the wall than you find yourself immediately drawn to it. If the room seemed comfortably warm before, now you check the thermometer to see exactly what its temperature is. If you get up in the middle of the night for a drink of water, the cold floor, you suddenly find, won't tell you half as much as a chilly walk to a new thermometer.

The first thing, you'll be watching the television weather programs, although it is impossible to understand (and why should you?) the high pressure centers, the low pressure centers, and all the crooked lines and straight lines. That high pressure ridge over Montana may have some meaning, who knows? It doesn't mean anything like a thermometer means. The person with the new thermometer from Johnson's Coal and Ice Company will learn about fahrenheits, centigrades and, perhaps, even Reaumurs.

On being late

No QUESTION about it, the meanest people in this world are those who are always late. Undoubtedly if these same people are employers, they are the very executives who keep salesmen and applicants waiting.

Being late is the most annoying of all social habits. Apparently the folks who always come late are unafraid of gossip because nothing will inflame the folks more than the couple who forget the world has a clock.

Psychologists have suggested that the inability to keep appointments, the inability to make a train, the inability to be punctual is related to a childish impulse. Children, especially babies, think they are omnipotent since all their wants are quickly satisfied. The child imagines it controls the world. The latecomers imagine they control time.

The curious thing about tardiness is why so much attention is paid it. At Carnegie Hall and the Metropolitan Opera they pay no attention to it. Of course, in both places the management closes all the doors to the auditorium promptly once the music starts and those who come late have to wait for the intermission. Maybe that's why very few people come late to the opera or the concert. In the salons of Europe, dinner starts when scheduled and the servants close the dining room door. If Mr. and Mrs. Late miss the shrimp, they wait for the soup, and if they miss the soup, they come in for the beef.

The only remedial action the punctual can take against the offenders is to be just that, punctual. If you never tolerate lateness and do what you want to do on time, you make your point and win it.

Publicity and trial

IF A Lee Harvey Oswald had assassinated Prime Minister Macmillan it would have created a sensation in the British
press, but a sensation concerned only with the enormity of the
crime, and the universal sorrow. But not a word about Oswald,
no photographs. And no one but the authorities would have
even seen him until he finally entered the courtroom for his trial.

I think the point that is missed is that the pretrial sensation-
alism not only denies the accused a fair trial but is the most
corrupting influence on those "outside," including the public
and the public officials: district attorney, juries, the judge, and
the communications media itself. The publicity is corrupting
in the sense that the newspapers are playing a cynical game,
which they know to be a cynical game.

I watched this very carefully across the years:

QUEEN OF THE BROTHELS REFUSES TO TALK.

This was hogwash, and the DA, the judge, the police, and all
the communications media knew that it was nothing. They
knew it would have only one result—it would send a poor, unfortunate woman to the women's prison at Beacon for five years,
instead of to Bellevue Hospital, where she belonged. A second
result: it sells papers.

And it is a continuing corruption. What happens when this
prostitute becomes the "Queen" of the brothels?

Everybody relaxes. With the "Queen" in tow, it means the
end of brothels. No more whores. DISTRICT ATTORNEY DIRECTS
CLEANUP is the headline.

Immediately, the pimps and whores of Newark, Camden,
Trenton, Philadelphia, and Hartford swarm into New York
because the coast is clear. You can't very well arrest a different
"Queen" every day. It would make a joke out of the whole thing.

The library

EVERY YEAR, around April 1, I receive a large communication from the National Library Week program. Every year I dutifully include such statistics as I think relevant to herald the library during its very own week. Every subsequent year I notice that National Library Week has not relieved the strain on libraries, that proportionately less per card holder is spent every year although there are proportionately more card holders and that fewer than 40 percent of the nation's libraries meet minimum standards.

So this year, to contribute a columnist's mite to whatever remedies may some day be available, I have decided to run the column after National Library Week and maybe pep up a few of the dispirited but loyal librarians around the country.

It is asking too much of people to implore that they spend as much time in the library as they do before their television sets, but if they were to pay a tenth as much to the library as they pay for television repair jobs—why, the librarians would take over the world in no time.

It strikes me that one of the reasons for the decline in library services is the tremendous growth in audio-visual materials. These materials are wonderful aids to science and technology but they are often perverted because they are used as a substitute for reading. This I have no doubt will call upon me a murrain from the audio-visual people, but they have called murrains on me before and I have survived.

No school or college or municipality should have an audio-visual director or an audio-visual room until it is spending five dollars for books per pupil and until it has installed in at least one of the schools a librarian.

Is this outrageous?

Will any materials or teaching methods ever serve the cause of education as well as books?

Chicago never had a library until after the great fire. At that time the British Parliament passed a charitable bill providing a certain sum of monies for the townsfolk of Chicago to replace the books they had lost when their libraries burned up. To Chicago's everlasting good sense it didn't replace any books, it built itself a library.

I think it is too extreme to suggest we burn all the towns and thus get libraries. Britain has been on its uppers for awhile and Parliament may not come through with the same sizable donation. Maybe it's time we did something for those generations yet unborn.

On becoming a writer

A FRIEND of mine, a more than successful and better than good writer, asked me for a favor. His son, who had completed his freshman year at one of our Carolina universities, had decided not to return to school. The boy had wangled a job on a Charlotte daily and had aspirations of becoming a writer.

A man will dispense nothing quicker than he will dispense his own advice. So this young fellow stopped at my office and we discussed school and writing.

"Do you think you're a genius?" I asked.

"Oh, no," he said.

We were on the right track.

"If you're not a genius the chances of becoming a writer as good as your father are slim indeed whether you go or do not go to college. But if you're not a genius, you've got a better chance with a formal education."

"Newspaper work is very exciting," he said.

"Is covering the Trade Fair really that exciting? Charlotte has, at best, two murders a year. With the exception of auto racers who kill themselves with regularity, what else happens? Most of your work will be covering the Chamber of Commerce luncheons and you know as well as I the reporters don't get the free drinks. They're lucky if the management saves them a couple of sandwiches."

"Didn't save us anything last week," he agreed.

"If you want to be a reporter, you should work on a news-paper. You want to be a writer, you should read books— Plutarch, *Madame Bovary, Don Quixote,* Balzac, Hardy, Dickens, and Dostoevsky."

"But what about life?" he asked.

"At nineteen years old, you are going to have no trouble about the quality of life. Life is wonderful for the young. It's not al-ways so hot when you reach my age because you're running out of tomorrows."

He went back to college.

Long-distance calling

THE LONG-DISTANCE call is perhaps one of the most excit-ing events of the day. Bad news usually comes by mail and tel-egram, good news by telephone. My heart leaps up when I be-hold my secretary announcing, "Long distance." I always figure I will hear how I have inherited the estate of some long-lost relative or that some important editor, director, or agent needs my services immediately. No suspense is equal to that which is generated when you have missed a long-distance call. If they call back, you know it's important. And if they don't, what made them change their minds?

Mature adults only

MOVIES now advertise on their marquees, "Recom-mended for Mature Adults Only." How the cashier tells a mature adult from an immature adult is a mystery but ap-parently she does for the pictures do a land-office business. I suspect the truly mature adult is not at the cashier's cage at all. He has thrown off his shoes, poured a drink, picked up the latest copy of the *Carolina Israelite* and enjoyed it at home.

Test of survival

JAMES W. HIGGINS is one of the first robbery suspects who ever called for the police himself. After an alleged holdup of a beauty parlor, Higgins found himself suddenly embroiled with the ladies, who charged him wielding their spiked heels on high. The cops rescued him in time to save him for trial.

What he didn't know is that one of the ways the British trained commandos was to make them charge through a ladies' turkish bath. Those who emerged alive were accepted for the dangerous missions.

With the best motives in the world, no sensible man would dare the rigors of a beauty parlor.

Again—profitwise

So FAR I've resisted printing letterheads with the declaration "From the desk of Harry Golden." I always smile when I get one of these "From the desk of . . ." memoranda. Why couldn't it say "Joe Doaks," with the address and telephone number? Everything is bound to be written or manufactured on some desk or table. I would consider "from the kitchen of Harry Golden" or maybe "from Louis's Bar," but never "from the desk of . . ."

And the New York taxi driver tells me on the way to the airport, "I've been lucky this year—weatherwise." I get the cold shivers when I hear it. "Profitwise I would say . . ." One fellow down here discussing his plans for his factory for the ensuing year started off one sentence, "Ladies hosiery-wise . . ."

Are we decadent?

Curing a headache

I REMEMBER as a kid the system the elderly Orthodox women from eastern Europe had for curing a headache. They would cut a potato into half-inch slices, put one on the forehead, and tie handkerchief around it to keep it in place. This was quite general and I wonder where it came from.

Joy unconfined

THERE IS no fun like getting out of the hospital. A lot of living is to be caught up with, and there is a sense of delirious freedom. To take a pill or not take a pill is our own business and no officious person is around to write down Gestapo-like reports on whether we went to the bathroom or not. Everything is our own business now. Getting out of the hospital is tops in human experience and happiness.

Playtime

MY RESEARCH assistant Martha Huntley was perturbed. She and her minister-husband and their child were leaving me for the greener pastures of Presbyterian mission service in Korea. She had been advised to take with her a five-year supply of toys, as none were available in Korea.

She left the office cheerily, expecting a happy afternoon spent among children's toys. She reported that the experience was disillusioning indeed. For boys there were jeeps, tanks, and guns of all descriptions—any weapon of death the most sadistic among us would wish. For girls there were expensive replicas of all mother's gleaming materialistic possessions down to miniature electric knives and can openers plus sexy dolls which come with bras, fur coats, and their own beauty shops and college campuses—the latter including a soda shop, drive-in movie, dormitory room, and football field, but no classrooms.

This is wholesome play? She said when she got home she wanted to take some of the baby's orange-flavored Miltown.

The meaning of "school"

A SCHOOL is a place or institution for teaching and learning.

Underneath this definition in every standard dictionary is another definition: School is a large number of fish of the same kind swimming together in the same direction.

On unemployment

Times slow? Hire everybody! When work is scarce, the wise Chinese take it for granted that more workers should be put to work. They do this by dividing the work, sharing evenly, and thus ride out the work shortage until happy days are here again. Mr. Yee Wo, a wise old friend, says China has had this custom for four thousand years, and it is expertly sane and logical to keep hands busy, mouths fed, and skills from becoming rusty until times pick up.

My fair lady

WE NEED a blessed changeover from the topless, bottomless, skirt-bobbed, blousy-blouse whimsies of present-day fashion to gowns of great artistry in line and color.

I was a messenger boy and the sexiest woman I ever saw was in the lobby of the Hotel Astor—a gown covering her from top to bottom and a large picture hat—and she was gorgeous. I thought of her for a long time.

Councils of crisis

I FEEL certain that there was a moment when a council was held in a big cave and one primitive man told the others that they would have to do something; that if the population kept increasing, the food supply would run out. Columbus found no more than say two and a half million Indians on the entire North American continent including the islands of the Caribbean. From two to three million from the tip of Alaska down to the tip of South America was all the Indians there were. Up in Red Bank, New Jersey, where I lived once, we dug a new foundation and we found literally three solid feet of clamshells. These Indians ate clams and when the clams were exhausted they started moving on to another place. I'm sure there were councils held all over the American continent: "What to do—if the birthrate continues as it is, soon the food supply will be down to dangerous proportions and something should be done." The human brain is a fantastic mechanism. We've only now begun to discover its vast capabilities, we have only tapped the surface.

Man has momentary fears before he discovers agriculture or before he invents the wheel or before he knows how to transplant his oyster and clam beds in the sea.

Man is resourceful and as Sandburg once wrote in one of his poems, "Let them keep coming on."

Long live old age

ELDERLY PEOPLE are always a little surprised to find themselves having lived to advanced age, and well they might be, for they beat tremendous odds. Four persons in a hundred thousand live to be a hundred.

What would we like to take into extreme old age? Good health, good humor, a keen mind that will not admit to having reached the last frontier, a faith that tells us that we will find ourselves eventually in a new and better life. But most of all we would take into old age affection and a passion for the young.

The wise guy is the sucker after all

SOME OF the smartest people who ever inhabited the United States built and operated the railroads. In the process men like Hill, Harriman, and Vanderbilt amassed vast fortunes. They used to align themselves against measures like workmen's compensation. They resisted and indeed, the railroads never did have workmen's compensation, insisting upon the 1908 negligence statutes.

But along came fellows like Melvin Belli, the San Francisco lawyer, who won $250,000 in damages for injured trainmen. Now the railroad men realized that the negligence statutes were not so favorable after all. Where an engineer or a conductor would have collected $25,000 when he sustained the loss of a leg, he was now collecting $250,000. The juries can't wait to give him his award. The railroads plead, "Give us that good old workmen's compensation."

The unions say, "No, you made your bed, you sleep in it."

Diamond Jim Brady was right: the wise guy is the sucker after all.

Civil disobedience

THE 106th General Assembly of the Presbyterian Church, U. S., Southern, which met at Montreat, North Carolina, resolved that any church refusing to accept Negro members denied the Gospel of Jesus Christ. Even more startling was the Assembly's resolution which affirmed approval of "civil disobedience as a measure of last resort against injustice otherwise irremediable, or when existing laws do not express the best in our fundamental concept of justice."

This was good news. During that same week, I was privileged to serve on a panel on Law Day at Duke University in Durham, North Carolina. The subject was "Civil Disobedience in a Society of Law." The panelists were John Pemberton, Jr., Executive Director of the American Civil Liberties Union; Theodore R. McKeldin, Mayor of Baltimore; Robert F. Drinan, S. J., Dean of the Boston College Law School; Malcolm Seawell, former Attorney General of North Carolina; and Sylvester Petro, Professor of Law at New York University. Father Drinan and I were unreserved in our defense of civil disobedience.

If a boy burns his draft card protesting the draft, he has no squawk when he is arrested, convicted, and imprisoned. Civil disobedience courts punishment, as Gandhi and Thoreau courted punishment. That is how the point is made. Civil disobedience is public, never secret, it is nonviolent, and it demands sacrifice.

Negro demonstrators who go joyously to Southern jails are true examples of what civil disobedience incurs as well as what civil disobedience gains. The Negroes go to jail because they call attention to an evil law—segregation—and they hope to impress both Congress and the public with the injustice segregation perpetuates.

Many people associate civil disobedience with Negroes but that is simply a lack of historical perspective. Thoreau refused to pay taxes to the Government because that Government tolerated slavery. White Anglo-Saxon matrons, descendants of *Mayflower* stock, go off to the paddy wagon on occasion, too. One group of suffragettes, I remember, chained themselves to a hydrant while picketing the home of a senator who had declared himself opposed to women's suffrage.

Socrates, who was tried by the Athenians for impiety, laid down the tradition. He told his jury of 501 men if they wanted to give him his just deserts, then they should reward him. He deserved no less for the service he had rendered Athens in making the youth reflective.

"If you say to me, 'Socrates, this time we will let you go, on this condition, however, that you no longer spend your time in this investigation or in philosophy, and if you are caught doing so again you shall die'; if you should let me go on this condition which I have mentioned, I should say to you, 'Men of Athens, I respect and love you, but I shall obey the god rather than you, and while I live and am able to continue, I shall never give up philosophy. . . .' "

David and Goliath

RALPH NADER, a young lawyer turned safety expert, took on the greatest industrial organization in the world—General Motors.

You can't fight City Hall, eh? Well, Nader had them dead to rights on auto safety in his book *Unsafe at Any Speed*. General Motors decided the way to deal with this upstart was to try to investigate him personally. But it was a bad decision. Nader made them sorry they ever started up with him. The president of General Motors felt compelled to hire a lawyer with the prestige of Ted Sorensen and come to Washington and apologize before a Senate Investigating Committee to this young lawyer Nader who could take care of himself in a fight.

And he didn't even have a slingshot.

Ralph Nader may even make our lives safer. The car companies may make needed safety improvements in their vehicles. He certainly shook up the auto industry. They called back thousands of new cars to make adjustments.

I think we ought to deplore the lengths General Motors went to. They hired private detectives to pry into Nader's private life. These silly investigators figured Nader was a Lebanese therefore he had to be an anti-Semite. He wasn't. He was a bachelor. Therefore he must be a deviant. He wasn't. They even told Senator Robert F. Kennedy why they thought Nader suspect. He was a lawyer, they said, without an office, the only one they ever heard of.

"Meet Number 2," said Senator Kennedy.

But we ought to cheer Nader's determination and bravery. I have seen computers at the Massachusetts Institute of Technology which can play chess. There's a computer at the Eastern Airlines office in Charlotte which can tell a clerk within seconds how many seats are vacant on each and every flight no matter what part of the country the airplane is at . . . yet one man with a brain and determination can best them all, corporations, computers, and private detectives.

Freedom of speech

SOME OF the more liberal regimes in eastern Europe have recently introduced the idea of freedom of speech.

But we'll have to wait and see. Freedom of speech is fine but what is far more important is freedom *after* speech.